Henley-in-Arden 1991
had been published
in a Limited Edition
of which this is

Number 792

A list of original
subscribers is printed
at the back of the book.

*FRONT COVER: Henley-in-Arden Market Square and Cross in 1910.
(WI)*

HENLEY-IN-ARDEN

AN ANCIENT MARKET TOWN

AND ITS SURROUNDINGS

BY

THE LATE

WILLIAM COOPER, F.S.A., F.R.Hist.S.

AUTHOR OF
The Records of Beaudesert ;
Wootton Wawen — Its History and Records ;
The History of Lillington, Leamington Spa ;
Contributor to The Victoria History of the
County of Warwick, Vol. III, etc.

BARRACUDA BOOKS LIMITED
BUCKINGHAM, ENGLAND
MCMXCII

ORIGINALLY PUBLISHED IN 1946
& IN THIS AMENDED FACSIMILE EDITION
IN 1992
BY BARRACUDA BOOKS LIMITED
BUCKINGHAM, ENGLAND

PRINTED BY
REDWOOD PRESS LIMITED
MELKSHAM, WILTSHIRE
AND BOUND BY
WBC BOOKBINDERS LIMITED
BRIDGEND, SOUTH WALES

LITHOGRAPHY BY
DEREK CROXSON LIMITED
CHESHAM, BUCKINGHAMSHIRE

JACKETS BY CHENEY & SONS LIMITED
BANBURY, OXON

ADDITIONAL TYPESETTING BY
KEY COMPOSITION
NORTHAMPTON, ENGLAND

ISBN 0 86023 500 9

CONTENTS

PREFACE TO 1991 EDITION

By Clive Birch FSA FRSA

FOR many outsiders, Henley means river and rowers, champagne and strawberries, Oxon and Berks — in short, the Regatta. For them, too, Arden prompts images of a misty, undefined paradise somewhere in the pages of the past, perhaps of a place that never really existed. Thus, mention of Henley-in-Arden often prompts puzzlement and disbelief, much to the irritation of those who live there, and especially those to whom it is their place of birth and upbringing, for this is a Henley equally steeped in tradition, with its own significant place in the past, and clear sense of identity. It is also an extremely pleasant place to visit and in which to live.

I was born in Arden sixty years ago — not Arden in Warwickshire, but a house in Edgware which bore that name because my mother chose it. She chose it because it reminded her of paradise, and reflected the family's Shakespearean tradition — her grandfather was the great elocutionist, manager and producer, Charles Fry, whose pupils included Lewis Casson, Sybil Thorndike and Edith Evans. Thus Arden held meaning and memory for me.

When Cooper's book arrived on my desk, Henley — and Arden — took on form and substance and, when George Wilson invited me to his home, to meet local people and to get to know the town, I was not disappointed, for Henley-in-Arden has much in common with paradise, past and present. Such a town demands its own record, and in Cooper's text, that record exists, but his book has been unavailable for years.

George Wilson suggested this new edition, and William Cooper's son readily approved; George Wilson, David Lodder and Bernard O'Donnell made available both knowledge and pictures of the past, and local people supported the project. On their advice, we have not tampered with Cooper's text, resisting the temptation to add what has been learnt since his day, in order to preserve the intention and flavour of the original. The pictures in the first edition were not reproducible, so an entirely new selection has been made, and spread throughout the book. These are separately indexed, and have replaced the appendices.

In offering William Cooper's work to a new generation, we hope Henley-in-Arden will once more take its place on history's bookshelves, local people will take pleasure in their town's past, and visitors will better understand this pleasant place.

KEY TO CAPTION CREDITS

DL   David Lodder
O'D   Bernard O'Donnell
GW   George Wilson
WI   Women's Institute

ACKNOWLEDGMENTS

I HAVE to acknowledge with gratitude the help I have received in the preparation of this book. First, I recall the names of three friends, since passed away, Mr. F. C. Wellstood, Mr. A. C. Coldicott and Mr. C. E. Mercer, to each of·whom I owe a special debt. To Mr. Philip Styles I am under a deep obligation, not only for reading the proofs and making valuable suggestions, but for the loan of some transcripts of documents from his collection. I am also indebted to the following for various items of information : Professor Hamilton Thompson, Mr. L. F. Salzman, Mr. J. W. Bloe, Mr. H. M. Cashmore, City Librarian, Birmingham, Mr. L. Edgar Stephens and Mr. W. A. Sutton, Shire Hall, Warwick, and Mr. John Burman of Solihull. The Misses M. M. and J. Smythe have generously contributed towards the cost of preparing the manuscript for the press, and others who have aided me in one way or another are mentioned in the text, in footnotes, or in the list of Illustrations. To all I owe warm thanks, gladly given. The use I have made of Dugdale (Thomas's Ed.), of Wellstood's *Records of the Manor of Henley-in-Arden*, and Hannett's *Forest of Arden* is gratefully acknowledged.

WILLIAM COOPER.

LULWORTH COURT,
LEAMINGTON SPA.
11 *November*, 1945.

ADDENDA

Since the type was set up Mr. J. P. Nelson, J.P., was elected High Bailiff on 14 November 1945, on the resignation of Dr. Willoughby Agar.

It is with regret that I have to record the death on 24 September last of Mr. G. F. Lodder, for many years Steward of the Manor.

INTRODUCTION

Henley-in-Arden is situated in the very heart of England, eight miles north of Shakespeare's Birthplace at Stratford-on-Avon and fourteen south of the great industrial city of Birmingham. This part of Britain was, during the Roman occupation, a densely wooded, sparsely populated country contained within a rough triangle of three Roman roads : Ryknild Street, the Fosseway and Watling Street, the Warwickshire portions of which are still traceable, and from these roads track-ways led to the interior such as the one passing south along the present Edge Lane towards Wootton Wawen. An alleged fragment of Roman pottery was found on Beaudesert Hill in 1807,[1] and there is little doubt that excavation work here would have its reward.

In Anglo-Saxon times it was in the kingdom of Mercia, and our mother parish of Wootton Wawen was the centre of an important estate in the reign of Ethelbald. By the time of the Norman Conquest, the northern portion of Warwickshire, in which Henley is situated, had many long-established settlements, although woodland remained its chief characteristic.

The Forest of Arden is not mentioned before the Conquest but in the Middle Ages was a dominant, geographical feature of the central Midlands. Like all medieval forests, it was far from being a continuous expanse of woodland. It was of large extent and was continued to the west and north by districts of similar character which formed the royal forests of Feckenham, Kinver, Morfe and Cannock, while to the north-east it was barely separated from Leicester Forest and Charnwood. Though never a forest in the technical sense, as being a royal preserve, it is clear from ancient charters that Arden was nevertheless deserving of that description whether strictly or not, and from its sylvan scenes and forest life, Shakespeare would receive many of his early impressions. Of it Leland, *temp.* Henry VIII, tells us " the most part of Warwickshire north of the Avon is called Arden, and this countrye is not so plentifull of corne, but of grasse and woode." And Camden in 1586 speaks of the woodland and its being covered mainly with woods, " though not without pastures, corn fields and iron mines." Dugdale in 1656 states that the parts of the county lying north of the Avon were in the woodland in contrast to the Felden, open country to the south of the river.

The district of Arden, as distinct from the forest, extended from Yardley on the North to Henley-in-Arden on the South, and as far East as Weston in Arden. In the 18th century the woodlands diminished owing to the need for timber to supply the

[1] *V.C.H. Warw.* I. 244.

ix

ironworks, resulting in a larger acreage for tillage and pasture, but it still retains remnants of the old forest and has an abundance of trees.

Henley sprang up under the protection of the de Montforts' great castle of Beaudesert which afforded the necessary security for its markets and for traders, becoming an important market town in the later Middle Ages and afterwards. In its early days it was much in the public eye owing to the prominence of its lords, one of whom, Peter de Montfort, was for a time, among the most powerful men in England. Two-thirds of the town was surrounded by the Great and Little Parks, in the latter of which stood the Castle on its hill, and the remainder was occupied by the Common Fields. Being on the main road from Stratford-on-Avon to the north would favour its development. Its picturesque High Street (three-quarters of a mile long) with its wealth and variety of ancient timber-framed and later style houses speak of its past history and bygone people and except for one or two instances of over restoration, it retains its old-world charm unimpaired by modern additions.

There is scarcely more beautiful scenery of the gentle, undulating kind to be found anywhere in Warwickshire than in its immediate neighbourhood, and many happy hours the writer has spent in the richly carpeted meadows and by the little river, in the leafy lanes and on the hills round Henley, thrilled as he ever was by the romantic story of its past.

It has been his endeavour to present as complete a history as possible of this ancient place from the far off days, when a knight with his men-at-arms might often be seen passing to and fro, to the present age of the motor car speeding along the main street. He has also included all he has been able to discover about Ullenhall and in each case no known documentary source has been left unexplored. Some of the information has already appeared in his earlier book, *The Records of Beaudesert*, now out of print. If readers derive some measure of the interest and pleasure its preparation over a number of years has afforded him, he will feel amply repaid.

THE MANOR AND TOWN

THE place-name Henley is derived from *hean* meaning high, and *leah*, a clearing in a wooded country, i.e., 'at the high clearing'[1] in reference to the high ground behind it, though the old town itself is in a valley. Arden derives from a stem *Ardu*, high, steep, which is appropriate to the comparatively high ground of the district which bears this name.[2] Henley is not mentioned in Domesday Book, being included with Wootton in that survey.

Wootton at the Conquest was bestowed on Robert de Stafford as tenant-in-chief and he granted the manor of Henley to Thurstan de Montfort of Beaudesert *temp*. Stephen[3] who held it of him as a sub-tenant.

About the year 1140 Thurstan obtained from the Empress Matilda during one of her brief periods of power the right to hold a market weekly on Sunday at his Castle of Beaudesert. The Charter[4] of which this is a translation reads as follows :

'Matilda the Empress,[5] daughter of King Henry, to Roger, Earl of Warwick, and to all her faithful [subjects], French and English of Warwickshire, greeting. Know ye that I have granted to Thurstan de Montfort that he may hold a market on Sunday at his Castle of Beaudesert. I will, therefore, and steadfastly decree that all coming to, standing in and returning from the Market aforesaid shall have lasting peace.

Witness Milo de Glocestria, at Winchester.'

Markets in those days could only be held in fortified places owing to the danger of robbery, so this Charter would bring prosperity to Beaudesert and no doubt occasioned the building of houses in Henley for traders and to accommodate people attending the market, lying as it does at the foot of the hill on which the Castle stood. The first known mention of Henley, however, is in a manuscript at Wollaton[6] where 'Rogero de Henle' occurs about the year 1180, but the earliest document of any importance is that of *c.* 1185, when Thurstan's son Henry granted a mill at Henley to the monks of Wootton in these terms :

'To the abbey of Castellion [i.e., the parent house of Wootton Priory] and the monks there serving God the mill of Henlea with the dwelling before the mill to the west and with

---

[1]*Place-names of Warwickshire*, 1936, *p*. 244.
[2]Ibid. p. 12.
[3]Dugdale, p. 805 ; *Red Bk. Exch.*, pp. 264 and 268.
[4]Dugdale, p. 798 (Translation). It was not exceptional for markets to be held on Sundays in those days.
[5]Married (1) The Emperor Henry V (2) Geoffrey, Count of Anjou.
[6] *MSS. of Lord Middleton* (Hist. MSS. Com.), p. 15.

the acre of land adjoining the mill to the east, between the land of John de Preston and the bank which comes from Lincroft, by which they shall take turves, when they will, to improve the mill without blocking the road there and without hindrance to the men of Henlea, with all appurtenances of the said mill in waters, in pools, etc., free from all damage by himself or anyone else as freely as he himself had held it in demesne. This grant which is made for the weal of his soul and [those] of his father Thurstan and his mother Juliana and all his friends and relatives, he and his heirs will warrant for ever.[1] '

About five years after the signing of the Great Charter evidence of the increasing growth and importance of Henley is afforded by the grant of a charter by Henry III in 1220 to Peter de Montfort, great-grandson of Thurstan, for a weekly market at Henley on Monday and a yearly fair ' on the even and day of the Feast of St. Giles ' to be held there.[2]

Peter also obtained on 10 Feb., 1227, when he had come of age, a charter for a market on Monday and a yearly fair ' on the night feast and morrow of St. Giles ' at his manor of Beaudesert[3] and thenceforth the history of the two places, which adjoin, was very much the same.

The right to hold a market and fair was a valuable privilege and one much sought after by manorial lords who derived profit by letting the ground to the traders who came to sell their wares, and by the tolls paid on all cattle and goods sold there. The lords, their tenants and others also benefited indirectly by the convenience of a market near at hand for the produce the neighbourhood had for sale, including also things made by local craftsmen, and for goods it wished to buy. Booths and stalls were set up in the market by the traders, but some would merely spread their goods upon the ground.

The fair was like a very large market except that it lasted continuously for several days. In the Middle Ages much of the business of the country was done at these fairs and all kinds of goods were traded in, including articles of clothing, food, drink and luxuries, which were carried from place to place on pack horses or by pedlars on their backs.

Special courts were instituted to settle disputes which arose. They were presided over by the bailiffs and were known as Courts of Pie-powder from *pied poudr'*, or dusty foot ; itinerant merchants often being called ' dusty-foots.'

The amusements of the people were not forgotten and minstrels and jugglers would be there, together with Morris Dancers and those who provided morality plays. All classes attended from far

---

[1]Round, *Cal. Doc. France*, p. 138.
[2]*Rot. Litt. Claus.* (Rec. Com.), 463, Cf. Assize R. 951, m. 1.
[3]*Cal. Chart. R.*, 1226-57, p. 5.

and near wearing a variety of costume in material, fashion and colour which must have made up a picturesque scene.

We learn from an Exchequer Roll[1] that in 50 Henry III [1265-6] the fairs at Henley bought in £15 a year rent and the tolls and escheats[2] were worth five marks, a fairly considerable sum when the value of money was something like thirty times what it is to-day.

In the Barons' War the de Montforts sided with the popular party and an event which had far-reaching consequences for Henley was the Battle of Evesham on 3 August 1265, when Peter was mortally wounded fighting against the King under his great namesake Simon de Montfort, who was also slain. After the battle the town was burnt down[3] probably in revenge for the part its lord had taken against the King, but it appears to have soon recovered, for in 13 Edward I [1284-5] Peter's son, who was named after him, claimed divers liberties held by his ancestors including right of gallows[4] and assize of bread and ale[5] as well as market and free-warren[6] all of which were allowed[7].

In an extent of John de Montfort's land, dated 24 of the same reign [1296] Henley is styled a *BOROUGH* having then sixty-nine burgesses who paid £7 18s. 10½d. rent, a park and two water mills, pleas and perquisites of court amounting to £1 18s. held of Edmund Baron of Stafford, by payment of 3s. or a pair of scarlet hose[8], so that by this time there were sixty-nine tenants of the lord holding their properties by a money rent instead of by servile tenure.

In 19 Edward II [1326] the town is stated to consist of ' a messuage called La Parksshepene,[9] three water mills, 300 acres of wood within the Great Park, £10 5s. rent service to be received from all and singular the Burgesses, tenants of the Borough of Henlye, together with the whole Borough of Henlye with tolls and all other liberties pertaining to the said manor.'[10]

As evidence of the continued progress of the town the inhabitants on 10 August 1336 obtained leave from the King to take toll of all corn and other commodities brought into the market for sale for the space of three years to meet the cost of paving the streets[11] : this not proving sufficient two subsequent renewals of the patent were granted for the same purpose, namely on 28 January 1343 for three years[12] and on 28 January 1383 for five years.[13]

When Parliament granted Edward III a tax on moveables in 1332[14] for the war in Scotland, twenty-five people headed by Peter de Montfort were assessed at Henley compared with forty-six at

[1]Dugdale, p. 806. [2]Property which fell to the lord of the manor through lack of heirs or forfeited for felony. [3] *Cal. Inq. Misc.*, I, 931. [4]Goods and chattels of those who were hanged. [5]A monopoly of the lord of the manor who derived profit from the exaction of fines for its breach. [6]The right to hunt the game which would otherwise belong to the king. [7]*Rot. Hund.* (Rec. Com.), II, 228. [8]*Cal. Inq. p.m.* III, No. 59. [9]The second element is from the Anglo-Saxon Scipen, a cowshed. [10]Cott. Ch. xxvii, 137. [11]*Cal. Pat. R.*, 1334-8, p. 310. [12]Ibid, 1343-5, p. 3. [13]Ibid., 1381-5, p. 225. [14]*Lay Sub. R.*, (Dugd. Soc. vi), pp. 2 and 5.

Stratford-on-Avon. No goods of less than ten shillings in value[1] were taxed, so that the poorest persons were exempt. The list of names shows the following industrial occupations here at that early date : a linen draper, ironmonger, shoemaker, smith, tanner, dyer and a tailor.

In February 1333 Peter de Montfort [iii] granted to Fulk the Armourer and Edith his wife the lease of a shop in Henley for their lives and the following is a translation of this interesting document which formerly belonged to Sir Simon Archer the friend of Dugdale :

' This Indenture[2] bears witness that I Peter de Montfort have granted, yielded and demised to Fulk le Armorer and Edith his wife a certain shop in the town of Henlegh situate next the shop of John Tymme opposite the house of Geoffrey Lyon To have and to hold the said shop of me and my heirs or assigns to the said Fulk and Edith his wife so long as they shall live or to the one of them who shall survive, freely, quietly, well and in peace with their appurtenances and easements, the said Fulk and Edith his wife so long as they shall live rendering thence annually to me and my heirs or assigns three shillings of silver at two terms of the year viz. at the feast of the Annunciation of the Blessed Mary and at the feast of St. Michael by equal portions and they shall maintain the buildings in the same condition in which they shall find them or in a better one And they shall do two suits in the year at the Lord's court for all secular service, exaction or demands. In witness whereof to the present indented writing remaining in my possession the said Fulk and Edith have affixed their seal.

These being witnesses—William Ive, John Hemery, Edward de Heyford, Symon Scarlet, Richard Faber, William le Hunte, and others. Dated on Sunday next before the feast of the Purification of the Blessed Virgin Mary in the 7th year of the reign of King Edward III from the Conquest.'

From this it is more than likely that Fulk performed the all important service of equipping the de Montforts and their men at arms in their mail and arms.

The Catesby family, who were lords of Lapworth, held a number of fee-farm rents in Henley and the immediate neighbourhood in the 15th and 16th centuries[3] and an interesting ' Rental of Margaret Catesby ' for Michaelmas 1446 is included on page 170. Margaret, the widow of John Catesby, was the daughter and co-heir of William de Montfort, son of Richard, and grandson of Peter de Montfort of Beaudesert by Lora Astley of Ullenhall. Her direct descendant, Robert Catesby of Bushwood Hall, was the

[1]At least £12 in present-day money.
[2]Saunders MSS. at Shakespeare's Birthplace.
[3]Various Catalogues of Anct. Deeds.

notorious Gunpowder Conspirator who with other Roman Catholics attempted unsuccessfully to blow up the King and Parliament in 1605.

An outstanding event in the town's history was the Charter granted by Henry VI on 16 May 1449 to the then lord, Sir Ralph Boteler for the benefit of himself and the inhabitants, which document now hangs in the Guildhall with the great seal attached. The impress is 'from the matrix which was used successively by Henry IV, V and VI although the last mentioned sovereign had added for the sake of distinction, a small quatrefoil in the cusped bordering.'

The Charter begins by reciting and confirming the liberties and franchises enjoyed by his ancestors, former lords of the manor, including View of Frankpledge[1] held at Henley twice a year and waifs and strays[2] and all pertaining to the said View, and a market there weekly on Monday. It grants to him the same, albeit he and his ancestors 'had not, nor ought to have had, the liberties and franchises aforesaid, or any of them, or did not fully use them.'

It further grants :

' That no sheriff, under sheriff, coroner, bailiff, or any other minister of us or our heirs shall enter into the said town or manor or the precincts of the same to do or execute anything there in anywise nor intermeddle in aught within the same, unless in default of the same Ralph or his heirs aforesaid. That the aforesaid Ralph and his heirs may have Infangthef[3] and Outfangthef[4] and all Chattels of Felons, Fugitives, or Persons in any wise condemned or put in exigence for treason or felony and the Chattels of outlaws whether it be at the suit of us or our heirs or at the suit of a party, the Chattels of self-slayers, and non resiants and of others resiant within the town and manor aforesaid . . . So that if anyone of them ought to lose his life or limb for his offence, or shall flee and not be willing to stand his Trial . . . it shall be well lawful for the same Ralph and his heirs by themselves or their ministers to seize those Chattels . . . and apply them to their own proper use etc.' 'And that no buyer or purveyor for the household of us or our heirs do take any goods from the aforesaid Ralph his heirs or from any tenants of the same . . . without the will of the same Ralph and his heirs and tenants aforesaid.'

'And that all and singular the tenants of the same Ralph and his heirs shall forever be quit of toll or tollage, stallage[5]

[1]See p. 25.
[2]The right of impounding (and keeping if unclaimed) lost property—waif applying to dead chattels and stray to live beasts.
[3]The liberty of trying a thief granted to the owner of an estate for a robbery committed within it.
[4]The privilege of judging any thief brought before the lord.
[5]Rent for erecting stalls or booths in a market or fair.

pontage,[1] paviage,[2] weighage,[3] murage,[4] keyage,[5] cheminage,[6] in all places as well by land as by water throughout our whole realm of England and elsewhere within our dominions and power. We have granted also to the same Ralph and his heirs that they shall have within the town aforesaid every Year two fairs, namely, one fair to be held on Tuesday in the week of Pentecost and the two following days, and the other Fair to be held on the day and feast of St. Luke the Evangelist and the two following days with all and singular things to such fairs appertaining.'

The Charter was witnessed by the Archbishop of Canterbury, the Bishops of Carlisle and Chichester, Humphrey, Duke of Buckingham, William, Duke of Suffolk, Richard, Earl of Salisbury, Thomas, Earl of Devon, Sir Ralph Cromwell, Sir James Fenys Lord de Say, and others, and is signed ' Rous.'

Edmund Brereton, who was made the King's bailiff of Henley in 1485, presented his accounts two years later when the rents of assize of the free tenants[7] amounted to £8 19s. 8d., rents and farms outside the town £17 6s. 6d., and the perquisites of the court £1 15s. The bailiff received 2d. a day and 17s. 10d. was paid to the steward and other officers and tenants for holding courts and procuring and preserving the good government of the demesne.[8]

From the reign of Edward IV in 1477 to that of Edward VI in 1547, during which the manor was in the hands of the Crown, there are some interesting references amongst the various rolls to the officials and others connected with it, namely, the steward, overseer, bailiff and receiver, the woodward or keeper of the parks, the master of the game and the master of the hunt. Complaint is made in 1532[9] about ' the waste done in Hendley parks and of the deer ' and that ' if Sir Edward Willoughby, their keeper, continue in his room the woods will be clearly undone.'

In 1546 Henley is stated to be an important market town.[10]

On the 13 May, 1557, the rents and fees amounted to £57 5s. 7½d. including the Great Park with the lodge, £26 13s. 4d., and the herbage of the Little Park, £19.[11]

---

[1] Toll paid on bridges.
[2] Paviage, a duty payable for passing over the soil of another.
[3] Rate paid for weighing of goods.
[4] Repair of walls.
[5] Quayage, payment for use of a quay.
[6] Repair of streets.
[7] Fixed rents payable for freeholds.
[8] Hannett, *The Forest of Arden*, p. 34, citing Papers ' Warwick ' at P.R.O., Wellstood, op. cit. p.x.
[9] P.R.O. Letter from John Grevyll to Sir Wm. Paulet dated 17th November, 1532 (cited by Wellstood).
[10] L. and P. Hen. VIII, xxi (1) 966.
[11] Harl. MS. 606 (cited by Wellstood).

In a survey of the manor made in 1608[1] Thomas Spencer is named as holding of the Crown by indenture ' All the manor of Henley with rents of assize both fee and customary[2] ; a water mill with a horse mill[3] and a pasture called Milnehame ; all the Little Park of Henley with a barn of three bays, a lodge of three bays and warren, inclosed with spikes and ditches, 200 acres, rent £30 2s. 4½d.' The annual fair was then held on the Feast of St. John the Evangelist and the Monday market fortnightly ; the tolls and profits went to Thomas Spencer as farmer under the Crown, who appears to have bought out William Harmon.

The bounds of the manor are then defined as running from ' the Little Parke Corner' (East of Henley Mill) to Blackford Bridge, down the stream to Hobdaye's Mill *alias* Nethermill (now Blackford Mill), by the Mille Lane to Stratford road and so by Gallowes Slade to Mayoes Lane (running past May's Hill Farm), up the lane to Newenton Ponde, to Fulses Bridge (near junction of Oldberrow Road), then northwards for half a mile to the Great Park and along its south edge to a close called Parke Shipton[4] stile and to the lane opposite Little Park Corner.[5]

There were sixty-one free tenants, six tenants-at-will and two tenants by indenture. Only twenty of the free tenants held any land other than the gardens, orchards, etc., belonging to their houses, and of these sixteen held a total of 118 acres in the Common Fields, and ten held among them twenty-three acres of closes, common meadow or pasture, some holding both. In addition one held ' divers lands on a lease for lives.' The proportion of land holders in the Common Fields is unusually small and may perhaps be accounted for by the manor being surrounded on three sides by Beaudesert, which left a very limited area for common field cultivation. It also seems to point to Henley having retained its original status of a predominately trading centre.

Returning to the Survey we find that the free tenants held eighty-four houses, the tenants-at-will six, and the tenants by indenture two, either by descent or purchase. At least twelve of the sixty-five tenants had bought their houses during the preceding twelve years, while a further eight or so appear to be holding by descent tenements which their predecessors had acquired by purchase. Most of the tenants of the manor were inhabitants of Henley and only nine appear to have been non-resident.

As mentioned in *Wootton Wawen* (pp. 76-77), Henley had close associations with Stratford at the time of Shakespeare and the

[1]Land Rev. Misc. Bks., 228 ff., 63 and 64.

[2]Rents of freeholders and of copyholders (*i.e.* servile tenants who had commuted their services for money payments).

[3]Both under one roof, granted by Letters Patent to Rd. Carpenter and others Feb. 6th, 1591. Now (1608) held by Indenture by T. Gibbs (f. 62).

[4]No doubt ' La Parksshepene ' of 1326.

[5]The boundaries of the manor were the same in 1820 but new details occur. See *Records of the Manor of Henley-in-Arden* by Wellstood, p. 134.

Whateleys, Kirbys, Wheelers, Barnhursts, Bakers, Kyrdalls, Slys, Hemmings and others had representatives in the poet's native town. Henley was the birthplace of Alderman George Whateley, the woollen draper, who was a neighbour of the Shakespeares ; also probably of Alderman Nicholas Barnhurst, a fellow recusant with John Shakespeare, father of the poet, and of Daniel Baker, the Puritan, who in 1602 opposed the travelling players at Stratford. William Quyny, son of Shakespeare's friend, Richard Quyny, settled in Henley and served the town in several public offices.

In the Muster Roll of 1599, when there were renewed threats from the Spanish Fleet and other threatening dangers, the names of five 'ablemen' are recorded for Henley, three of whom had among them two pikes, one steel cap, or skull, and one morion, i.e., an open helmet without cover for the face—in addition there are four supernumeraries.[1]

On Sunday, 23 October 1642, Richard Baxter, the Puritan Divine, was disturbed in his preaching at Alcester by the booming of cannon at Edgehill and knew that the terrible conflict between King and Parliament had begun. Among those who fought for the King on that memorable day was Captain John Smith, a member of the ancient Wootton Wawen Catholic family of that name, who was knighted by his sovereign on the field for recovering with his own hand the lost standard. We do not know how far Henley was affected by this indecisive battle, but about six months later the King ordered his nephew, Prince Rupert, to ' open a communication ' between Oxford and York. The Prince's detachment consisted of from 1,500 to 2,000 men with four drakes (a small piece of artillery) and two sakers (a piece of ordnance of $3\frac{1}{2}$ inches bore). Passing through Stratford-on-Avon the forces reached Henley, about which they hovered for four days ' pillaging the countrie extremely as their manner is.' Continuing their march to Birmingham they attacked and captured the town, afterwards robbing the inhabitants and treating them with the utmost severity[2] in consequence, it is said, of their having supplied the Roundheads with arms.

At the time of the Commonwealth, Henley seems to have been Puritan in sympathy, nevertheless, the inhabitants brought upon themselves the following presentment at the Easter Quarter Session in 1655. The Court ' being informed that usually heretofore there have been at Henley in Arden severall unlawful meetings of idle and vain persons about this time of the yeare for erecting of May Poles and May Bushes and for using of Morris Dances and other heathenish and unlawful customs, the observation whereof tendeth to draw together a great concourse of loose people, and consequently to the hazard of the publique peace, besides other evil consequences, do order the same to be suppressed.'[3]

---

[1]Bloom, S.-on.A. Odd Volumes, No. 1.
[2]Warwicks. Antiq. Mag., p. 290.
[3]Sessions Order Book, 1650-57, pp. 271, 272.

These merrymakings were very popular with our ancestors, and we can well understand how loth they were to give them up. They were eagerly resumed at the Restoration and although they have not been held at Henley for a good many years,[1] in some parts of Warwickshire May Day is still celebrated in the old-time way.

To make up the deficiency in the revenue granted to Charles II[2] after the Restoration of the Monarchy, a Hearth Tax of 2s. on every hearth and stove was imposed in 1662. The return which appears on page 173 shows that in the third year after the King was restored there were sixty-two houses in Henley with a total number of hearths of 108 liable for the tax, which was generally payable by occupiers, not owners. These figures include a few houses then empty.

Exemption was granted to everyone who ' by reason of poverty or the smallness of his estate ' was exempt from Church and poor rates, or the annual value of whose house was not more than 20s., and thirty-one cottages of one hearth each are recorded under this head. The Act was greatly disliked, as it touched many who had up to then escaped direct taxation, and when the inquisitorial visits of the ' chimney-men ' (as the assessors and collectors were called) began after the third Hearth Tax Act in 1664, they were deeply resented as being an invasion of the privacy of the home. The roll is interesting as showing the names of householders in the town at that period and to some extent their social position.

A list of those who took out certificates in 1797 for the use of hair powder in the parish of Wootton Wawen, including Henley, gives the names of forty-one such persons and will be found on page 175. The practice of powdering the hair which began in England in the early 17th century used up so much flour that it caused a shortage of bread, and in 1795 to remedy this state of affairs a duty of £1 1s. per annum was levied on everyone who continued to use hair powder.

Elsewhere in this book it has been shown in the Churchwardens and Overseers' accounts what active preparations were made to meet the menace of Napoleon and it can easily be imagined what a relief it was to the people of Henley and district when peace was declared in 1814. William London, senior, a native of the town, had promised that if peace came during his lifetime he would erect at his own expense a Triumphal Arch across the King's highway under which the coaches could pass. He was as good as his word and the arch was erected in front of his house, which was nearly opposite the Yew Trees. It was brilliantly illuminated with gas from a gasometer placed in the back of his premises which supplied a range of tubes of more than 200 lights in addition to twelve dozen lamps. This was fifty years before the gas works was established in

[1]See p. 14.
[2]Incidentally it was at Bearley Cross on 10th Sept. 1651, when he was fleeing for his life after the Battle of Worcester, that he narrowly escaped capture.

Henley. An enthusiastic description of it and of the general illuminations, by a spectator, follows :

"On Tuesday 14 June 1814, there was a splendid illumination with some good fireworks at Henley-in-Arden, several appropriate and beautiful transparances were exhibited in the fronts of many houses and there were many tasteful arrangements of both plain and coloured lamps, particularly the ancient stone pillar standing in the market-place, the upper part of which was entirely cased with variegated lamps, which gave in a pleasing and beautiful manner the appearance of the decayed shaft and its pinnacle. So unbounded was the zeal of the inhabitants to vie with each other in splendour of their representation, which happily was governed by the most perfect unanimity, that no effort was disregarded in rendering the scene one of enchantment. The morning was ushered in at an early hour by an effective band of numerous musicians who assembled on the church tower, performing the most popular and loyal airs ; which was succeeded by the ringing and slamming of the bells, the firing of small cannon, etc., which took place at alternate intervals during the day. The preparations for the illumination also commenced early in the morning, and gave the town an unparalleled busy and bustling occupation, the great diversity of fancy so tastefully and originally displayed, the ingenious devices, and grotesque exhibitions that presented to view by mid-day was truly astonishing to the numerous visitors who were flocking in to the town at that early period, and called forth the remark that magic must have lent aid to art ; but the principle attraction of the evening was the uncasing and opening to view of a Grand Triumphal Architectural Arch which occupied the whole width of the street, it was thirty feet high, and thirty-two feet wide in its whole extent, and twenty feet wide, and eighteen feet and a half high in the interior ; erected at a very considerable expense by Mr. William London, senior, joiner and cabinet maker, opposite to his house across the great road from London to Birmingham (it was designed and painted by his eldest son, Mr. Richard London) it proved a fine specimen of architectural skill and artistical talent ; this erection was constructed to front each way of the line of the street, consequently the north and south views were alike, was illuminated on each side of the range or apex of the cornice by a double row of gas lights, and rows and clusters of variegated lamps ; on one side of it in large gilt letters on the frieze, were the words ' England triumphant. America despondent.' On the other side, ' George Alexander, Francis Frederick William Charles.' The four columns supporting the arch formed a compartment on each side, and represented four of the principle Pillars of the British Constitution, and were entwined with wreaths having the following inscriptions : ' Nelson, Conqueror of the Nile, Copenhagen and Trafalgar ; Wellington, Britain's hero, liberator of Portugal, Spain and the south of France ; Pitt to whose councils England owes her glory and Europe her safety ; Castlereagh, the friend of Pitt, and the concilliator of Europe.' The soffit of the arch represented panelling with carved mouldings and rosettes, the spandrels of the same formed between the compartments and the cornice extended the whole width, each spandrel was executed with an emblematical design in bas-relief, they were indicative of commerce by a representation of the sea, shipping, the beach with bales of goods, etc., etc. Agriculture by groups of various implements, science by a display of astronomical instruments, etc., and the fine arts by appropriate emblems ; in the inter-column compartments were displayed whole length figures well executed, of the two most eminent commanders in the good cause, each of gigantic stature, standing on tessellated flooring, which were Wellington and Blucher ; beneath these immortal heroes on marble pedestals were the initials, G.R. III., G.P.R.P.O.I., XVIII, in brilliant characters about two feet in dimensions. The platform over the arch was surmounted by three very striking full-size figures being a representation of Bonaparte between the emblems of Time and Death, very effectively executed ; Bonaparte was receding in a state of despondency from the arrow of the skeleton pointed at him, but was approached by the figure of Time, holding in one hand his scythe, and in the other the emblem of eternity ; as represented by a viper forming a circle by the tail being inserted into the mouth ; this hieroglyphic so prophetical, needs no comment ; over the figures was the Latin inscription, *Bonna-rapta pone leno*, on the flank of one of the sides was represented the Eye of Providence surveying the globe, and a full-size female figure of fame in a graceful attitude sounding the golden trumpet of victory over that part representing Europe holding in her left hand a blue flag, bearing the inscription ' Peace ' ; on the other flank was a bust of the immortal Nelson guarded by the British Lion couchant, with a similar flag inscribed ' England has done her duty,' this arrangement balanced the whole of its parts in the greatest harmony and terminated the grandeur of the design.

The tout-ensemble had an astonishing, grand, novel and enchanting effect and appearance, and reflected great credit on the loyalty, taste, ingenuity, and industry of the parties concerned in designing and executing it. Many of the passengers of the various coaches that went under it (while being lighted up) seemed transported with surprise and delight, and gave vent to their estatic feeling in the loudest hurras, among those of the surrounding multitude."[1]

The inscriptions therein recorded refer of course to contemporary events. To cut off supplies from France we had imposed restrictions on neutrals which almost ruined the foreign trade of America, who in 1812 declared war upon us, but the downfall of France in 1814 left the two countries with nothing to fight about and

[1] A copy of a contemporary report from the late Mr. A. C. Coldicott's collection.

the American war soon came to an end. In the following year, however, great consternation was caused by the news of Napoleon's escape from Elba, but after his utter defeat at Waterloo Europe entered upon a long period of peace.

William London, senior, died 9 June, 1832. His son, Richard, who was sometime Low Bailiff of Henley, died eighteen years later and lies buried on the south side of Beaudesert churchyard. His gravestone, which is no longer to be found, bore this inscription:

'To Richard London of Henley-in-Arden, a man of genius and ability who died June 13 1850, aged 69. Erected by a few friends that his memory may not sink into oblivion. I have been what thou art, I am what thou wilt be.'

In a valuation of Lord Archer's estate in 1812[1] the manor of Henley, with tolls, storehouse and market-house, is stated to be worth:

Tolls about £15 at 20 years' purchase	£300
Quit Rents, £6 9s. 10d., at 20 years' purchase	130
Cottage Rents, 17s. 8d., at 20 years' purchase..	17
Royalty, small	150
	£597

Fairs were then held on Lady Day, Whitsun Tuesday and St. Luke. The charges made were as follows: Each horse sold, 4d.; each beast, 2d.; each sheep, 1d.; standings, 6d. to 1s. 6d. each.

It is stated in 1850 that the fair at Lady Day was for cattle and sheep and that on Whit Tuesday a pleasure fair. On 11 October was held the statute fair for hiring servants and on 29 October a large fair for hops.[2]

The fairs continued to be held until well on to the end of last century, and of the one held on 29 October, 1890, called 'The Runaway Mop' we read that it was 'considerably larger than the last but there was very little hiring done.'[3] Formerly it was the custom for those who wished to be employed as servants to line up in the street, men in one row and women in another. Each man wore some symbol of his calling, for instance, a cowman a wisp of cowhair, a waggoner a piece of whip cord, a shepherd a lock of wool and so on. On engagement the employers handed them a shilling, which made it legally binding for one year.

The only survival now is 'The Mop,' a pleasure fair with roundabouts, swing boats, etc., held on 11 October each year at which tolls are still collected by the lord and lady of the manor for 'standings.' The Monday market is also a thing of the past, but auction sales of cattle are held fortnightly and of dairy produce, etc., weekly.

[1]MS. formerly in possession of the late R. Savage, cited by Wellstood.
[2]*White's Directory*, 1850.
[3]*Stratford-on-Avon Herald*, 31 Oct., 1890.

Quit rents of varying small sums are still payable by sixty-nine burgesses as in the past and amount at the present time to £4 8s. 2¾d. Cottage rents are due from four cottagers at Littleworth[1] and amount to 4s. These rents are still (1938) collected yearly in September.

Despite local prejudice against the manufacturer and the artisan, Henley seems to have gone forward under the stimulus of the Industrial Revolution and, while agriculture and business connected therewith continued its main concern, a number of industries flourished in the High Street in the first half of the 19th century and later. These included the making of nails, needles and fish hooks.[2] Among the nail shops was a large one at the rear of the present Nos. 162-4-6 and the last to survive was a small one kept by Simon Harris known as ' Tinker Harris,' who is still remembered by old inhabitants, and whose forge at the back of No. 233 was in existence until recent years. Needles and pins were made in a shop which stood north of and adjoining No. 223, and pins in a shop behind Nos. 172-4-6 and in another at the back of No. 169.

Besides the above, candles were made at No. 104 (now Henderson's)[3] and there was tanning at what is still known as the old tanyard, the entrance to which is north of The Bell. A malt-house stood on a site at the rear of the Central School and another where the present Nos. 146 and 148 have since been built ; brewing, basket-making and flax-dressing were also carried on in the town.[4] Spinning was done by many of the inhabitants in their own homes as in other places at that time. The coaches, post-chaises and post-horses mentioned in another chapter increased the demand for inn accommodation. There was rope-making at Mount Pleasant and there were brickyards at Buckley Green, Kemp's Green and Wootton.

At the rear of the Yew Trees was the tenter-grounds,[5] where in olden times cloth was stretched. The wool from the sheep was first dyed then woven into cloth. The cloth was then scoured with a special kind of clay known as fuller's earth to remove the grease, after which it was taken to the tenter-grounds to be stretched and dried, and, finally, it was combed all over with teazles and its surface trimmed ready for use. The phrase ' to be on tenter-hooks,' is a survival from those days.

The Crimean War undertaken by England and France in defence of Turkey against Russia evidently met with the enthusiastic support of Henley people as the undermentioned old poster now in the Gild Hall will show. Feeling must, however, have changed

[1]From ' Lytel ' meaning small and ' worth ' a farm. In the Subsidy rolls of 1327 it occurs as Luttleworth.

[2]*Pigot and Company's Directory* (1835). Nails were made here as early as 1651.

[3]Needles are also said to have been made here.

[4]These trades are mentioned in the Parish Registers, and the writer is indebted to Mr. C. E. Mercer for obtaining information from old inhabitants and other sources.

[5]Charities Report, 1826, Kempson's Charity.

as tne sufferings of our army from cold and disease became known, and the ultimate victory of the allies would come as a great relief here as elsewhere. It reads as follows :

> ' A grand pic-nic party for the wives and children of soldiers ordered to the seat of war will take place on Beaudesert Mount by permission of Mr. T. Middleton on Wednesday, 28th June, 1854[1] and the anniversary of Her Majesty's Coronation. The entrance will be through a triumphal arch surmounted by a pictorial banner, and the Mount will be inclosed round the old ramparts and surmounted with a variety of flags among which the cognizances of the De Montforts, Dudleys, Beauchamps, Botelers, Archers, Smythes, Musgraves and other lords of the soil will be conspicuous, whilst the united standards of England, France and Turkey will tower high over the ground where once the banner of the Baron of the old castle fluttered in the breeze. A spacious marquee will be erected at the north end ; a richly-decorated Maypole at the south ; and in the centre a floral court for the dance. Various amusements will be provided. Gates open at three o'clock and tea to commence at five. A band of music will be in attendance during the afternoon and evening. A quadrille and country dance band will be formed. At eight o'clock a variety of old English sports will be introduced. At half-past nine a display of fireworks will be exhibited by a neighbouring gentleman and at ten Montgolfier[2] Balloons sent off, when the evening's amusements will terminate by a representation of the old signals in time of war : The Beacon Light, answered from hill to hill. Admission by ticket, 2s. each. Refreshments of all kinds supplied during the evening at moderate charge.'

It will be seen how the spirit of old England lingered here in those early Victorian times. Henley's historic past is recalled, and the people enjoyed themselves with the maypole, old country dances and sports, ending the day with the ancient beacon light which may often have been seen there in times of danger through the ages.

The Public Hall and Institute in Station Road was built in 1908 mainly through the efforts of Dr. W. E. Nelson, who with Sir William Jaffray and others promoted a company for this purpose with a capital of £1,500. It has a concert hall to seat 400 persons with gallery and stage, reading-room, billiard-room, cloak-rooms and miniature rifle-range. At the opening ceremony on 31 December 1908, Mr. C. Couchman, High Bailiff, at first presided, after which the Marquis of Hertford, Lord Lieutenant, took the chair ; a large number of people being present. The first performance was given on 4 January, 1909 by Oscar Asche and Lily

---

[1] The bridge over the Alne in Beaudesert Lane was built in this year.

[2] Toy balloons named after the brothers Montgolfier, two Frenchmen, who invented a balloon in 1783 which took up a passenger.

Brayton and a small company, who presented the wooing scene from
' The Taming of the Shrew.'

During the Great War, 1914-18, a voluntary aid auxiliary
hospital was established there on 28 November 1914 and continued
to do excellent work until 5 April, 1919, when it ceased to be used
as a hospital. The open-air wards were the first of their kind to be
introduced, and the larger one known as the Muntz Ward with the
administrative block was the gift of Mr. F. E. Muntz of Umberslade
early in 1917. They were afterwards removed to Bramcote near
Nuneaton to serve as an annexe to the County Tuberculosis Hospital.

An extension was opened at Wootton Hall in the music room
there in June, 1917, through the kindness of Mr. and Mrs. R. D.
Guinness, which provided thirty beds in addition to the fifty-two
at Henley and proved a great benefit to the Henley Hospital as it
enabled cases to be transferred from there.

The number of wounded and others who were treated was
1,576, only two of whom died.

The late Dr. W. E. Nelson, O.B.E., was the commandant and
medical officer and Mrs. Nelson the assistant commandant. The
matron was Sister N. Stevenson, A.R.R.C., and the Lady Super-
intendent Mrs. G. F. Lodder.

Miss N. Fieldhouse (now Mrs. Barnard) was the commandant
and Mrs. Guinness the honorary assistant commandant at the
Wootton Hall Extension.   In addition there were many others
from among the inhabitants who gave their services as nurses and
as officers of various kinds in connection with the establishment.

Peace was celebrated on 19 July 1919 by the ringing of the
church bells, after which a procession was formed at the Market
Place consisting of the High and Low Bailiffs and officers of the
Court Leet, the members of His Majesty's Forces, the various
public bodies in the town and the general public. The procession
marched to the then recently consecrated ground on the hill
adjoining Beaudesert old churchyard, where a service was held, the
officiating clergy and ministers being the Rev. F. D. Lane (Rector),
the Rev. L. G. Schofield (Baptist) and Mr. T. R. Perkins (Methodist).

A dinner was afterwards provided at the ' Golden Cross ' for
all the members of His Majesty's Forces. In the afternoon a public
entertainment in the open air was given for the benefit of all the
inhabitants and the children were invited to a children's tea.   A
further open air entertainment was given to the public after tea,
followed by dancing. The day was brought to a close by the firing of
rockets and the lighting of flares on Beaudesert Mount. It was
decided not to have a bonfire, which had been usual on such occasions
in the past, owing to the necessity of conserving fuel at that time.

In 1563 the number of families in Henley was 113[1] which had
only increased to 115 families by the year 1730[2]. The population

[1]Harl. MSS. 595, cited by Hannett.
[2]Dugdale, p. 808.

in 1811 was 1055, and there were 242 houses. Ten years later the
number of people had increased to 1,249, houses to 261, and the
number of families was 291, of whom 186 were employed in trade.
This large increase in so short a time was probably due to the nail
and needle industries which were then very active in the town.
By 1861 the number of inhabitants had fallen to 1,069 owing most
likely to Henley's industries being removed to Birmingham and
other larger towns. During the next twenty years the population
increased by fifty, but by the end of the century it was only 1,009.
At the census of 1921 it had again risen to 1,192, this time due
partly to the influx of residents from Birmingham, and since then
it has gone on increasing a little from the same cause.

New houses began to be built in Station Road about 1920 and
building then continued into the Cherry Orchard. The Barley
Close houses were erected between 1926 and 1931 and Rose
Avenue was completed in 1931.

*Drakeley's Electric Galloping Horses appeared 'at the shortest notice' at
fêtes and fairs — in this case at the 1915 Mop or Hiring Fair, an annual
'labour exchange' centred on Market Square. (WI)*

THE MANOR AND TOWN

THE TOWN IN EARLY DAYS

THE first houses built at Henley were probably of wood and plaster, unglazed but with wooden shutters for the night-time, and thatched roofs.[1] During the days of the de Montforts at the castle, the town would consist mainly of this type of building but all have long disappeared. A good number of timber-framed houses dating from the 15th to the 17th century remain, some of which have overhanging storeys and many have gabled roofs. These examples give us an idea of what the town looked like in those times, and it probably covered not much less ground than the present High Street. In the 15th century the present Church and Gild Hall were built, forming a prominent feature in the centre of the High Street, as now, and the Market Place, with the then newly-erected cross and the stream running past it, was the centre of the town's activities.

As early as 1390 a shop is mentioned as standing in ' boveria,' i.e., in the cattle market,[2] and the site of another in ' the old meat market ' is referred to in 1461.[3] In 1470 we read of ' a shop with a chamber built over it '[4] and this shop would be open to the street, without a window, but closed with oak shutters at will. At the back was probably the workshop or store-room and the chamber in the overhanging upper storey served as the dwelling for the tradesman and his family ; any apprentices would sleep below. Frequent mention is made of selds, or shops, and of the shop-row in the 15th and 16th centuries,[5] all of which would be situated around or near the market place, and, as was then usual, close to the church. Each shop had its coloured picture sign hanging before it to show the trade followed by its inhabitants, for comparatively few could read or write.

Reference is often made in the 14th century to the ' barregate ' which appears to have been situated on the Henley-Beaudesert boundary leading to the castle. A small area near this gate was called ' at la Barre '[6] The name of Gilbert ' infra barra ' occurs in the subsidy roll of 1327. There was also in the Middle Ages a bargate at the south end of the street[7] and probably one at the north end where, after the road was turnpiked in 1725, a toll-gate house was built (see page 90). It is clear from mediæval documents that there was a ford at the lower end of the town before a bridge

[1]*Cat. Anct. Deeds*, B.8201 (1325).
[2]Ibid., B.4054.
[3]Anct. Deeds, B.S. 347.
[4]*Cat. Anct. Deeds*, A.7617.
[5]Ibid., A.7614, A.7619 and others.
[6]*Beaudesert*, p. 2 (1358).
[7]*Cat. Anct. Deeds*, A.13228.

was built over the brook there. In 1648 the inhabitants were indicted and fined at Quarter Sessions[1] for ' not keeping a sufficient bridge at the nether end of the town,' and four years later for ' not repairing Rale bridge leading from Henley to Birmingham.'

Outside the town on the main road south, just beyond Arden House, and near the small pool is Gallows Slade,[2] where in former days hangings would take place. Every town and almost every large manorial lord had the right of hanging. Executions took place in public and the gallows with a body hanging from it was a common sight, for even sheep-stealing and pocket-picking were capital offences.

In the de Montfort Charter of c. 1185 (see page 1-2), the witnesses' names consist mainly of ' de ' names where the second part is the name of a place : de Offurde, de Hulehale, de Cherlecote, de Preston, showing that they came from villages in the neighbourhood. The only remaining two names besides those of the grantor, the chaplain, and the man who wrote the charter, Master Anketill, are Robert filius Nicholai and William filius Engenulfi. This latter form, ' son of ' was an early way of distinguishing the lesser folk but its use was not found satisfactory and it gradually declined. In the documents included on pages 169, in the Feet of Fines and Lapworth Deeds[3] a number of early Henley names occur : During the early part of the 13th century the ' de ' names are still in evidence, de Bosco ' of the wood ' probably from a Norman name ' de bois,' de Crowenhale ' of Crewenhale ' in Tanworth parish, meaning ' Crow's nook,' de la Le ' of the lea,' de Sancto Jacobo ' of St. James', Durvassal a Norman name occurring in Spernall parish temp. Henry II, and Carbon probably ' a charcoal burner.' Some later 13th century names are le Gaunter ' the glover,' Brice, an ancient baptismal name, Marshall, ' a horse servant,' and le ffaukener, ' the falconer.'

The middle of the 14th century gives us Hemery, the same as Emery, which may be traced back to the Anglo-Saxon ' Amalhere,' le Lyndraper is of course ' the linen draper,' le Pultere, one having charge of poultry, le Taillor, ' the tailor,' Corviser, ' shoemaker,' Coccus, ' cook,' le Armourer, ' the armourer,' Porreye, possibly from Perreye which comes from Pyrige a pear tree, Ive from ' Ivo,' an Anglo-Saxon personal name, Faber ' blacksmith,' le Hunte, ' the hunter ' and at a later date Barcar, a man who stripped the bark off trees for tanning.

It does not necessarily follow that these second names had all become hereditary surnames, even those occurring in the middle of the 14th century, but many of them were becoming so and they afford an example of how our modern surnames originated.

---

[1] *Warw. Co. Rec.*, vi, 82.
[2] Bounds of the Manor 1608 and 1820. At the latter date the pool was called ' The Lawyer's Pool.'
[3] Hudson *Memorials of a Warwickshire Parish*, 1904

THE PARKS

THE Great Park lay immediately north and north-west of the Henley boundary, that is of a line running from the old weighing machine house down the back of the High Street to the Bear Lane, and then south-eastwards to where it touches Ullenhall parish[1]. It will be seen below how extensive it was, and the land occupied by the present Park Farm must have been included in it. Although situated in Beaudesert, it was generally called the Great Park of Henley. South of it and west of the town lay the Common Fields of Henley.

The Little Park surrounded the Mount on which formerly stood the de Montforts' castle, and extended north to Buckley Green.[2] Between 1376 and 1411 its area was increased by the inclosure of some meadows for which allowances seem to have been made to the tenants.[3]

The Park of Edmund de Stafford at Henley (i.e., the Great Park), is mentioned in 1296, when it was broken into while he was in Scotland on the King's service by some persons who hunted there and carried away his deer.[4] Thirty years later we read of the Great and Little Parks, the former including 300 acres of wood, both of which Peter de Montfort was then holding.[5] In the Account Roll of the constable of Beaudesert Castle made in 1411 a sum of 53s. 4d. was received for the pasture of the Great Park and a like sum for the pasture of the Little Park, let for the time of the account, i.e. from 8 May until the morrow of the Feast of St. Michael the Archangel, 1411.[6] The herbage of the Little Park, value £6, was in 1487 ' retained in the King's hands for the support of his colts and mares there, called the stud.'[7] A moor within the Little Park is mentioned in 1444.[8] Sir Charles Brandon was, in 1513, appointed by the King master of the hunt in the parks,[9] and in 1535 the keeper of the Great Park was ordered to deliver a doe to Edmund Connesbe one of the grooms of the King's chamber.[10] These parks were for a long period empaled for deer but in 1547 the Great Park is then described as being disparked and ' remains in the hands of the King for the sustentation of his foals and mares,' its value being £4. The herbage of the Little Park at that time in the King's hands for the same purpose is stated to be worth £6.[11] It appears that the parks were first used by Henry VIII for his studs about 1540.[12] His son, Edward VI, in 1550, leased for twenty-one years the herbage of ' the Little Park of Henley in Arden *alias* Beaudesert,' to John Dudley, Earl of Warwick.[13] In

[1]Bounds of the Manor, 1608 (See p. 7). [2]Rental S.C. 12/16/20 P.R.O., Dugdale, p. 804. [3]*Beaudesert*, p. 4. [4]*Cal. Pat. R.*, 1292—1301, p. 218. [5]Cott. Ch. xxvii, 137. [6]*Beaudesert*, p. 4. [7]Hannett, op. cit., p. 34. [8]*Cat. Anct. Deeds*, A.4567. See ' the 'Moores ' on p. 107. [9]*L. and P. Hen. viii*, i, 3880. [10]Ibid., viii, 59. [11]Dugdale Society, vol. II, p. 160. [12]*L. and P. Hen. viii*, xv, 410. [13]*Cat. Anct. Deeds*, E.615.

Saxton's map of Warwickshire for 1603 neither of them is marked
as being empaled, but it is clear from the survey of 1608 already
mentioned that the Little Park of 200 acres was at any rate then
fenced with spikes and ditches if not technically empaled. A levy
made by the overseers of Beaudesert on the Great Park in 1680
produced a sum of £10.[1] In conclusion the map of 1695 in the
back cover is of interest as showing the Little Park with the Mount
and inclosed fields at that later date, when the whole acreage was
232a. 0r. 33p.

*Early cricket at The Mount, with horse racing and swing-boats, on a
football pitch with what looks like a beer tent and a queue in the background.
The bicycles suggest a later date than the style of the drawing reflects. (O'D)*

[1]*Beaudesert*, p. 27.

THE COMMON FIELDS

THE Midland Open Field system has been explained briefly in dealing with Ullenhall (see page 121), but it may be well to add to the information there given. The cultivated portion of the manor consisted of large open arable fields without the hedges with which we are familiar to-day. Each field was divided into smaller portions called shots or furlongs, these being sub-divided into small narrow strips[1] each of an acre or half-acre or sometimes less.

The normal holding of the villein (i.e., man of the vill) was thirty acres of strips, and these were distributed in such a way that no two strips belonging to the same person lay side by side, to avoid any one man getting all the good or bad land. At first there were probably two large fields, later three, and the holdings would be divided equally between each field. Much of the work was of a co-operative nature, for the villein rarely owned more than two of the eight oxen necessary for a plough team. All were obliged to farm according to a common plan, the strips being so intermingled, and each man had to sow the same kind of crop as his neighbour and reap it by a specified date. Originally the occupiers were not tenants in our understanding of the term, they were land holders whose holdings descended to their children but they could not leave the manor or sell their lands. At first they performed certain services for their lord by way of rent, but as time went on these were commuted for a money payment and by the time of the Rental of 1446 (see page 170) a number of tenants were holding their selions, or strips, of land in the Field of Henley of Margaret Catesby by payment of fee-farm rents, some also paying a rental to the chief lord of Henley.[2]

In this rental one field only, ' the Field of Henley,' is mentioned, but in the Court Rolls of the 17th century and in various deeds of that and the following century the Great Backfield and Little Backfield are often referred to,[3] no others being mentioned.

There is no sign here of the three-field system which was common by that time but it must be borne in mind that Wootton Wawen was the principal manor out of which Henley sub-manor was formed about the middle of the 12th century, and it would seem that the area of the open fields as an integral unit was that of the original manor of Wootton. In other words the agricultural unit of two or three fields was in existence before Henley manor was created, and such creation would probably have no effect upon the field system.

[1]Strips were usually a furlong in length and two or sometimes four poles wide according to whether they were half-an-acre or an acre.

[2]This rental only includes a portion of the arable land but it is clear that there was then only one field in Henley Manor.

[3]At Birm. Ref. Lib. and Shakespeare's Birthplace.

The Great Backfield was situated west and south-west of the lower part of the town. In 1674 it was stated to include Harper's Hill,[1] and it extended back to what in the Inclosure Award is called the Portway road, that is the road from the top of Wootton Hill through Ullenhall to the Portway. Little Backfield lay west of the Swan and immediately south of the former Great Park and a part of Ullenhall parish.[2] Between these fields and the premises at the back of the houses in the High Street lay what in the Court Rolls are referred to as ' lands ' and in 1619 it was ordered by the Court that all those holding such lands should keep sufficient mounds between them and the two fields so long as the latter had any corn in them. The penalty for not scouring the ditches and making these mounds in 1656 was 3s. 4d. each offender. Near the Henley-Hunger Hill[3] brook there were meadows, including Lammas Meadow, and this latter would in early days at any rate be divided into strips like the arable for the purpose of the hay crop.

It is interesting to find that what was called Watery Lane formerly ran along the course of this stream, and when flooded it was quite impassable. In 1769 the land to make the present ' New Road ' was bought at a cost of £59 1s. 3d., which sum was paid by James Baker, Overseer of Highways, in consideration of his being granted land called ' Dockey Meadow ' in Henley Little Back Field, free from all right of common.[4]

In 1774, when £150 was needed for paving the streets, sufficient land in the common fields and meadow or pasture lying in Harper's Hill Field, the Great Backfield and Little Backfield was dis-commoned.[5]

It is clear from the allotments made to owners of certain lands with common right in Henley, Whitley and Wootton under the Inclosure Award of 1776 (p. 174) that not only the Backfield but other commonable land in Henley parish was inclosed and hedges, ditches, etc., ordered to be made. At this late date the earlier regularity of the open fields had vanished owing to gradual inclosure, and of the strips then remaining no doubt a number of exchanges and purchases towards their amalgamation had been made.

As mentioned in an earlier chapter relating to a Survey of 1608 (p. 000) only twenty of the sixty-one free tenants in Henley at that time held any land other than the gardens, orchards, etc., attached to their houses, and of these, sixteen held a total of 114 acres[6] in the Common Fields and ten held among them twenty-three acres of closes, common meadow or pasture, some holding both ;

[1]Birm. Ref. Lib. Deeds 192624.
[2]Court Rolls. For the Great Park see p. 19.
[3]Hangandehull in Feet of Fines, 1212. Hangra is a wood on the slope of a hill.
[4]High Bailiff's Book.
[5]Ibid.
[6]In addition there were four acres in Wyndemill Field in Whitley but which, in 1757, are stated to be part of the Common Fields of Henley [Shire Hall, U.24].

in addition one held ' divers lands on a lease for lives.' It will thus be seen that the majority of the burgesses were landless men, who would be engaged exclusively in trade or handicraft. Five plough teams only were kept at Henley in 1730, whereas at Wootton there were twelve.[1]

When the Award of 1776 was made 95a. 0r. 3p. were inclosed in the Backfield[2] so that about nineteen acres had been inclosed since 1608, i.e., in a period of 168 years. In 1717 it is found that Over New Close, Nether New Close, Clay Piece, Watt Close and Houses Pleck, all in the Backfields, had lately been inclosed.

The foregoing figures are small but the whole of Henley manor was but 340 acres including the town, being formed out of Wootton for the benefit of the de Montforts as an adjunct to their principal manor of Beaudesert and to allow the town of Henley to be built at the foot of their castle. After the inclosure the owners were able to change their scattered strips into compact holdings for better tillage, the wasteful part of the common fields being ploughed up and hedges planted. This made for more economical farming and the beauty of the countryside was enhanced by the hedgerows, but on the other hand the loss of ancient rights in the land was felt severely, more especially by the smaller tenants.

From the Court Rolls[3] of the 17th century it is clear that, as we should expect at that time, the tenants were copyholders, that is men who possessed land with certain rights and messuages, which were entered as theirs on the manor rolls. For these they paid a customary rent to the lord in lieu of services and the holdings descended to their children. As well as entries of property passing to heirs there are a large proportion of cases where it was alienated to others outside the family, and in addition to the annual chief rent a ' relief' (usually equal to a year's rent) had to be paid when a tenant died or when alienation took place.

Typical entries are these :

1637. ' The Jurie presente the death of Ed. Goosetree and doe finde Will. Goosetree to be heire unto the said Edward, and tenaunte to ye Lord and y^t releife of a yeares rent [is] due to ye Lord.'

1656. ' The Homage aforesaid doe present that William Whately, shoomaker, who late held of the Lord . . . freely in socage a messuage and backside in Henley in Arden w^thin the said manor by fealty, suite of Court[4] and the yearly rent of ijs. ijd. since the last Court dyed thereof seised whereby there hapned to the Lord for a relieffe the somme of ijs. ijd. and the said Homage does further find that Peter Whateley eldest sonne of the said William is his heire and the next tennant of the premises, wch said Peter

---

[1]Dugdale, p. 808.
[2]This included Great and Little Backfield.
[3]All the subsequent information is from these Rolls.
[4]Attendance at the lord's court.

being present in Court paid the aforesaid relieffe and did his fealty.'

1656. 'An alienation by Foulke Bellars, cousin and heir of Foulke Bellars, deceased, of a messuage, three cottages and a barn near the house of John Clarke, a close called Lettes croft, a close called Surrey croft, with certain parcels of arable land lying in the common fields of Henley and two closes called New Close and Wadd Close to Foulke Whateley, the lord of the manor claiming a relief of two shillings'.

Before a man was admitted tenant he did fealty, i.e., took an oath to be faithful to his lord. As late as 1840 several free tenants were presented by the jury for ' not coming into Court and doing fealty to the lady of the manor by being sworn to become true tenants.' Every occupier of uninclosed land in the common fields was allowed to pasture his cattle and sheep over the rest of the field after the corn was cut and carried and when it lay in fallow. In 1629 it was ordered that 'no sheep or other cattell or horses be kept in the back feildes before they be clearly rid of all corne and every on[e] making default [to pay] xs.' Six years later Richard Whately was amerced 40s. for ' putting sheep into the Little Bakfield before the field was clearly rid of corne.'

The cows would be driven daily by the herdsman to the green commons or, after the hay had been gathered, to the Lammas Meadow which was down by the Henley-Hunger Hill brook. It is said that formerly there were sheds at the top of the Milking Lane where the cows were milked.

We read that John Barrett was elected herd and common hayward in 1618 and his duties would be to look after the cattle and sheep, also the woods, the corn including the sowing, and the meadows. All straying cattle were driven to the pound and kept there until the owner paid a fine to redeem them. The wife of one Richard Key was amerced 12d. in 1607 for ' having forstalled the highwaye when the heyward was drivinge her husband's beastes to the pounde.' Two field reeves, to superintend the cultivation of the arable land, were appointed in 1656.

Sowing was by hand, scattering the seeds, reaping with the sickle, threshing with the flail and mowing with the scythe. The old farming methods which had been practised for so many centuries have now been superseded by machines. This is a great gain so far as production and hours of labour are concerned, yet for some reasons we may regret the passing of the old order.

THE COURT ROLLS, 1592-1819

THE Court Rolls of the manor[1] throw an interesting light upon the life of the town at the close of the 16th and during the succeeding century. The system of government was by Court Leet and Court Baron.[2] The Court Leet with View of Frankpledge[3] had jurisdiction over petty offences and civil affairs and inflicted fines[4] and punishments. The Court Baron dealt principally with the transfers of property from one tenant to another. From the year 1592 and probably earlier these courts at Henley were held together twice a year.

Besides the usual presentations for assaults, for breaking the assize of bread and ale,[5] for not clearing watercourses and others of a like nature there occur the following items :

The inhabitants were amerced 12d. in 1592 for not practising the use of bows and arrows at the butts. Although gunpowder was in use at this time the guns were cumbersome and not very satisfactory and archers were still a necessary part of an army. Every town and village in time of war was expected to provide a certain number of archers, gunmen, pikemen and billmen.

In 1596 the whole of the inhabitants of ' this liberty ' were presented for breaking the statute in not wearing woollen caps on Sunday and Holy Days. This vexatious enactment, which was intended to encourage the declining woollen industry, was resented by the ultra-Protestants as an interference with their liberty and as emphasising social distinctions. Shakespeare refers to them in *Love's Labour's Lost :* ' Better wits,' says Rosaline, ' have worn plain Statute Caps.'

It was ordained in 1595 that the price of ale and beer be $3\frac{1}{2}$d. the ' galland ' new and 4d. stale, the fine for exceeding these charges being 12d. In 1607 the alehouse keepers were ordered to make small drink for the poor at ' one penie a gallant ' only, for beer was then considered a necessity. Three innholders were fined 12d. in 1637 for not selling a quart of ale for 1d. according to the statute.

Efforts were made to keep Henley street clean, but nevertheless, as appears from the following extracts, its condition must have been anything but satisfactory.

Among the ' pains ' in 1592 it was ordered that no pig troughs should stand in the street, and in the following year that no

---

[1]Transcribed by F. C. Wellstood.

[2]As at Birmingham until it was incorporated in 1838.

[3]From at least as early as Norman times people were formed into groups of ten or twelve who under the control of a tithingman, or chief pledge, were mutually responsible for the good behaviour of one another. Not only was there actual view of the tithings but presentments were taken. By this time (1592) the frankpledge system had fallen into disuse.

[4]The fines and fees would go to the lord of the manor.

[5]A certain quality and maximum prices were fixed for these necessities.

' tymber, mucke or soyle' should lie in the street.   In 1641
' Wydowe Danfor' was fined 3s. 4d. for making a 'miskin' therein,
that is a dungheap.

Formerly a brook ran down the street from the mill at the north
end, passing along the Back Lane as far as the church, under
which it was carried by a watercourse provided with floodgates,[1]
whence it probably flowed into the brook at Littleworth.   For many
years it has been arched over.

On 8 October 1596 all the inhabitants were ordered to pay
' a penney a pece towardes scowringe the towne brooke.'   Upwards
of eighty years afterwards it was laid down that ' every inhabitant
of Henley who hath planted any trees in the streets there or who
claymeth any right or title to such trees shall cutt the same down . . .
the said trees beinge a nusance as well to the said streete as to the
brooke runninge through the same.'

Frequent references relate to acts of personal violence and the
inhabitants of those days appear to have been much more quarrel-
some than they are to-day.   Presentments of blood being drawn
' with a dagger,' ' with a stonne pott,' and with a ' bering cudggel,'
occur on 23 October 1616.   Seventeen years earlier it had been
ordered that all the householders should provide a club to be kept
in their houses to aid the constable or any other officer in case of
need.

For wilfully breaking the town stocks in the night time one
Richard Knight was, on 22 October 1622, fined 3s. 4d. and com-
mitted to sit in the stocks for one day.   These stocks stood near the
Market Cross.

It was ordered in 1607 that no one shall sell corn in the market
before the market bell had rung.   This was to prevent forestalling,
that is, buying up the whole stock of goods before the market opened,
to sell again at higher prices.   And in 1619 that the ' forren bakers
shall bring theire bread to the market crosse ther to be tried and
wayed[2] before they put the same to sale.'   In those days all persons
not resident in Henley would be regarded as foreigners even if they
lived only just outside the boundaries of the manor.

An interesting reference occurs to one of Shakespeare's con-
temporaries, Francis Collins, the lawyer and Town Clerk of Stratford,
who drafted and witnessed the poet's will.   Francis alienated a tenement with a garden and orchard in Henley on 23 October 1616 (the
year of Shakespeare's death), to Humphrey Harrison and another.

The penalty for those prosecuted as common scolds was harsh
and the references to them are somewhat frequent.   On 21 October
1618, Elizabeth Smith, the wife of Thomas Smith, cutler, was

---

[1] Court Rolls, 1673.

[2] The High Bailiff's Book in 1801 mentions ' One Standard Bushel Brass
Scales ' as then belonging to the town.   In the Quarter Sessions Records of 1835
there is a record of the appointment of Wm. Cooper, of Henley, Road Surveyor,
as Inspector of Weights and Measures for the Hundred of Barlichway.

ordered to be ducked in the cucking stool, the then usual method of punishment.

Two years later Eleanor Powell was presented for ' that she is a scold and liveth unquietly. Judgment that she shall be cooked.' In 1635 no less than eleven married women were presented for common scolds, everyone to pay 3s. 4d. or be ' cooked in the cookestoole.'

These duckings would take place in the brook, the victims being exposed to the scorn and derision of the people.

Although Henley was a seigniorial borough with market and fair it was never an incorporated town and it occupied a small portion of land within the lordship of the same name, the remainder of the land being known as the ' foreign.' As we have seen, there were sixty-nine burgesses in 1296 paying money rents to the lord instead of doing villein services of a servile nature and we may assume that this process of commuting their services for money payments had been going on for a long time before. We can picture a small rent-paying community concerned more with industry than with land and having special privileges of trading within the borough, so that the chief profits of the lord would come from the markets and fairs and the rents of the tenants.

The charter of 1449 already quoted in detail confirmed the ancient liberties and franchises and conferred additional privileges upon the lord and his tenants, and it was under this charter that the town continued to prosper.

The officers of the Court as given in 1656 were a high bailiff, a low bailiff and thirdborough, a constable, two aletasters, two chamberlains, two brooklookers, two leathersealers, two field reeves and two affeerers. Of these the high bailiff was, of course, the chief official, who among other duties collected the rents, revenues and other profits of the lord, supervised the weekly markets and the fairs, and was responsible for the correctness of the weights and measures used in the town ; the low bailiff was his assistant and also acted as thirdborough, or under-constable, in addition he probably appointed leet juries. The duties of the aletasters were to see that the brewers brewed wholesome ale of the right strength and purity, that they did not charge excessively for it nor use false measures. The brooklookers were responsible for seeing that the river Alne and other water courses were kept free of refuse, and for preventing, amongst other things, the laying of hemp in the river, a common offence in those days. Leathersealers tested the leather to see that the quality was up to standard and as a mark of approval impressed a seal upon it.

Lastly the affeerers were sworn to fix the amount of the amercement or fine at what seemed a reasonable amount for the particular offence.

It appears from among the ' pains ' in 1593 that all who had served the office of high bailiff and constable were under an obligation to meet at the Town Hall on Wednesday after Michaelmas, annually, to choose the officers for the ensuing year. All these officers had no doubt remained the same since the charter of 1449 and had probably existed in a somewhat similar form for two or three centuries before. At first the bailiffs were simply the lord's officials and although they continued to remain under the lord, at any rate nominally, as time went on and freedom was gradually gained they came more and more to represent the whole body of the inhabitants.

Those who were elected bailiff and refused to serve were fined and John Wheatley, who was presented for that reason in 1593, had to pay 3s. 4d.

Among the lists of ' Paines and orders ' for 1619 occurs this amusing warning : that no one shall ' abuse Mr. Baylife in calling him knave or giving him any other unmanerly wordes,' the fine for so doing being 40s.

All who had been bailiffs or constables had to attend upon the bailiff on fair days to make the King's proclamation or in default pay a fine of 3s. 4d. This would be done at the market cross and the last time it took place was in 1840, when Thomas Wowen Jones[1] was high bailiff.

It is interesting to record that the lords here continued to hold their courts, though sometimes at long intervals, until the present time[2] but the duties of the several officials are now merely nominal except those of the high bailiff, who takes the lead in all public matters in the town. He also receives and distributes the rents of the various charities and looks after the expenses of the repairs to the property belonging thereto.

The present office holders are a high bailiff, low bailiff, constable, aletaster, butter-weigher, two brooklookers, two affeerors, a mace-bearer, and a town-crier.

The procedure for electing the Court Leet is as follows : The high bailiff calls a meeting of the townspeople, who nominate the high bailiff, whose name is then submitted to the lord of the manor and if approved he is appointed to the office. The other officers are appointed by the town alone.

A list of the high bailiffs from 1477 down to the late Dr. William Ernest Nelson appears in Mr. F. C. Wellstood's book.[3] Since then Mr. W. T. Taylor, J.P. (1922-26), Mr. Harry Hawkes, J.P. (1926-30) and Dr. Willoughby Agar, who was elected in 1930, have severally held the office.

The present low bailiff is Mr. N. Welch, who succeeded, in 1944, Mr. R. L. Newcombe, J.P. (sometime chairman of Stratford-on-Avon Rural District Council) ; Mr. G. F. Lodder has been steward of the manor for many years.

Since the local government reforms of last century the powers

[1]Surgeon, of The Turrets, Henley.
[2]Even since the recent extinction of such courts.
[3]*Records of the Manor of Henley-in-Arden.*

and duties of the Court Leet have passed to a number of administrative and other bodies too well known to mention here.

As a precaution against the accident of fire all those inhabitants holding real property of the yearly value of £4 or personal estate of the value of not less than £50 were, in 1675, ordered to provide a substantial leather bucket for quenching the same.

It appears that the old prison had gone to decay and had been taken down so that in 1799 there was no ' prison or lock-up house for securing felons vagrants and disorderly persons.' The jury undertook to arrange that one should be erected and stated that there was a convenient building belonging to the lords of the manor in the possession of Wm. Baker, which might be converted into a prison at small expense.

In 1819 it is presented that ' there is no common pound [1] within this manor and that the lord of the said manor ought to set up a proper pound and support the same.'

Evidently nothing was done, however, for we find the inhabitants were indicted at Quarter Sessions six years later for not setting up a common pound and a pair of stocks.

Formerly there was a pinfold for impounding cattle on the Ullenhall Road west of the railway arch. It stood opposite the stepping stones used years ago by people taking the track over the brook southwards to join a path which connected Arden House Lane with the Wootton to Ullenhall Road opposite Mays Hill Farm.

HIGH BAILIFF'S CHAIN OF OFFICE.

This chain was presented by Mr. W. J. Fieldhouse (lord of the manor) in 1919 in commemoration of peace to the then high bailiff, Dr. W. E. Nelson, for himself and his successors in the bailiwick. It is composed of eight shields emblazoned with the arms of eight principal lords of the manor from the de Montforts, in Norman days, to Mr. Fieldhouse, together with the badge of the Beauchamps, the bear and ragged staff, [2] and nine smaller shields engraved with the names of prominent high bailiffs beginning with Edward Brereton in 1485 and ending with Dr. Nelson. The links are in the form of a red rose and Stafford knot alternately. The former was the badge of Henry VI who granted the Henley Charter. The de Beauchamps held the manor by the presentation of a red rose and it is the symbol of St. John the Baptist, patron saint of the church and joint patron of the gild. The latter, the Stafford knot, is the badge of the de Staffords, formerly lords of Wootton and overlords of Henley. The pendant bears the badge granted to Mr. Fieldhouse for the use of the manor and consists of a red rose and sprig of mulberry, the stems passed through a coronet on the rim of which are the red rose and cross of St. John alternately. Behind this, in saltire, are represented the town mace and the gild master's staff.

[1] Wm. Baldwin, lord of the manor, was indicted in 1649 for not repairing the common pound—*Warw. Co. Rec.*, vi, 89.

[2] See p. 96.

THE MANOR LORDS

HENLEY does not occur in Domesday, its land being involved with Wootton, neither is Beaudesert mentioned in that survey, but it seems to have been included in Preston Bagot. The Saxon Britnod's five hides therein recorded[1] appear without doubt to have been the present day Beaudesert.[2] Britnod's portion passed from the Count of Meulan to Henry de Newburgh, the first Earl of Warwick of the Norman line, who granted it to his great-nephew Thurstan,[3] the first de Montfort to settle at Beaudesert, where he built a strong castle (see p. 112) which continued the chief seat of his descendants for several generations. During the lawless reign of Stephen, in the spring of 1141, the Empress Matilda granted to Thurstan a weekly market on Sundays at Beaudesert[4] (see p. 000). Some time before this he had succeeded to Preston, Co. Rutland, on the death of his eldest brother Robert.[5] In 1166 we find he was holding $10\frac{1}{4}$ knights' fees, including Beaudesert, of the Earl of Warwick, $\frac{1}{4}$ of a knight's fee of Robert de Stafford in Henley-in-Arden, and $3\frac{3}{4}$ of Roger de Mowbray in Yorkshire.[6] He attested several charters of Roger and one of William, Earls of Warwick, to the college of Warwick, his name generally following immediately after those of the Earl's own family. He also attested a grant to Margaret, Countess of Warwick, to the Canons of Kenilworth.

Though he appears to have been very ready to witness the signatures of others he seems to have been less free with his own when it meant parting with any property, and at first he refused to confirm the grant of ' a moiety of the vill and of the church of Wing, Co. Rutland, and the mill there,' which he and his late brother, Robert, had made to Thorney Abbey. After being threatened by King Stephen, however, he, ' for the health of his soul, with the souls of his wife and sons, and especially for the soul of his brother Robert, and all his ancestors and successors,' did what he was commanded and the abbey continued to enjoy these possessions.

His wife was Juliana, daughter and co-heir of Geoffrey Murdac, and no mention of his name occurs after 1170.

Thurstan was succeeded by his son Henry[7] who with Alice de Harecourt, widow of his brother Robert, granted to Walter, son of Thurstan de Cherlecote (alias Montfort), the village of

---

[1] *V.C.H. Warw.*, i, 317.

[2] *Records of Beaudesert*, pp. x-xi, and *V.C.H. Warw.*, i, 313, in a note to ' Donnelie.' Beaudesert is a Norman-French name meaning the beautiful waste.

[3] *Red Bk. of Exch.*, 325.

[4] Dugdale, p. 789, citing a charter in possession of Sir Simon Archer.

[5] For this and some of the other information about the De Montforts the writer is indebted to Cockayne's *Complete Peerage*.

[6] *Red Bk. of Exch.*, pp. 264, 268, 324, 325, 420. A knight's fee was land given on condition of military service, that of a fully armed horseman, or knight, and the estate which had to provide one such knight was called a ' knight's fee.'

[7] Round, *Cal. Doc. France*, p. 138.

Charlecote which grant was confirmed by Richard I and John. He gave land in Beaudesert to Reinbald de Charlecote,[1] the mill at Henley to the monks of Conches,[2] the parent house of the Priory of Wootton Wawen, and land and the mill at Beaudesert to his son Thurstan.[3]

He also granted the right of fishing in the river Avon at Hillborough, near Bidford, to the monks of Bordesley.[4]

Thurstan de Montfort, his son and heir, was a minor when he succeeded his father in or before 1199.[5] In 1205 King John received his homage and gave him his land on the condition that he demised it for two years to William de Cantilupe. In the summer of 1206 he was abroad in the King's service and four years later he was serving his sovereign in Ireland. He was with the King in Poitou in 1214 and was excused scutage[6] because he fought there himself, and he bore for his arms : *Bendy of six or and azure.* King John returned defeated from the war in Poitou and in the following year Thurstan appears to have joined against him in the rebellion which resulted in the King being forced to sign the Great Charter. To the nuns of Pinley he gave ' the tenth part of the provision in victuall for his household, viz., bread, beer, flesh, fish, and other things pertaining to his kitchen.'[7] He died before 21 November 1216 and was succeeded by his son Peter, a minor whose wardship and marriage were granted to William de Cantilupe.[8] The influence of his guardian probably led to his association later on with the Barons in their movement against the King. This boy was destined to become the most powerful of all the de Montforts of Beaudesert, and Dugdale states that in him the family reached the meridian of its glory. During his minority he had a grant of a market and fair at Henley (see page 2).[9] In 1236 he went on a pilgrimage to Santiago in Spain (the traditional burial place of St. James) with William de Cantilupe, his lord. He was with Henry III in the unsuccessful expedition to Poitou in 1242. For attending a prohibited tournament at Cambridge his lands were taken by the King but were restored to him 1245. It was under the cloak of these meetings that the Barons plotted their disloyal practices.

In the autumn of 1248 he went abroad with Simon de Montfort, who had been appointed Seneschal of Gascony. Later in the same year he appears to have accompanied Prince Edward to Spain for his marriage with Eleanor of Castile and was one of the sureties

<hr>

[1]Harl. MS., 506 f. 122.
[2]Round, *Cal. Doc. France*, p. 138.
[3]Harl. MS., 506 f. 122.
[4]Dugdale, p. 800.
[5]*Curia Regis R.*, i, 70.
[6]Scutage : A money payment in place of knight's service.
[7]Dugdale, p. 800.
[8]*Rot. Lit. Claus.* (Rec. Com.) 278, 298. His brother Walter was Bishop of Worcester, 1237-66.
[9]*Rot. Lit. Claus.*, p. 463 ; *Cal. Chart. R.*, 1226-57, p. 5.

for the King's debts in Bordeaux. Peter took an active part in Henry III's wars with France and was also ambassador to that country. In 1257 he was appointed to guard the Welsh Marches in Montgomery and to keep the counties of Salop and Stafford with the castles of Shrewsbury and Bridgnorth, and played a conspicuous part then and later in defending the borders against Llewellyn.

He was one of the twelve magnates chosen by the Barons to represent them on the Council of Twenty-four which formulated the Provisions of Oxford in 1258, when a council was set up for the better government of the kingdom, more especially to enforce the Great Charter. When the King, in 1261, made known the Pope's absolution regarding his oath to keep these Provisions, Peter was elected by the Barons one of the three arbitrators to negotiate with him on this and other affairs. He was now beginning to side definitely with the Baronial party and in 1262 the sheriff of Warwickshire was ordered to prevent him fortifying his castle of Beaudesert.[1] In 1263, during the Barons' activities in the west of England, he is named among those who took the city of Worcester, when they are said to have plundered all they could find outside the church, including the Jewish quarter. At Northampton, where the Barons in 1264 rose in arms against the King, Peter and his sons Peter and Robert were taken prisoner and confined in Windsor Castle. After the Barons' victory at Lewes on 14 May 1264 Peter and his sons were set free and Peter was elected one of the Council of Nine who had the whole power of government in their hands. Dugdale says of these nine that 'there was a more especial power given to our Peter than to any of the rest, that is to say that whatsoever he should swear to do the King must be bound by it.' He accompanied Simon de Montfort into Wales, being joint keeper of the royal seal with which Simon sealed a pact with Prince Edward. Not long afterwards the Prince, who had been confined in Hereford Castle, escaped, raised a powerful army and on 4 August 1265 came upon the Barons at Evesham ' like terrible thunder.' Earl Simon, realising the strength of the royal forces against him and recognising in the orderly advance of his enemies the proof of his own training, cried, ' Let us commend our souls to God for our bodies are the foes.' In the fearful slaughter which followed, Simon and our Peter, who was fighting under him, were slain.

During his lifetime he received many marks of favour from Henry III and may be called a rebel for the part he took on more than one occasion against his sovereign, but it may be pleaded that it was in the cause of freedom against the arrogant pretensions of the King. Dugdale, however, describes him as a man ' puft up with blind ambition which prompted him to a confederacy with the rebellious barons of that age.'

Some other local-affairs in which he was concerned are these :

[1]Close, R., 46, Hen. III, m. 10d., 22 June, 1462.

He granted to the monks of Bordesley common of pasture within his lordship of Edstone for ' xv beasts, two horses for draught and cc sheep according to the large hundred.'[1] In 34 Henry III he was granted a charter of free warren, or full rights to kill the ground and small game as distinct from the red deer, on his demesne lands at Beaudesert, Henley and other places.[2] For the health of his soul and that of Alice[3] his wife, and also for the souls of his father and mother and ancestors whose bodies lay buried in the Priory of Studley, he gave to that house all his demesne lands called the Vineyard situated within his lordship of Studley.[4]

Six months after his death, namely on 11 February 1266, a commission (in which he is described as the King's enemy) was directed to the Abbot of Bordesley and the Prior of Studley to make an extent of his Warwickshire manors of Beaudesert, Whitchurch, Wellesbourne and Edstone.[5]

His eldest son and heir, Peter (ii), was wounded and taken prisoner at the Battle of Evesham and placed in the custody of Thomas de Clare, to whom his forfeited lands were granted ; but having ' appeased the King's indignation and rancour of mind,' he was, on 28 June 1267, pardoned and his inheritance restored to him.[6]

Following his father's example he went on a pilgrimage to Santiago in 1272 and again in 1275. On 10 June 1272 he received confirmation of the additional manor of Ilmington from John, lord of Harcourt, knt,[7] and the same year he was appointed sheriff. He was in high favour with Edward I and in November 1276 was one of the council held at Westminster which was concerned with Llewelyn and Welsh affairs. In April 1282 he was summoned to serve in person with the King in the invasion of Wales, which resulted in the defeat and death of Llewelyn.   In 1284 he was allowed right of gallows, assize of bread and ale, market and free warren within his manor of Henley, all of which had been held by his ancestors (see p. ooo). He married about 1260 Maud, daughter and heir of Matthew de la Warre, and died before 4 March 1286-7.[8]

The manors and estates then descended to his son John,[9] whose marriage had been granted to Queen Eleanor in 1280. Of him we read that in April 1294 he was going overseas by the King's command with Eleanor the King's daughter, and in August of

[1]Dugdale, p. 828
[2]Ibid., p. 800.
[3]i.e., Alice, daughter of Henry de Audley.
[4]Cotton Ch. xi, 28.
[5]Cal. Pat. R., 1258-66, p. 658.
[6]Ibid., 1266-72, p. 148.
[7]Cal. Chart. R., 1257-1300, p. 182.
[8]Cal. Fine R., i, 235. This Peter changed his arms from bendy of six to bendy of ten.
[9]Feet of F. Div. Co. Hil, 14 Edw. I.

the same year he with his brother William was in the Earl of Lincoln's company in Gascony.   He was summoned to Parliament by writ on 24 June 1295 by which he is held to have become Lord Montfort of Beaudesert.   He married between 1286 and 1289 Alice, daughter of William de la Planche and died before 11 May 1296.   His son John, second Lord Montfort aged five, at his father's death, is named as the heir to the castle of Beaudesert, and the borough of Henley held of Edmund, Baron Stafford.[1] On 26 July 1313 he was summoned to Parliament.   He was one of the knights concerned in the execution of Piers Gaveston, the hated favourite of Edward II, on Blacklow Hill, but was pardoned for this offence and for being an adherent of Thomas, Earl of Lancaster, on 16 October 1313.   He died fighting for the King against the Scots at Bannockburn on 24 June 1314, when the English army was defeated, and being unmarried most of his manors, including Beaudesert and Henley passed, to his brother Peter (iii)[2], third Lord Montfort.   Having entered the church as a secular priest he was instituted to the rectory of Ilmington on 14 June 1312, being described as ' clerk '[3] but on succeeding his brother he became a knight.   He stood loyal to Edward II when Thomas, Earl of Lancaster, rebelled against him, and on 30 November 1321 was ordered to assemble horse and foot in Warwickshire to resist the insurgents,[4]   Early next year he was guarding the Welsh Marches and was given the joint custody of the City of Worcester.   The King, who was at Henley from 4 to 10 January 1324,[5] probably stayed with him at Beaudesert Castle.   During the minority of the Earl of Warwick's heir he had the custody of Warwick Castle in 1326.   He was summoned for military service against the Scots in 1327 having already seen service there in 1316 ; he also served in Gascony and Flanders.   Under Edward III he was summoned to Parliament from 1336 to 1349.

In respect of his lands in Warwickshire and five other counties he was assessed to contribute twelve men-at-arms for the war of 1346 in France,[6] and was one of the commissioners of the county for arraying 160 archers at this time who helped to win the decisive victory over the French at Crecy.   Nine years later he was one of those commissioned to put into operation the Statute of Labourers which sought to check the rise in wages following the Black Death.

Peter was patron of the living of Preston Bagot[7] and in the

---

[1]John held Beaudesert with a hide of land in Brailes by one knight's fee of Sir Wm. de Beauchamp ; Henley by service of 3s. or a pair of scarlet hose, and Whitley by one knight's fee, both of Edmund de Stafford. *Cal. Inq. p. m.* III No. 364.

[2]Dugdale, p. 803.

[3]Dugdale Society, ix, 154.

[4]*Cal. Pat. R.*, 1321-24, p. 39.

[5]Pat. Rolls and Close Rolls, 4-10 Jan., 1324.

[6]The Fine Rolls tell us, however, that he was discharged of seven of them and paid 50 marks for the remaining five.

[7]Dugdale, p. 796.

Norman Church there he founded a chantry in 20 Edward II for a priest to celebrate Mass daily at the altar of Our Lady, for the health of his soul, and the souls of his ancestors and successors.[1]

In his youth he had two illegitimate sons by Laura, daughter of Richard Astley of Ullenhall. The elder one, John, married Joan, daughter of Sir John de Clinton, lord of Coleshill, and founded the family of the de Montforts of that place. The younger son, Richard, married Rose, daughter of Hugh de Brandestone, and with his wife became possessed of half the manor of Lapworth.[2] Peter died before 24 January 1369-70 on which day his will was proved.[3] In it he bequeathed his soul to Almighty God and the Virgin Mary and his body to be buried in the Church of the Friar Preachers at Warwick, to which he left £10 for the Friars to pray for his soul. To the nuns of Pinley he left 10 marks for the same purpose, and to Lora de Astley, ' his old paramour ' as Dugdale calls her, then a nun there, £5. By his wife Margaret, daughter of Lord Furnival, he had one son named Guy, married to Margaret, daughter of Thomas de Beauchamp, Earl of Warwick, upon whom, in 1349, the manor and castle of Beaudesert and the manor of Henley were settled in tail male with contingent reversion to the Earl of Warwick.[4] Guy,[5] having died in 1361, leaving no issue, the manors passed by reversion at his father's death about eight years later to Thomas de Beauchamp, Earl of Warwick, who was one of the principal commanders under the Black Prince at Crecy in 1346, where the English bowmen gained such a notable victory over the chivalry of France ; and at the victorious battle of Poitiers, ten years later, when as Dugdale says ' he fought so long and so stoutly that his hand was galled with the exercise of his sword and pole-axe.' He afterwards fought under the banner of the Cross and won fresh laurels in the Holy Land. The Earl, who was one of the original Knights of the Garter, died of the plague at Calais on 13 November 1369, and was succeeded by his son Thomas,[6] Earl of Warwick, K.G. This nobleman was appointed by Parliament governor of the young King Richard II, then aged about twelve, but not long afterwards we find the King taking others into favour against the Earl. Whereupon the latter took up arms with Thomas Duke of Gloucester and forced King Richard to call a Parliament. For this action he was several years afterwards seized at a feast given by the King, tried and condemned to death. The sentence was commuted to banishment to the Isle of Man but later he was taken

[1]Dugdale, p. 798.
[2]Ibid, pp. 1009 and 787.
[3]P.C.C. Whitleseye, 111.
[4]Feet of F. Div. Co. East, 23 Edw. III.
[5]Guy's widow, Margaret, became a professed nun. *Cal. of Inq.*, xii, 309, 20 Nov., 1369. The Earl of Warwick was then overlord of Beaudesert and the Earl of Stafford overlord of Henley.
[6]*Cal. Inq. p. m.*, xii, p. 309.

to the Tower and imprisoned there until the accession of Henry IV, when he was reinstated in all his honours and possessions.[1]

In 1376 he granted the manors to his brother Sir William de Beauchamp for life at the rent of a red rose.[2] On the death of his cousin, John Hastings, Earl of Pembroke and Lord Bergavenny, who was slain in a tournament in 1390, Sir William succeeded, by reversion, to the estates and Barony of Bergavenny, with the arms of Hastings. These arms *or a maunch gules* were in Dugdale's day in one of the north windows of the chancel at Wootton Wawen. In 1392 he was summoned to Parliament as a baron and during the first year of the reign of Henry IV was created a Knight of the Garter. He died on the 8 May 1411 and was buried in the Black Friars, at Hereford.[3]

The manors were then divided between William Boteler of Sudeley and Baldwin Freville,[4] son of Sir Baldwin Freville, knt.,[5] of Tamworth Castle, who were descended respectively from Maud and Elizabeth, sisters of the last Peter de Montfort. The Boteler inheritance consisted of the castle of Beaudesert and the park in which it stood and part of the manor of Beaudesert, together with the Borough of Henley.[6] Thereafter it was known as the manor of HENLEY-BEAUDESERT. The remainder of Beaudesert passed to the Frevilles[7] and will be referred to later.

William Boteler's holding came to his brother Sir Ralph Boteler in 1442-43 on the death of his mother Alice, widow of Sir Thomas Boteler[8] who had died in 1398.

Sir Ralph, on 10 September 1441, being then Chamberlain of the Household, was created by letters patent Baron Sudeley of Co. Gloucester, with the fee of 200 marks annually from the county of Lincoln, for the better support of his dignity. About the same year he was made a Knight of the Garter. He became Treasurer of the Exchequer in 1443, Lord High Treasurer from 1444 to 1447 and Joint Governor of Calais from 1450 to 1455.

This lord was a staunch adherent of the House of Lancaster and took an eminent part in the stirring events of the reigns of Henry V and VI. Besides serving the King with distinction in the French wars he was one of the firmest supporters of the Lancastrian cause at home. He fought for Henry VI in the first battle of the Wars of the Roses, when, at St. Albans in 1455, the King was

[1]The information about this lord and his father is from Dugdale, and Burke, *Dormant and Extinct Peerages*, 1866.

[2]Cott. Ch. xi, 70.

[3]Joseph Edmondson, *Family of Grevile*, 1766, p. 39.

[4]His father, Sir Baldwin Freville, held a knight's fee in Henley of the Earl of Warwick in 1372 : *Chan. Inq. p.m.*, 46, Edw. III (1st nos.), 62.

[5]*Chan. Inq. p.m.*, 13, Hen. IV, No. 38 ; B.M. Cott. Ch. xxiii, 12.

[6]Dugdale, p. 804.

[7]Ibid.

[8]*Cal. Fine. R.*, 1437-45, p. 254. At the same time Sir Ralph inherited lands in Sussex, Gloucestershire and the adjacent marches of Wales. See also *Cal. Close R.*, Hen. V, I, 136.

defeated and taken prisoner by the Duke of York. After the accession of the Duke of York as Edward IV, Lord Sudeley excused himself from attending Parliament by reason of his advanced age, and had letters patent of exemption from the duty during life, but later he was taken to the Tower and kept there until he agreed to alienate his castle of Sudeley with all its lands to the King. As he was departing from his seat he cast a lingering look back and exclaimed : ' Sudeley Castle, thou art the traitor, not I.' This castle is said to have been rebuilt out of the spoils he had obtained from the wars in France. In the civil war it was ordered to be ' slighted ' and lay desolate for two centuries but was then again rebuilt. Fuller thus quaintly speaks of it in the days of its magnificence, ' It was of subjects' castles the most handsome habitation and of subjects' habitations the strongest castle.'[1]

So far as his local activities were concerned by far the most important to Henley were his obtaining a Charter from Henry VI in 1449 and his refounding of the Gild (see p. 67). He died without issue on 2 May 1473,[2] when the Barony by patent became extinct and he was succeeded by his nephews Sir John Norbury and William Belknap,[3] who were forced to sell the manor to Edward IV in 1477.[4] From the Patent Rolls it appears to have remained with the Crown[5] until Edward VI granted it in 1547 to Sir John Dudley,[6] who was born in 1502. In the thirty-first year of the reign of Henry VIII he was appointed Master of the Horse to Anne of Cleves. The following year he was one of the principal challengers at the jousts at Westminster, where he appeared in great magnificence, his horse being accoutred with white velvet, but on this occasion he was unhorsed. Upon the accession of Edward VI he was created Earl of Warwick, and in 1551 Duke of Northumberland. His influence over his sovereign was very great and he became the most powerful man in England. After the death of the young King he endeavoured by force of arms to put Lady Jane Grey (the wife of his son, Lord Guilford Dudley) upon the throne. For this he was brought to the block on Tower Hill in 1553 and after uttering the words, ' I have deserved a thousand deaths,' his head was struck off, and all his estates were forfeited.[7]

Sir Ambrose Dudley, Earl of Warwick, K.G., known as ' the good Earl of Warwick,' was the eldest surviving son of the last

[1]*G.E.C. Complete Peerage*, vii, 296-7 ; Burke, *Dormant and Extinct Peerages*, 1866 ; Dent, *Annals of Winchcombe and Sudeley*, 1877.

[2]His arms were 1st and 4th gu. a fess chequy arg. and sa. between six cross-crosslets or (Boteler) 2nd and 3rd or two bendlets gu. (Sudeley).

[3]Inq. p.m., 13, Edw. IV, No. 58.

[4]Close R. 17, Edw. IV, M.18 ; Add Ch. 5836.

[5]Various appointments to officers in connection with the manor.

[6]*Cal. Pat. R.*, Edw. VI, i. 171, where the manor is stated to be ' parcel of the possessions of Richard, Earl of Warwick [i.e., the Kingmaker] attainted.' This seems to show that the Warwick overlordship continued throughout the Middle Ages.

[7]F. L. Colvile, *Worthies of Warwickshire.*

mentioned lord. Having been involved with his family on behalf of Lady Jane Grey he was sentenced to death but obtained a pardon. In 1561 he was created Earl of Warwick by Queen Elizabeth, who granted to him the manor of Henley-Beaudesert in 1562 [1] and restored to him other lordships of which his father had been deprived. During the Queen's eventful reign he held many high offices of state, but was never concerned in any of the intrigues of that time. He is said to have been a person of faultless character and great sweetness of temper, so that he was much beloved.

He died without issue in 1590 and was buried in the Beauchamp Chapel in St. Mary's, Warwick. [2] His Renaissance tomb of alabaster shows the effigy of the Earl in ornamental armour reclining on a rush mat, one end of which is rolled up to form a pillow. On his left leg is the Garter, and he wears the mantle and insignia of that exalted order. At his feet is a muzzled bear, and on his head is a coronet of iron, gilded. The effigy rests on a tomb-chest of alabaster and black marble. [3]

Two years after his death the Queen leased the manor to William Harmon. [4] From 1592 to 1609 Thomas Spencer is named as lord, being farmer under the Crown. [5] In 1611 Anne of Denmark, Queen of James I, was holding it as her jointure. [6] From 1614 to 1629 William White of Shipston on Stour, [7] and from 1637 to 1650 William Baldwin [8] are stated to be lords. The last named in the first year of the Commonwealth is found to be holding the manor with a park at a yearly rent of £28 2s. 3½d. [9] In 1656 Richard Walker was farmer of the manor. [0]

Dugdale says ' in our time ' the site of Beaudesert Castle and the Park wherein it stood were purchased by ' Alderman Cawdwell, a Londoner,' that is Sir John Cordell of St. Lawrence, Jewry, London, who died 5 March 1649. [11] He was succeeded by his son Sir Robert Cordell, bart., of Melford, Co. Suffolk, Sheriff of Suffolk and M.P. for Sudbury, who with his wife Margaret was holding the manor in 1669. [12]

Sir Robert and his wife sold it in 1672 to Thomas Archer of Umberslade, in the adjoining parish of Tanworth, by the name of the manor of ' Henley in Arden-Beaudesert.' [13] Some time between

[1] Pat. R. 4, Eliz., Pt. 4.
[2] *Worthies of Warwickshire.*
[3] P. B. Chatwin, *Birm. Archæol. Soc. Trans.*, lvii, 110.
[4] Pat. R. 33, Eliz , Pt. 2.
[5] F. C. Wellstood, *Records of the Manor of Henley-in-Arden* (Court Rolls, Sub Annis).
[6] Pat. R. 9 Jas. I, Pt. 9.
[7] Wellstood, op. cit.
[8] Ibid.
[9] Parl. Surveys Warws., No. 13, P.R.O.
[10] Wellstood, op. cit.
[11] G.E.C. *Complete Peerage*, III, 52.
[12] Ibid., and Feet of F. Div. Co. Trin, 21 Chas. II.
[13] Feet of F. Mich, 24 Chas. II ; Recov. R. Mich. 24, Chas. II, No. 163.

this date and 1734[1] the Archers sold the portion of Beaudesert and site of the castle which had been joined to Henley manor to the Smiths of Wootton Wawen, who then became lords of the whole of Beaudesert, as will be seen later.

The other portion of the manor of Beaudesert which was not united with Henley passed from Baldwin Freville[2] at his death in 1418 through his sister and co-heir Joyce, the wife of Roger Aston, to their son Robert Aston[3] of Parkhall and Haywood, who was aged four in 1419. He was afterwards knighted and by his wife Isabel, daughter of Sir William Brereton of Brereton, Co. Stafford, had a son, Sir John Aston, who in 16 Edward IV [1476-77] was High Sheriff of Stafford. Sir John married Elizabeth, daughter of Sir John Delves of Doddington, Co. Chester, and dying in 1483-4 was succeeded by his son, Sir John Aston, K.B., of Tixall, Co. Stafford, a soldier of eminence in the reigns of the first two Tudor sovereigns. He was with Henry VIII in the French War of 1513 and was made a banneret[4] for his valorous conduct at the Battle of the Spurs.

He also greatly distinguished himself at the sieges of Terouenne and Tournay. Sir John, who was High Sheriff of the counties of Warwick, Stafford and Leicester, married Joan, only child of Sir William Littleton of Frankley, Co. Worcester.[5]

At his death in 1523 he is stated to be holding this manor of the Marquis of Dorset as of his manor of Wootton.[6] His son, Edward, then aged 30, was his heir and later was made a knight. This Sir Edward Aston built a stately mansion at Tixall, the ruins of which are still standing. By his wife, Joan, daughter of Sir Thomas Bowles, one of the Barons of the Exchequer, he had a son, Sir Walter Aston of Tixall, who succeeded him and who married Elizabeth, daughter of Sir James Leveson of Lilleshall. Dying in 1589 he was followed by his son Sir Edward Aston of Tixall, then aged 38,[7] who is said to have possessed estates of the value of £10,000 a year in the counties of Warwick, Stafford, Derby and Leicester. His wife was Anne, only daughter of Sir Thomas Lucy of Charlecote.[8] Sir Edward was the last of the Astons[9] to

---

[1]Thomas Archer (afterwards 1st Baron Archer) was then holding the manor of Henley without any portion of Beaudesert Manor. [Gamekeepers' Deputations, Shire Hall, Warwick.]

[2]The arms of Freville are : *or a cross patonce gu.*

[3]Chan. Inq. p.m., 6 Hen. V, No. 47. The manor had first been divided between Baldwin's three sisters as in 1435 one third was settled on Sir Hugh Willoughby and Margaret his wife (the second sister) : Feet of F. Div. Co. Trin. 13, Hen. VI.

[4]A knight who for some brave deed was entitled to bear a banner instead of a pennon.

[5]Information about the Astons where not otherwise stated is from Burke, *Dormant and Extinct Peerages*, pp. 13 and 14, and Clifford, *Parish of Tixall*, 1817.

[6]Chan. Inq. p.m. (Ser. 2), xl, 43.   [7]Chan. Inq. p.m. (Ser. 2), ccxxii, 43.

[8]Before whom Shakespeare is said, without foundation, to have been brought for deer stealing.

[9]The arms of Aston are : Arg. a fess and three lozenges in chief sa. Information about this family, where not otherwise stated, is from Burke, *Dormant and Extinct Peerages*, 1866, pp. 13 and 14, and Clifford, *Parish of Tixall*, 1817.

hold this manor, which he sold to Francis Smith of Wootton Wawen in 1594.[1] It descended with the manor of Wootton and on 14 April 1880 was, with the other portion of Beaudesert already referred to, sold by Sir Charles Frederick Smythe, Bart., to Thomas Cattell, the father of Mr. Samuel K. Cattell of Packwood, who now holds it.

Incidentally there is in the Quarter Sessions records for 1810[2] an interesting reference to the grandfather and predecessor of this last of the Smythes to hold Beaudesert, where it states that Lieut. John Trapp, 2nd Foot, is ' bound by recognisance to appear to answer what shall be objected to him by Sir Edward Smythe for endeavouring to provoke him to a duel.'

The manor of Henley as shown above descended with the other portion of Beaudesert and the castle until the time of the lordship of the Archers, an ancient and honourable family, who had been settled at Umberslade from the reign of Henry II. As already mentioned it was purchased by Thomas Archer, the son of Sir Simon Archer, the antiquary and friend of Dugdale, in 1672.[3] Thomas served as a colonel in Cromwell's army at the beginning of the Civil War and raised a troop of horse at his own expense, but as soon as he discovered the designs of the Parliamentarians he threw up his commission and went abroad. On the restoration of the monarchy he returned to England and afterwards represented Warwick in Parliament. He was buried at Tanworth on 24 October 1685, being succeeded by his son Andrew,[4] who was M.P. for the County of Warwick and married Elizabeth, daughter of Sir Samuel Dashwood, sometime Lord Mayor of London. Andrew rebuilt Umberslade Hall in the Palladian style, and died there on 31 December 1741, aged 82. His eldest son, Thomas, who was born on 21 July 1695, was Whig M.P. for Warwick 1738-41, and for Bramber 1741-47, also Recorder of Coventry. On 14 July 1747 he was created Lord Archer, Baron of Umberslade. He married on 11 August 1726 at the Chapel Royal, St. James's, Catharine, daughter and co-heir of Sir Thomas Tipping, first Bart., by his wife, Anne Cheke, niece of Edward Russell, Earl of Orford, who commanded the English Fleet at the victorious battle of La Hogue against the French. To Henley and other manors he added that of Birmingham by purchase in 1746. He died at Pirgo, his wife's estate near Havering, Essex, on 19 October 1768 and was buried at Tanworth. Andrew, his only son, who succeeded him as second Lord Archer,

[1]Feet of F. East. 36, Eliz.
[2]Shire Hall, Warwick.
[3]On 23 Oct., 1677, the homage find that ' Sir John Clopton, Kt., who formerly held his Manor of Clopton of the Lord of the Manor of Henley as of his castle of Henley for the service of one knight's fee and by fealty, suit of court and a yearly rent of 4s., now holds the same as of his castle of Henley in free and common socage, suit of court and a yearly rent of 4s. by force of an Act of Parliament.' Wellstood, *Records of Manor*, p.xxii.
[4]Wellstood, op. cit.

was born at Pirgo 29 July 1736, and married on 27 July 1761 at that place Sarah, daughter of James West of Alscot, Co. Gloucester. Before succeeding to the barony he was Recorder of Coventry, and Whig M.P. for that city 1761-68. This last of the Archers was a good friend to Lady Luxborough of Barrells, almost the only one of her own dignity she had in the neighbourhood. He died without male issue on 25 April 1778, and lies buried with his ancestors at Tanworth. His monument in the Church there is of white marble, and consists of a small draped female figure leaning on a pedestal on which is a bust of Lord Archer, the whole surmounted by an urn—characteristic of the 18th century. Arms : *Az. three arrows or.* Motto : *Heu pietas, heu prisca fides.*[1]

The manor went to his daughters as co-heirs,[2] viz., Sarah married first the Earl of Plymouth, secondly the Earl Amherst ; Ann Elizabeth married Christopher Musgrave of Eden Hall, Cumberland ; Maria married Henry Howard of Corby ; Harriet married Edward Bolton Clive of Whitfield, Herefordshire. It was then held jointly by the husbands of these co-heirs but in 1812 Christopher Musgrave alone is named as lord.[3] In 1840, however, his wife herself is stated to be holding it, and she was followed by her son, Capt. Christopher Musgrave, who was in possession of it in 1850.[4] From him Darwin Galton, J.P., D.L., of Claverdon Leys (lord of the manor of Claverdon) purchased it in 1873. As his name suggests he was descended from two distinguished families—his father, Samuel Tertius, J.P., D.L., of Duddeston, was the son of Samuel John Galton, F.R.S. (1753-1832) of that place, a manufacturer who became a contractor on a large scale for the supply of muskets to the army during the Napoleonic wars. The family had been Quakers for many generations. His mother was the daughter of Erasmus Darwin, M.D., F.R.S. (1731—1802) the eminent scientist and poet, grandfather of Charles Darwin the originator of the theory of man's evolution. Darwin Galton (whose brother was Sir Francis, the distinguished anthropologist and founder of eugenics) was born on 18 March 1814, and married as the first of his three wives Mary Elizabeth, elder daughter of John Phillips (then deceased) of Edstone Hall. In 1850 he was High Sheriff of Warwickshire, being then described as of Edstone Hall, and was sometime a captain in the Warwickshire Yeomanry.[5] He was an active magistrate, sitting on the Bench at Henley from 1840 and for many years was its chairman.

[1]Information about the Archers is derived mainly from G.E.C., *Complete Peerage*, I, 188 ; Burke, *Dormant and Extinct Peerages*, 1866 ; and J. Burman, *The Story of Tanworth*, except where stated otherwise.
[2]Wellstood, op. cit.
[3]Ibid.
[4]Ibid.
[5]The foregoing information about the Galtons is from Sir Francis Galton, F.R.S., *Memories of my Life*, and Burke's *Landed Gentry*, 1937. Sir Francis was buried at Claverdon.

In him the Bench had a jealous upholder of its dignity in the days when a county magistrate stood for a good deal in the life of the countryside. A stern man, he was feared by those brought before him, but was upright and just in this and all his dealings. He was fond of hunting and shooting and kept a coach-and-four.

His brother, Sir Francis, writes thus :[1] ' My elder brother Darwin was a great favourite among his friends from his early life onwards. He used me as his fag when I was a boy and taught me to be fairly smart. I imbibed many commonsense maxims from him, but our ideals of life differed to an almost absurd degree ; he had not the slightest care for literature or science, and I had no taste for country pursuits. Our differences of temperament became more marked the older we grew. When I finally left Shetland, which was after the grouse season, I took as a present to my brother for the large pool at Edstone a crate full of many different kinds of sea birds, which I was assured would live in fresh water and pick up snails in the garden, as tamed gulls do. The railway people put the crate in a very exposed truck on a chill autumn night, which killed three-quarters of them at least. The remainder throve at Edstone for a while, the last survivor being an oyster-catcher who came to his end thus : It had been freezing hard in the night, followed by soft snow, and then re-freezing. Next morning they found the tracks of a fox on the snow-covered ice, going to a place where the yellow legs and nothing else of the bird remained frozen in. The oyster-catcher's legs had been entrapped by the frost, and his body had been snapped up by the fox.'

Darwin Galton died on 4 January 1903, aged 88, and was buried in a vault in the churchyard at Wootton Wawen, his memory being perpetuated by a tablet in the chancel there.[2] The manor then passed to his widow, Penelope Maria Elisabeth, eldest daughter of Richard Edward Cumberland of Middlecave, near Malton, Yorks, and descended to Edward Galton Wheler[3] his nephew, who, in accordance with the terms of his uncle's will, obtained Royal Licence to use the additional surname and arms of Galton.[4] The last named sold it in 1914 to William John Fieldhouse, C.B.E., J.P., of Austey Manor, a benefactor to Henley and district. Mr. Fieldhouse died on 28 October 1928 and left the manor to his son and daughter, Ernest Francis Fieldhouse and Olive Nancy, the wife of Major C. W. Barnard, M.C., of Oldberrow, who now hold it jointly.

[1] In his book, *Memories of My Life*, pp. 84 and 114.
[2] *Wootton Wawen*, p. 115.
[3] To his widow, Mrs. Mary L. Wheler-Galton (daughter of the late James Dugdale of Wroxall Abbey), I am indebted for some of the information about the Galton family.
[4] The arms of Galton are : *Quarterly 1st and 4th argent a chevron ermines between in chief two popinjays and in base a like popinjay upon a perch issuant from the base all proper.*

ABOVE: High Street, when the Bear and Ragged Staff was in action — a free house; beyond is the projecting arm of the old King's Head sign; the Market Cross, secured by iron supports early this century, and railed off at the end of the last one, features in Henley printer E. J. Stephens' postcard of around 1910. BELOW: The long gone White Horse on the left, and Stinson's (undertakers) on the right, dominate this late 19th century photograph of High Street. (Both O'D)

ABOVE: An early view of High Street includes the entrance to the tanyard on the right. The writer says 'I have bn to Chaple an come home and fine that I have not got a stamp . . . so I got a post Card . . .', which is our good fortune. BELOW: South End looked like this in the twenties. (Both O'D)

ABOVE: Station Road now runs where there was once 'Good accommodation for cyclists'; the house on the left survives as Filbert's Restaurant Francais, and was even then a teashop in the late 19th century.
BELOW: Another casualty of progress was Green Gates, where Mrs Watkins lived with her children, Jack and Evelyn — here early this century. The baker's shop was on the left. (Both O'D)

ABOVE: Alder's Garage has not survived — it was opposite Johnson's Coaches, on the site of Ye Old Forge. (O'D) BELOW: The Post Office has; here in the late 19th century it was also the telegraph office and savings bank beside Miss Chetter's stationer's shop. Today it is G. F. Lodder & Sons, solicitors. (WI)

ST. JOHN'S CHURCH—FORMERLY ST. JOHN'S CHAPEL

HISTORICAL NOTES.

As early as 1262, a felon named Geoffrey de Lynde took sanctuary in ' the church of Henley '[1] which would thus afford him security until he had decided whether to surrender or quit the realm.

In 1297 ' John, parson of the church of Henle ' is mentioned[2] and again in 1302 it is recorded that Henry de Burmyngham, chaplain, was instituted to ' the church of Henleya by Roger chaplain of the same, his proctor.'[3]

It is almost certain, however, that these all refer to Beaudesert as there is no record of a church being built in Henley until 1367, when we read :

' The Chapell here (dedicated to S. John Baptist)[4] was built about the 41 year of King Edward III as appears by the confirmation thereof made by William Witlesey, Bishop of Worcester ; in which is exprest, that it was erected at the sole charges of the inhabitants, in regard of the large distance, the foul ways in winter-time, betwixt this village and the parish church of Wootton Wawen ; and by the consent of William de Senye then Prior of Wootton (unto which religious house the said mother Church of Wootton was appropriated) and Will. de Perton the then Vicar, which inhabitants and their successors had authorite then given them by the same Bishop to provide and maintain a fitting Priest at their own proper charges for celebration of divine service there, so that the Vicar of Wootton, for the time being, might wholly receive and take all oblations, arising in the said Chapell, upon Christmass day, Candlemass day, Easter day, and S. Peter's day (being the day of the dedication of that Church) and for Churching of women, at any time, in the said Chapell. But of all other profits arising upon the said days, or any other throughout the year, the Vicar to have two parts only and the Prior the third. And that the Priest belonging to this Chapell might have power, so often as occasion should be, to Church women there, to administer the Sacrament to such old and decrepite people as could not go to the said Parish Church, and to perform all other parochiall rites therein, buriall for the dead only excepted. For the performance of all which the Priest for the time being, at his first admission thereto was to oblige himself by his corporall oath, in the presence of the Prior of Wawens-Wootton and the Vicar,

---

[1] Assize R. 954 m. 59 d.
[2] *Cal. Pat. R.*, 4 Apr., 1297.
[3] Reg. Sede Vacante I,65.
[4] Register Wittlesey however states that it was built in honour of St. John the Evangelist, but since 1545, at any rate, it has been St. John the Baptist (see p. 66).

lest the said Church of Wawens-Wootton should be dampnified. And that all good people might be the more stirred up to contribute towards the charges for the fabrick hereof ; as also for the bells, books, lights, vestments, and other ornaments belonging thereto, the said Bishop by that his publique instrument, which bears date at Hertlebury, 5 Cal. Aug. Anno 1367, granted to everyone that would be open-handed therein, an indulgence[1] of xl days ; all which was confirmed by the Prior and Monks of Worcester.'[2]

In 1369 William Fifhide of Henley, draper, obtained a licence for one mark paid to the king, ' for the alienation in mortmain by him of three messuages in Henley in aid of the sustenance of a chaplain to celebrate divine service daily, in a chapel to be built by him for his good estate, for his soul when he shall be taken from the light and for the souls of all benefactors of the chapel.'[3] It is stated in the inquisition which preceded the licence that the chaplain's name was Thomas Veysy and that it would be no ' damage ' [to the King or others] to allow Fifhide to assign the tenements. The reason for such an inquiry was that once property had passed to the use of a church it was inalienable and not subject to ordinary feudal dues.

Presumably the building referred to would be a small chantry chapel built within the new parochial chapel but no trace of these buildings remains.

Notwithstanding the safeguards afforded by the document of 1367 cited above it is evident that the new parochial chapel soon began to affect the income of Robert de Wikwant, vicar of the mother church of Wootton, for in 1370 he petitioned Pope Urban V that ' although his parish is large and populous his portion is insufficient and is diminished by the existence of a chapel newly built at Henley within the said parish, for the convenience of those who had been wont to hear Mass on Sundays and Holy days in the parish church.'[4] Whereupon a mandate was issued to the Archdeacon of Oxford to deal with the matter[5] but no further reference to it occurs in the records.

What this chapel was like we have no means of knowing but most likely it was a smaller building than the existing one which replaced it in about the middle of the following century.

[1]An indulgence was not, as is often supposed, a papal permission to commit sin, nor was it really a pardon for sin already committed. The commission of a sin involved two consequences, guilt, which put the sinner out of right relations with God, and was removed by absolution ; and punishment, which had to be worked out either by penance in this life, or in purgatory. An indulgence was the remission of the whole or part of the punishment thus due, and was acquired by the performance of certain specified good works with a right disposition, and the payment of a certain sum of money in commutation of the required acts of penance. *Hist. of Church of England* by H. A. Wakeman, p. 194.

[2]Dugdale, p. 806, citing Reg. Wittlesey f. 17b.
[3]*Cal. Pat. R.*, 1367-70, p. 232.
[4]*Cal. Papal. Reg.*, 4 Kal. Apr. 1370.
[5]Ibid.

As to this later chapel we have evidence, from the will of Wm. Reynolds in 1507, and other sources, of the appearance of its interior before the Reformation, as will be shown presently.

It remained subordinate to Wootton but was so closely identified with the gild (see p. 65) that it was seized into the hands of Henry VIII in the 37th year of his reign, at which time there were 324 communicants, or as they are called, 'houseling[1] people.' In consequence of which the inhabitants in May 1546 petitioned the King that they should still be allowed to use the chapel in the town which had been built by their predecessors, setting forth that owing to the distance from their parish church—'children may die un-baptised, the dying may be deprived of the last sacraments, and the dead may have to lie unburied' if these misfortunes came to them at the time of floods.[2] Even when there were no floods the distance from their homes increased the danger of robbers attacking them, or of fires arising in houses left so long untended, and of children falling into the mill streams which ran through the middle of the town, and being drowned.[3] The commissioners of Edward VI, on 4 November 1548, reported that 'The said town of Henley is severed from the parish church (being two miles off) with a brook which in winter so riseth that none of the people may pass over it without imminent danger of perishing. Wherefore it is very necessary that the same chapel stand and the service therein be maintained.'[4] And so the inhabitants were allowed to retain it though no doubt many of its valuable ornaments had in the meantime been taken away and sold.

An order was made in 1534 by the Archbishop of Canterbury, Thomas Cranmer,[5] concerning the chapelries of Henley and Ullenhall and the mother church of Wootton. It is addressed in the pre-Reformation way :

'To all the children of the Holy Mother Churche,' and states that when the commissary and another came to the parish church of Wootton they found very many dissentions, strifes, variances, contentions and controversies, betwixt the churchwardens and inhabitants of Wootton on the one part and the churchwardens of Henley and Ullenhall on the other, concerning the repairing and building of the body of the parish church of Wootton and other things belonging to it. At length it was decreed that two representa-tives from each place should meet in the church of Wootton 'under the payne of three pound of waxe to the said church' of everyone absenting himself, and take some order for the repara-tions. If the expenses could not be discharged out of the common

[1]Housel, a middle English word meaning a sacrifice.
[2]Floods are still experienced but they would be more severe in those days owing to the greater number of trees and the undergrowth.
[3]*L. and P.*, Hen. VIII, xxi(i), 966.
[4]Certificates of Colleges, I Edw. VI.
[5]He abjured allegiance to the Pope in the following year,

chest then they should make levies on the inhabitants of all the three places.[1]

In a survey made by the Puritans in 1586[2] we read ' Mascall vicar and precher thogh he be growen Idle negligent and slouthfull, a man defamed and of tainted life be hath two charges beside Wooton, videlicet, Henley and Ownall wch he supplieth by his hirelinges : whereof one vpon a rumor of change of religion in mounsiers daies did shave his beard.' That is, the days when the Duke of Alençon, a Roman Catholic, was paying court to Queen Elizabeth ; clean-shaven priests being, of course, the rule in the Roman Church.

A vicar of Wootton Wawen, W^m. Lyvyng, by will dated 3 May 1495 leaves 6s. 8d. to the Chapel of Henley.[3] W^m. Reynolds of Henley bequeaths £10 in 1507 ' to wage a priest to celebrate two years next after my decease in the said chapel of Henley at the altar of Our Lady for my soul my wife's soul the souls of my father and mother and for all Christian souls.'[4] On 13 November 1547 Sir Roberte Pratt, priest, late vicar of Coughton, dwelling in Henley, bequeathes ' my soul vnto Almyghty God our lady Saynte Mary, wythe all the company of heavon to pray for me and my body to be buried within the paryshe churche of Wotten Wawyn.' To ' the Chapell of Hendley vj^s viij^d ' and ' for the space of one yere iiij^d ob. [4½^d.] in bread to be wikeleye [weekly] bestowed emonge the poore of Hendley.'[5] This last affords an interesting example of what has aptly been described as a ' spiritual bequeathing ' common to those days, but as time went on God and the soul were less and less remembered in wills until they ceased to be mentioned.

Catholic recusants at Henley appear to have been few, and in 1592 we hear of only three. John Symondes and Eleanor, his wife, were presented ' for willfuly refusinge to come to church,' when John was committed to Warwick gaol. On his humble submission and desire to resolve doubts and ' to conferre with a godlie and learned minister appointed to him by the commission,' he was released from gaol and allowed the liberty of his own house.[6] Also ' there is an olde Preeste called Sr Robert Wheatly who used to come to his ffriendes hee beeinge a man of fowrescorc yeare olde.'[7] This priest was brother of Alderman George Whateley of Stratford, who endowed the school in Henley in 1586.

During the sequestration of the Rectory of Beaudesert and in the period 1646-9 it was ordered that one, Mr. Griffin, should take all its profits and tithes for one year, ' his meyntenance for preachinge at the chappell of Henley and the Church of Bewdesert.'[8]

[1]Hamper's notes to Dugdale, B.M. C45 K2.
[2]A Survei of the State of the Ministrie in Warwickshire. *Dugd. Soc.*, x, 3.
[3]P.C.C. Vox 24.
[4]P.C.C. Adeane 23.
[5]Worc. Wills.
[6]P.R.O., Recusant Rolls, 1592.
[7]Ibid.   [8]Minute Bk. Sequestration Committee, Warw. 1646-9 (B.M.).

At Easter, 1650, Henry Browne and others of Henley were indicted for recusancy and abstaining from church for one month ; they were probably Catholics.[1]

The late Dean Hutton[2] possessed a curious work written by 'A friend to truth and peace' in 1651. This friend appears to have been Thomas Hall, a minister of King's Norton, who dedicates it to John Trapp,[3] pastor of Beaudesert. Hall complains of being threatened by the Episcopal party for non-conformity and of how deeply he has suffered from the Cavaliering party, but he feels impelled to write :

' The Pulpit Guarded to warn his people of the awful example of Henley-in-Arden that Private persons (though they be gifted yet) may not Preach in a constituted Church without a call.' He argues in presbyterian sort but will have no disparagement of bishops, and is sure that ' we have our ordinations from Christ by bishops and presbyters.' But, however, the point is what a fearful place Henley must have been when it thought otherwise. Thus Hall's title-page :

' The Pulpit Guarded with xvii arguments proving the unlawfulness, sinfulness and Danger of suffering private persons to take upon them publike preaching and expounding the scriptures without a call ; as being contrary to the Word of God, contrary to the practice of all Reformed Churches, contrary to the three and twentieth Article of Religion, contrary to two Ordinances of Parliament, and contrary to the judgment of a whole jury of learned, judicious, pious Divines, both forraign and domestick. Occasioned by a dispute at Henley-in-Arden in Warwickshire, Aug. 20 1650. Against Lawrence Williams, a Nailor-publike-preacher ; Tho. Palmer, a Baker-preacher ; Tho. Hinde, a plough-wright publike-preacher ; Henry Oakes a Weaver-preacher ; Hum. Rogers (lately) a Bakers-boy-publike-preacher. Here you have all their arguments (never yet compiled in one tract) retelled and answered, many Texts of Scripture cleared the quintessence and marrow of most of our modern authors (in reference to this controversie) collected, with references to such authors as clear any doubt more fully ; many incident cases resolved, the utmost extent of lay-mens using their gifts in eleven particulars demonstrated, and above thirty objections answered. In the close are added six arguments to prove our ministers free from Anti-christeanism.'

At the Easter Sessions 1653 John Miller, Edward Biggs, John Baker, Wm. Heynes, and Wm. Goostree, all of Henley-in-Arden, were indicted for ' a riotous assembly and for disturbing and hindering Mr. James Cooke from preaching the word of God at the public chapel there, he being lawfully appointed thereto.' They were ordered to traverse the indictment and give up the

[1] *Warw. Co. Rec.*, vi, 92.
[2] *Highways and Byways in Shakespeare's Country*, p. 276.
[3] Probably an intruded minister.

keys of the chapel, but at the next Court at Michaelmas it was stated that they had neglected to do so and were then ordered to at once deliver up the keys to Mr. Cooke, or the sequestrators of the Chapel appointed by Parliament, or answer their contempt.[1] Cooke was evidently a nominee of Parliament, and many similar scenes must have occurred throughout the country during the Interregnum, when those with Royalist sympathies tried to withhold possession of parish churches from Puritan ministers.

On the 3rd October of the same year Wm. Cooper, Richard Knight, John Fauks and Foulke Wheatley sent a petition to the Parliament about appointing a minister for Henley chapel.

This was handed over to the officers concerned with instructions that they should ' take care that the order . . . be observed and peace preserved.'[2]

A grant of £30 was made in 1658 by the Parliament for the maintenance of a minister.[3]

It seems that the influence of Puritanism remained at Henley until at any rate the early part of last century, for a communion table then stood in the middle of the chancel to enable the communicants to partake of the Bread and Wine sitting round it in accordance with an order which had been made by the Parliament in 1644.[4]

It is stated in 1847 that the floor of the chapel was fitted up with square high pews like horse-boxes[5] which would be rented to the leading parishioners. People too poor to pay for their seats were huddled together at the back or consigned to the gallery which stretched across the west end of the nave and aisle.[6] Over the altar against the east wall was another gallery containing a small organ, a violation of all ecclesiastical usage.[7] The three-decker pulpit for parson and clerk was a prominent feature. The almost invariable type of service which went with a church fitted up like this was evangelical. Long sermons were preached and prayers and psalms were said not sung.

All this unsightly woodwork was cleared out at the extensive restoration of 1856, for which we may be thankful, but unfortunately a few ancient objects of interest which then remained were also taken away. The cost of this ' restoration ' work which amounted to £900 was met to some extent by church rates varying from 3d. to 5d. in the £ extending over a number of years,[8] but the greater portion came from voluntary subscriptions. Every parishioner, except the

---

[1] *Warw. Co., Rec.*, iii, 195. James Cooke was probably the Warwick Physician who is said to have been the first Minister of the Baptist Church there.

[2] *Cal. State Papers Dom.*, 1653-54, p. 182.

[3] Ibid, 1658-59, p. 112.

[4] *Churches of Warwickshire*, p. 137.

[5] Ibid, p. 136.

[6] Ibid.

[7] Ibid.

[8] Vestry Rate Book.

very poor, would have to pay these rates including Nonconformists, with whom they were naturally unpopular, and about the middle of Queen Victoria's reign an act was passed forbidding them, after which the power of the Vestry declined.

When the Pope, by a Bull of 1850, proceeded to map out England into dioceses and to appoint bishops all over the country, the inhabitants here, in common with many elsewhere, were filled with indignation as this will show :

'Petition of the high bailiff and inhabitants of the Royal Township of Henley-in-Arden to Her Majesty Queen Victoria, praying the repression of the Bishop of Rome's Papal encroachment upon the rights and liberties of the established Church of England, 1850.

'That your petitioners consider this Papal Bull whereby the whole kingdom has been parcelled out into pretended provinces and dioceses to be an invasion of the rights of your Majesty's Crown, a violation of the constitutional laws of this realm and an infringement upon the liberties of your Majesty's free people.

'That your petitioners, owing allegiance to none under Heaven save to your Majesty, will never submit to the government or interference of any foreign person, prelate or potentate who (to use the language of the Oath of Supremacy) cannot have any jurisdiction, power, superiority, preeminence, or authority ecclesiastical or spiritual within this realm, that while your Majesty's petitioners regard with indignation the encroachment of the Bishop of Rome, they would ill fulfil their duty did they not express their alarm at the extensive introduction of Romish principles and ceremonies into the Church of England by many of its clergymen. They believe this has been one cause of the aggression of which they complain and that it is a far greater danger to our Protestant faith than any interference of a foreign potentate.

'Your petitioners therefore most humbly pray your Majesty speedily to adopt such measures as will at once effectually repress this and every other Papal encroachment upon the rights laws and liberties of England.'[1]

To this a reply came from Whitehall that Her Majesty was pleased to receive the petition very graciously.[2] It is evident from the later words of the petition that the Catholic Revival known as the Oxford Movement did not find much favour at Henley.

More than thirty years later feeling still ran high. When the Rev. G. E. Bell, in 1881, put the choir into cassocks and surplices there was an outcry and it was some years before he lived it down. Some of his parishioners cried ' Papist ' ! on meeting him in the street, and a few left the church never to return ; this in spite of the general esteem in which he was held. They were first worn at the funeral of the clerk's wife. On catching sight of the surpliced choir

[1]Shire Hall MSS.
[2]Ibid.

waiting at the churchyard gate one of the bearers set down the coffin in the road and walked off. It is said that the clerk never spoke to him again[1]!

The harvest festivals however for 1881 and 1882 were evidently very joyous occasions. The church was decorated in the traditional way and on the Sunday Holy Communion was at 8-0 a.m., matins and second celebration at 11-0 a.m. ; children's service at 3-0 p.m., and evensong with sermon at 6-30 p.m. On the following day, Monday, after a well-attended evensong, a public tea was held in a tent erected in the Market Place at which, in 1882, nearly 300 sat down ; the parishioners making gifts to it of provisions and money. A charge of 8d. each was made, but many of the poor were admitted free, and the profits were given to the church. Dancing began in the tent after tea, a piano having been lent for the occasion, and we read that ' the town band added greatly to the pleasure of the company both in the tent and throughout the evening, which was passed in social entertainment in the National School.' A visitor who looked in at the School towards the close thus describes the scene : ' The orderly country dance, to the accompaniment of a popular melody . . . the drum obligato by the delighted boys on the school-room floor, the contented faces of the lookers-on whose dancing days were over, or may be had never come, all testify how happily pastor[2] and people keep harvest-tide at Henley.'[3]

At the present the services at St. John's are of the moderate type, as indeed they really were in Mr. Bell's time, and at Beaudesert they are the same. Since the union of benefices the two churches have, so far as possible, been used alternately. The rector[4] is the Rev. Canon W. J. Easterbrook, R.D., and the organist is Mr. J. M. Pearse.

DESCRIPTION.

No trace of the chapel of 1367 remains and the main body of the present building is of the late perpendicular style of architecture of the middle of the 15th century. The north aisle is rather later in the same century ; the tower is earlier than the aisle, and appears also to be earlier than the nave as it is not placed symmetrically with either and encroaches on both with its buttresses. Local stone was used in its construction but less care seems to have been taken in its selection than in some other churches in the Forest of Arden, and the face of many stones on the exterior has scaled off and has had to be renewed. Apart from this the work appears to have been carried out with much care and skill.

The chapel consists of an undivided nave and chancel, north aisle, a stone porch and an embattled tower at the west end, and a

[1] Keble Howard, *My Motley Life.*
[2] The Rev. George Edward Bell.
[3] Parish Magazine.
[4] For details of rectors see *Beaudesert*, p. xxxviii.

vestry on the north side of the chancel. The chancel, which is raised above the nave, was formerly on the same level. The porch,[1] which is embattled, is entered by a plain obtusely-pointed arched doorway. The arch to the inner door is pointed and curved only at the haunches with bowtel mouldings. It is rather highly ornamented, and the hood moulding springs from corbels representing the heads of a king and queen, probably Henry VI and his consort. The ogee-headed niche in the north wall was probably a holy-water stoup, and the glass in the small window in the south side is a memorial to the Rev. G. E. Bell, B.A. (Oxon.), vicar of Henley from 1876 to 1914, who died in 1924, and Mary Sophia, his wife, who died in 1917.

The aisle is separated from the nave and chancel by four depressed four-centred arches, resting on tall octagonal pillars with moulded capitals and plain bases, and from the tower by a small pointed arch of two chamfered orders, the inner having moulded capitals. The hood mouldings over the arches and windows spring from corbel heads, some of which are interesting as illustrations of contemporary headgear. The corbels of the north aisle window are curious representations of a bat and frog respectively, and at the west end of the arcade a grotesque figure of an animal with wings which are outstretched. The north door,[2] which has been set inside out, has a pointed arch curved only at the haunches with bowtel mouldings, and was no doubt the entrance from the gild adjoining, after passing through a doorway of the same period in the wall which fills the space between the chapel and the gild hall.

The vestry, formerly the sacristy, is entered from the chancel by a similar pointed-arch doorway. It is lighted on the north side by a small oblong window, with a plain modern window above, divided by a mullion ; and on the east side by a similar oblong window, but somewhat larger. At one time the upper portion of the vestry was of brick masonry, and was higher than at present to allow a stairway to be carried up to the entrance to the gallery, which was over the altar. The old entrance may still be seen blocked up on the north wall. A partition then separated the stairway from the part used as the vestry. The doorway at the east end of the aisle probably belongs to this period. It does not appear that this vestry was ever a chantry chapel, as has been suggested. There is no sign of a piscina—and it could not have been built by Wm. Fifhyde for his chantry chapel, as has been supposed, for this formed part of the earlier building which was all pulled down when the present one was erected.

The chapel is lighted on the south side by five triangular arched windows of three principal lights cinquefoiled in the heads, and six smaller trefoiled lights above.

[1]Near the porch there stood until early this century an old yew tree.
[2]Outside this door on the right are the apparent remains of a stoup.

The east window has an obtuse arch, but is struck from two centres. It is of five principal cinquefoil-headed lights, with smaller panel lights of various shapes. At the west end of the nave is a four-centred obtuse-arched window of four principal lights cinquefoiled in the heads, with lesser panel lights above.

In the aisle the east and two north windows have obtuse-angle arches with three principal ogee headed lights cinquefoiled. Formerly these windows were filled with ancient stained glass containing the arms of various lords of the manor of Henley and Beaudesert and others, as recorded by Saunders[1] in the following description :

'In the chappell are these coates in the windowes. In the nethermost south windowe next the doore at the west end of the church these two coates : Freville ; Botetort. In the next windowe[2] these coates : Boteler-Sudley ; Archer of Tanworth ; Catisbye ; Harewell of Wotton-Wawen.

There is also the picture of one, Thomas Kockin, grocer, with this subscription : ' Orate pro anima Thome Kockin.'

In the next south windowe is this coate quarterly :
Boteler and Sudley quarterly as before.

In this windowe is also the picture of Thomas Kockin, grocer, with the former inscription repeated.

In the uppermost south windowe all the coates are gone.[3]

In the chancell est windowe these Coates :
Boteler and Sudley quarterly as before. France-England,[4]
Beauchamp Newburg quarterly, on an escutcheon of pretence Spenser and Clare quarterly.[5]

These two coates are in the next payne of the same est windowe :
Grocers of London. Boteler and Sudley quarterly as before.[6]

In the chancell windowe is the picture of Thomas Kockin with the subscription as before : It is likely he was a benefactor to this place.

In the est windowe of the chancel that was a Chantery place, (peradventure it was the Chantery of the Guild and Fraternity there), for there is the picture of one Stokes, and there was one Stockes, Mayster of the Guyld there. In this windowe are these armes : Boteler and Sudley, quarterly as before.

This coate is in the north windowe of the chancell : Evesham Abbey.

---

[1]Saunders' MSS.—Shakespeare's Birthplace.

[2]The arms of Aston are also said to have been in this window. See *Memorials of Families of the Surname of Archer* (1861), by an anonymous author.

[3]Dugdale also mentions the following coats in the south windows : Aston, Stafford, Camville and Burdet quartered, Trussel, Abbey of Winchcombe and Company of Mercers [Wm. Fifhyde already mentioned was a draper].

[4]Probably the arms of Henry VI.

[5]The arms of Richard Beauchamp, E. of Warwick after 1422.

[6]Dugdale also mentions : Butler [Boteler] impaling Norbury, and Abbey of Evesham.

> In the north windowe of the church are the coates of Boteler and Sudley, quartered together (baron), empaled with another that is broken out.[1]
>
> There is also in this north windowe and in its lowest payne these two coates empaled together after an antient manner thus : Freville as before.   Mountfort.'

The tower, which is embattled, formerly had a large gargoyle at the south-east angle.   The west window is pointed and of two trefoil-headed lights, with a quatrefoil above.   Over this is a pointed window of one light, and a little higher up is a small square window. Above is an obtuse-arched belfry window divided by a mullion and having a transom which divides the window into four principal lights, with lesser lights in the head.   The other sides of the tower are similar, but without the lowest west window.   Inside at the south-west angle is a stair-vice with a pointed doorway.

The main structure as it is to-day is essentially the same as when it left the builders' hands in the 15th century, but the interior has undergone many changes.

There is a great difference in styles between the Norman work at Beaudesert and the late perpendicular architecture to be seen at Henley Chapel.   At the Norman Church we have the massive walls and arches with sculptured detail, while the perpendicular style is light and slender, and the builders were concerned more with the broad contrasts of light, shade and colour.

By the time St. John's was built, the rood-screen, with its rood-loft,[2] and its representation of Christ on the Cross with attendant figures of St. Mary and St. John had become the most outstanding feature in churches.   Chancel-arches had been largely superseded as we find at Henley.   Windows were built as large as possible to show off the stained glass, which was generally in a setting of coloured wall-paintings, painted woodwork, and other objects.   With the destruction of its ornaments at the Reformation and after, the chapel was left with merely the framework from which the picture had been taken away.

William Reynolds of Henley, in his will dated 27 March 1507,[3] refers to the Lady Chapel, and expresses a wish to be buried in it ' before the image of Our Lady.'   He also makes bequests to the Gild of Henley to buy vestments to be used at the Lady Altar, and he leaves his third best mazer, or drinking cup, to Sir Thomas Bownall, one of the chaplains of the Gild.

The Saunders' MSS.[4] tell us that there was a ' Chantery place ' at the east end of the north aisle in the chancel, where the organ now

---

[1]Dugdale mentions the arms of Clinton of Coleshill as being formerly in this window.

[2]It is said that the loft in such a church would be used mainly for musical purposes, vocal and instrumental.

[3]*Records of Beaudesert*, p. 9.

[4]Shakespeare's Birthplace.

stands, and that the picture of one Stokes, sometime master of the
Gild, was originally in the east window there. This shows the
situation of the Lady Chapel and also that it was supported and
used by the Gild.[1] By her will of 4 November 1537, Joan Stookes,
or Stokes, gentlewoman and widow, bequeaths ' my sowle vnto
almyghty God to our lady Seynt Mary and to all the hooly
company of heavyn and my body too be buryed within the Gylde
Chapell off Henley in Hardeyn nyghe to the awlter off Seynt
Katheryne by my husband Rowland Stokes.'[2] This altar would
stand against the north wall and probably under the second window,
the whole of the north aisle being assigned to the use of the Gild.

From Saunders we can also gather an impression of the fine
heraldic and other ancient stained glass, already described, which
once filled the windows—most of the arms being blazoned in colour
in the MS. In 1847 it is also on record that there was then in one
of the upper lights of the east window of the chancel ' a small
fragment of ancient stained glass representing the head and upper
part of an angel clad in an alb, the orphrey or collar of which is
yellow.'[3] We are told by the late John Hannett in *The Forest of
Arden* that during the alterations of 1856 in removing a flat ceiling
over the nave and chancel, the canopy of the rood loft, gilt and highly
coloured, was found above the ceiling, corresponding with the
surbase below, from which the pillars of the screen, supporting the
rood, had been cut. On one part of the surbase, in old-English
lettering, was the following inscription : ' Nativitas Domini nostri.
Assumptio beatae Mariae. Resurrectio Domini nostri.'

A close examination of the octagonal pillar near the pulpit
discloses the holes—now filled in with stone—into which the
screen was fitted, and as these appear on the north and south sides
of this pillar, it is clear that the screen extended across the whole
width of the chapel, including the north aisle. It is also evident
that the screen was nearly as high as the capital of the pillar. This
coloured screen, which was probably of the open-work wooden
variety, with painted panels in the base, would thus divide the
sanctuary of the Lady Chapel from the aisle and the chancel from
the nave. There would probably also be a screen in harmony on
the line of the present organ front.

In addition to the High Altar in the chancel and the two altars
in the Gild chapel, there may have been another against the rood
screen near the south wall. To the same period belongs the roof
of the nave and chancel mentioned in 1847 in the *Churches of
Warwickshire*, where we read that ' the roof of the nave and chancel
is divided internally into five bays, the principals forming which
spring from sculptured demi-angels holding shields.[4] The roof of

---

[1]As at Tintenhull in Somerset.
[2]Worc. Wills, 373.
[3]*Churches of Warwickshire*, p. 136.
[4]These still remain.

the easternmost, or fifth bay, is richer in appearance than that of the other bays, an arrangement not unusual in our ancient churches ; it is nearly flat and divided by small ribs with carved bosses at the intersections, into forty-eight square compartments.' There seems to be no doubt that this roof would have been of wood and that it was coloured. It appears to have been removed at the restoration of 1856. The old timbers of the gabled roof are of the queen-post type, with tie-beams, which are arch-braced to the corbels which support them.

The aisle has a lean-to roof of four bays divided by cross-beams with curved braces (except one) resting on plain stone corbels. The only pre-Reformation memorial on record, except the stained glass windows, is that to Richard Stoke, or Stokes. This, according to Hannett, was ' a very thick slab '[1] bearing a Maltese cross five feet six inches in length and the words ' Orate pro ane Richardi Stoke.' The slab and a stone coffin were discovered about a foot underneath on removing the pavement of the chapel at the restoration before mentioned. Unfortunately they have now both disappeared. An altar slab, with a design upon it representing the waves of the sea, is said to have formed part of the vestry floor early this century, and it probably belonged originally to the chancel.

THE CHAPEL OF THE GILD, as already seen, embraced not only the Lady Chapel at the east end of the north aisle, where the organ now stands, but all the remainder of this aisle. The Lady Chapel contained the Lady Altar against the east wall, also the image of Our Lady,[2] before which a light was probably kept burning. There would also most likely be images representing the Holy Trinity and St. John, patrons of the Gild, before which candles would burn. The stained glass in the east window over the Altar contained the picture of one Stokes, Master of the Gild, also the arms of Sir Ralph Boteler its great benefactor.[3] In the north window were the arms of Evesham Abbey, to which the Gild formerly paid an annual rental of 4d.[4] The before-mentioned William Reynolds, in 1507, left a breviary to the Gild, to the intent that he and his son Roger be prayed for perpetually in the common beadroll, also his ' best piece of silver ' and his ' salt of silver ' to buy vestments for use at the Lady Altar. In 1546 ' wine, bread and wax, and for making of the same within the church ' cost 18s. 8d. per annum, and ' for washing the linen vestments, belonging to the Gild, 20d. per annum.'[5] In the following year we read that the Gild owned two chalices, weighing 20 ozs., and a cross of silver, weighing 59 ozs.[6]

All these ornaments were entirely separate from, and independent of, the High Altar, as also were the Gild chaplains independent of the chaplain of St. John's. These Gild priests would,

---

[1]This slab as late as 1905 was loose outside the north wall.
[2]*Records of Beaudesert*, p. 9.
[3]See p. 58.   [4]Certificates of Colleges, 37, Hen. VIII.
[5]Ibid.   [6]Certificates of Colleges, 1 Edw. VI.

however, be bound to attend mass at the High Altar on the principal feast-days, and they most likely assisted the chaplain of St. John's with some of the daily services.

The position of the other altar, that to St. Katherine, has already been shown and the Gild chapel as a whole resembled somewhat the chapel formerly in the north aisle of Holy Trinity, Stratford-on-Avon.

From the above we are able to recover some idea of the beauty and interest of the interior as it appeared in its early days, a great contrast with its later appearance, when there was an ugly gallery over the altar in the chancel, and another at the west end, with unsightly pews to match, all removed in 1856. Changes for the better, however, have been made of late years, and the panelling of the chancel in oak and the new oak choir stalls, completed in 1926, are a pleasing feature. If a suitable screen could be provided in the position of the old one, and the old chapel of the Gild brought into use once more as a side chapel, it would greatly improve the interior of the sacred building. If at the same time the windows could be filled once more with heraldic and other glass, as they were in the 15th century, the appearance would be still further enhanced.

The font is octagonal with a shallow bowl of the 17th or 18th century. It has a plain stem and chamfered base.

The pulpit is hexagonal and of the early 16th century. Each side has a panelled, traceried head and below exhibits in relief the linen-fold pattern. The oak top-rail and the stone base are modern.

The tower screen of oak is inscribed : ' In loving memory of John Keble Bell, ' Keble Howard,' June 8 1875—March 29 1928. This screen was erected by his wife.'

All the existing *stained glass* is modern and none is of particular merit except that in the porch. The two lights of the window here contain respectively a figure of St. Christopher and a figure of St. George, and the inscription reads : ' A.M.D.G. in memory of George Edward Bell, B.A., Oxon., Vicar of Henley-in-Arden 1876-1914, born 1833, died 1924, and of Mary Sophia, his wife, died 1917. The gift of their children.'

The east window is a memorial of 1879 to Nehemiah Hopkins by his son Daniel M. Hopkins, both of Henley. It depicts our Lord bearing the chalice, with the four evangelists. The tracery panels contain sacred monograms with the Agnus Dei and the descending dove, angels with harps and other instruments of music. Above are the figures of the archangels Michael and Gabriel with their respective emblems, the spear and the lily.

The west window is a memorial to John and Sarah Cooke and was given in 1882 by their children John Cooke and Sarah Heynes. It represents the adoration of the infant Jesus by the magi and shepherds. In the top lights are the words : ' Unto us a child is born, unto us a Son is given.' All the glass in the other windows is of conventional design without any inscription except the east window of the north aisle, which is inscribed : 'Presented to the church on Ascension Day, A.D. 1865.'

The Royal Arms of the Hanoverian period, now indistinct, are painted on a board in the tower, which would originally occupy a more prominent position, probably at the east end of the chapel. In the aisle are the Royal Arms in cross-stitch *temp*. Victoria.

There is an oil painting on the west wall of Christ bearing the cross inscribed : 'To the Glory of God and in loving memory of George Edward Bell (for thirty-eight years vicar of Henley-in-Arden) and Mary Sophia, his wife. This picture is the gift of Orlando and Monica Wagner.'

The clock cost £250, collected by subscriptions, and took the place of one which played tunes every three hours. It is the largest in the district and is inscribed : ' This clock was made in the year of our Lord 1868 by Alexander Sadler Simmons, a native of this town.' Simmons was then in business at Warwick.

The electric light was installed in 1931 and dedicated on Easter Day of that year ' to the Glory of God and in memory of Theodore John Cartwright, M.A., Oxon., Priest, Canon of Coventry, Rector of Beaudesert-cum-Henley-in-Arden, 1921-30.'

There is a board on the west wall recording the partial restoring of the church in 1900 at the cost of £1,100. This restoration included rather extensive repairs to the stonework of the exterior of the nave and chancel, and the mullions, tracery, etc., of the windows ; also some alterations to the vestry to which reference has been made above. Inside, it was necessary amongst other work to repair the arch covering the brook course which runs under the church, and to deal thoroughly with the floor and seating ; also to replace the decayed plaster on the walls. Sufficient funds not being available, the repairs of the tower had to wait until 1912, when the then churchwardens, Mr. F. T. Cooper and Mr. Robert Herring, issued an appeal, which brought in enough money to carry through the much needed restoration. The pinnacles, which were an addition of comparatively modern times, having become unsafe, were removed that year, and not replaced. The organ was provided by subscription in 1911.

There is no churchyard attached and burials generally took place at the mother church of Wootton Wawen, though some of the more prominent parishioners were, prior to the Order in Council of 1882, buried in the chapel. Since the union of Henley benefice with that of Beaudesert all burials have been in the churchyard of the latter. In 1610 it was ordained by the Court[1] that ' none of the buchers of this libertye shall pen up or put any kind of cattell in the chappell porche or in the entrye that leads from Thomas Fearfaxe shope vnto the Chappell at any time to forfeit for everi default xij[d].'

[1] Court Rolls.

Parish registers[1] :　Vol. I, 1679-1762 and one entry for 1766, Baptisms, Marriages and Burials mixed.　Vols. II, III, contain Baptisms only, 1772-1812.　Vol. IV Baptisms 1813-1839 ; Burials 1824, 1831 and 1861.　Vol. V, Marriages, 1816.　Vol. VI Baptisms 1839-1921.　Vol. VII Banns 1864-1921.

The Bells.[2]　There were formerly seven bells, but a small one was removed to the Market House in 1694 for the use of the free school there and the bell-framing shows clearly whence it was taken ;　it was probably the sacring bell, rung at Mass.　Those remaining are inscribed as follows :

1.—Gloria in excelsis deo 1727.　Below, arabesques all round.
2.—John Wever Chapel Warden 1707.　IHS.
3.—IHS.　IHS.
4.—1707.　On waist a coat of arms (see below).
5.—As No. 4.
6.—Above, scroll-border all round.

Thomas Baker[3] and Robert Morrell,[4] Church Wardens 1727.
Below, border of arabesques with cable-moulding above.
The treble and tenor are by Joseph Smith and the 2nd—5th by Clark and Bushell of Evesham.

The coat of arms on the 4th and 5th bells is that of Sir Ralph Boteler, Lord Sudeley, lord of the manor of Henley in the reign of Henry VI :　Quarterly 1 and 4 gules, a fess countercomponée arg. and sa., between six crosses pattées or, 2 and 3 or, two bends gules. It will be noticed that on the bells these arms are reversed, from which we may assume that the founders finding them on the old bells wished to preserve them but failed to impress them the right way.

BELL RINGING CUSTOMS.

1.—A bell is rung at 8-0 a.m. on Sundays and at 10-0 a.m. on weekdays for daily service.

2.—The death-knell is rung at 9-0 a.m., or later if more convenient.　The bells are rung in succession from the first down to the tenor as follows :　Each three times for a man, twice for a woman and once for a child.　The tenor is then rung up and then down again.　For a king or queen the same except that each bell is rung four times.　This custom was instituted on the death of Queen Victoria and the knell has since been rung at the death of Edward VII, Queen Alexandra, and George V, on all four occasions by the present leader of the ringers, Mr. W. E. Hemming.

3.—At funerals a bell is tolled at intervals of one minute for a short time and is known as ' the minute bell.'　For a person of importance or an old ringer a muffled peal is rung.

---

[1] At Shire Hall, Warwick, D.R.O. 21/1-5—Transcription of Vol. I in the writer's possession.
[2] *Church Bells of Warwickshire* by H. T. Tilley and H. B. Walters, 1910.
[3] High Bailiff, 1722-3.
[4] Ibid., 1727-8.

4.—For about a month before Christmas the bells are rung (including change-ringing) once or twice a week.

5.—At midnight on Christmas Eve and New Year's Eve, 12-0 o'clock is struck on the bell on which the clock strikes (as the bell is up the clock cannot strike it), then the bells ' slam ' twelve times (that is, all the six bells ring together) ; after that the bells are rung including change-ringing.

6.—A bell was rung formerly at vestry meetings but this has been discontinued.

A Benediction Service was held in the belfry by the Archdeacon of Warwick on 10 April 1910, after the rehanging of the six bells at a cost of £100.

Bell-ringing and the sound of bells have from early times been a source of pleasure to our people in town and country alike.

During Christmas week the hand-bell ringers visit houses or institutions by invitation and play selections of tunes on the hand-bells. In the past at Christmas hand-bells were rung up and down the main street.

Church Plate : The chalice was given by Edward Sale, Esq., in 1732 and has this inscription upon it : ' Ex dono Edwardi Sale 1732. In usum capellæ de Henley in Arden.'

There are two patens, one given by Mrs. Mary Roadnight in 1792, and the other by Mrs. Mary Horsley on 22 June 1848.

The flagon is inscribed ' Given in remembrance of God's mercies to the donor.' The date is not decipherable, but Archdeacon Lea in his book on church plate assigns it to the Restoration period [1660].

A silver paten, the work of the Warham Guild, is inscribed ' Presented by the members of the Convention, March 18-25, 1928, in thankful remembrance.'

The brass cross and pair of candlesticks on the altar were given by Miss Betts of Rowington in 1878.

There is a processional cross to the memory of the Rev. G. E. Bell, vicar (died 1924), and his wife, the gift of their grandchildren, Anthony[1] and Rosalind Wagner, which appears to be of Spanish workmanship ; and another given by Dr. W. E. Nelson of Arden House. On one side of this latter a figure of St. Nicholas is engraved, and on the other the Lamb and Flag of St. John the Baptist ; the idea being to symbolise the unity of the two parishes of Beaudesert and Henley, and so make it available for use in either church.

The rectory at the corner of Beaudesert Street dates from about 1700 and has a cemented front with gables, plain copings, and ball finials. It was given to the living by Miss Lea, late of Tanworth.

[1]The present Richmond Herald.

Monuments—North Aisle

Against the north wall.

A tablet.[1] Sacred to the memory of Mrs. Mary Horsley died November 9 1831, aged 81 years.   She bequeathed as a residence for the ministers of this chapel the house[2] at Henley in which she died full of years and highly and deservedly respected.

A marble monument : Arms : Or 3 bars az. in chief as many mullets of the second, impaling a chevron between 3 boars.   The colours on the sinister side are not blazoned.   Crest : A demi lion az. gorged with a collar or charged with 3 mullets of the first.   Hic jacet corpus Simonis Kempson filius et haeres Gulielmi Kempson de Hilborough in Com. War. Armig. qui postquam ad provectam in hoc oppido vixisset aetatem obiit decimo quinto die Julii An. Dom. 1719, aetatis suae 77. Hic etiam jacet Margareta uxor Simonis Kempson praedicti, quae Margareta fuit filia Wallastonis Betham de Rowington in Com. praedict. Armig. Dormivit in Domino vicessimo primo die Aug. Anno Dni. 1699, aetatis suae 63. Requiescant in pace.

Translation : Here lies the body of Simon Kempson, son and heir of William Kempson of Hilborough in the county of Warwick Esquire, who after that he had lived to an advanced age in this town, died on the 15th day of July in the year of our Lord 1719, aged 77.   Here also lies Margaret, wife of the afore-mentioned Simon Kempson, which Margaret was the daughter of Wallaston Betham of Rowington in the aforesaid county, esquire.   She slept in the Lord on the 21st day of August in the year of our Lord 1699, aged 63. May they rest in peace.

Against the north wall.

A tablet.[3]   Near this place he interred the remains of Hopkins Horsley sen[r].[4] late of this town, died 20 Feb[r] 1808 in the 84th year of his age.

Also Hopkins Horsley jun[r], son of the above, who died 7 Nov[r] 1824, aged 72 years.

Against the north-west corner.

A brass plate. To the honoured memory of John Hannett, author of *The Forest of Arden*, and for twenty years high bailiff of this town who died 12 April 1893, aged 89 and is buried in Beaudesert churchyard.[5]

On a board over the above brass plate :

Joseph Williams, formerly of Knightsbridge in the county of Middlesex, but afterwards of Stratford-on-Avon, gentleman, by his will dated 8 May 1796, did (by the desire of his wife), give and

---

[1]This monument was originally against the East Wall of the Chancel.
[2]This is the house on the South side of the Midland Bank.
[3]Originally against the East wall of the Chancel.
[4]He was a chandler and grocer—P.C.C. 305, Ely. High Bailiff 1757-58.
[5]See *Beaudesert*, p. 57.

bequeath to the chapel wardens of this town the sum of £50 the interest whereof should be disposed of Christmas Day yearly to the poor of this town one moiety thereof in money and the other in bread.

A flatstone on the floor near the north door.

To the memory of Mr. Edward Sale[1] late of this town, who departed this life June the 4th Anno Domini 1758, aged 66 years. To the memory of Anne, second wife of Mr. Edward Sale, and only surviving daughter of Mr. Francis Baker of this town, by Mary his wife, who departed this life July 10th A.D. 1730, aged 37 years.[2]

A flatstone nearly opposite Simon Kempson's monument.

In memory of Christopher Baker, late of this town, who departed this life 26th day of March 1717, aetatis suae 61.[3]

IN THE NAVE.

A flatstone on the floor near west wall.

Arms : A cross engrailed between 4 pellets impaling 3 bars in chief as many mullets.

Crest : An arm in armour embowed in hand a sword point downward.

Here lieth the body of Robert Clayton, alias Freeman,[4] of this town, gent., who departed this life the 30th day of April, in the year of our Lord, 1729, aged 49.[5]

On the south wall.

A tablet : In memory of Nancy Horsley, relict of the late Hopkins Horsley, who died 22 January 1861, aged 87 years.

A brass plate to the memory of the men of Henley who fell in the Great War, 1914-18. The sixteen names are recorded in *Beaudesert*, p. lvii.

On a flatstone[6] near the war memorial.

John Keble Bell, ' Keble Howard,' 1875-1928.

A board on west wall.

This church was partially restored A.D. 1900 at the cost of £1,100.

G. E. Bell, B.A., vicar.
Robert Herring, churchwarden.
Charles Couchman, high bailiff.

---

[1] High Bailiff, 1733-34.

[2] and [3] At one time these gravestones were in the passage outside the North door.

[4] Of Gray's Inn. Married Mary d. of Simon Kempson of Henley—Marr. Settlemt., 10 June 1706, Shire Hall MSS.

[5] At one time this gravestone was also in the passage outside the North door. It appears to represent a coffin lid.

[6] Underneath is a casket containing his ashes.

On a board near the above.

A benediction service was held in this Belfrey by the Ven. J. H. F. Peile, M.A., Archdeacon of Warwick on Sunday, April 10 1910, after the rehanging of the six bells in the tower at the cost of £100.

> George Edward Bell, B.A., Oxon., vicar.
>
> W. T. Taylor ⎱
> R. Herring ⎰ churchwardens.
>
> Charles Couchman, J.P., high bailiff.
>
> Laus Deo.

MONUMENTS FORMERLY IN THE CHURCH.

Recorded in a MS. vol. of W. Staunton,[1] *but all gone before* 1847.

' In the church lyeth buried Mr. John Bellers[2] and his sonne, under a stone. The inscription is worne out.

In the chancel is buried under a free stone Thomas Wheyham.

In the middest of the chancel under the communion table lyeth buried John Baker with this inscription : Here lyeth the body of John Baker who departed this life the 24 September An° Dni 1618.'

Preserved in Dugdale, 2nd ed. 1730, *p.* 808, *probably remaining in* 1847, *but illegible.*

On a flatstone in the chancel :

' Here lieth the body of Jonathan Wood of Shrewsbury, in the County of Salop, son of Jonathan Wood of Peploe, Gent., who departed this life January the 12 Anno Dom. 1699. Aetat. suae 23.

Mentioned in the Churches of Warwickshire, 1847, *probably removed in* 1856.[3]

' On the chancel floor : To the memory of Mary Gaches, niece of the late Revd. Daniel Gaches, who died March 2nd, 1809, aged 38 years.'

---

[1]*Churches of Warwickshire,* 1847, p. 137.
[2]High Bailiff, 1596-97.
[3]The Chancel was then paved with Minton tiles.

THE ADVOWSONS OF HENLEY AND ULLENHALL

IN early days the whole parish of Wootton Wawen, including what is now Henley and Ullenhall, would have its rector, a priest who ministered to all its inhabitants, supported by their tithes and oblations. The tithes as we know were payments of a tenth of all agricultural produce and oblations were voluntary offerings and payments made for special services such as baptisms, marriages and burials. In return the rector had not only to maintain himself and the chancel of the church but provide for the poor, and offer hospitality to pilgrims and other wayfarers. He would probably be assisted by a chaplain. At the Norman Conquest Robert de Stafford, patron of the living, bestowed it upon the Abbey of St. Peter de Castellion of Conches[1] who set up an Alien Priory in Wootton,[2] and a vicarage was instituted in 1178.[3] Thereafter the Priory would take the great tithes, i.e., of corn and hay, and the vicar the small tithes. The chapelries of Henley and Ullenhall were later formed out of this mother parish of Wootton.

As we have seen the first chapel at Henley was built in 1367 at the sole charge of the inhabitants, and authority was given by the bishop for them to provide and maintain a fitting priest[4] at their own expense. The Wootton terriers of 1585 and 1714[5] confirm this, adding that all tithes of the whole parish (including Henley and Ullenhall) except those of corn and hay, were to be paid to the vicar of Wootton, including oblations, tithe of wood, lamb, wool, pig, etc., and the tenth of all profits. At the Inclosure of 1776[6] a considerable number of proprietors and owners of old inclosed grounds and homesteads in Henley were at their own request exonerated from vicarial tithes by small annual money payments, the total of which amounted to £1 14s. 6d. only. Under the Apportionment of 1840[7] thirty-eight persons there commuted their tithes for small annual payments amounting to £1 16s. 10d. This sum was still being received in 1925, but the amount due under the Inclosure had then declined to £1 10s. 8d.

On 14 May 1914 Henley was constituted a separate

---

[1] It passed to King's Coll. Camb. in 1447, with whom it still remains. *Wootton Wawen*, p. 107.
[2] Ibid. p. 41.
[3] Ibid. p. 43.
[4] In 1475 Henry Sowthwike, Chaplain of Henley, was taxed to a subsidy 6s. 8d. Hamper citing Reg. Carpenter, II, 67.
[5] Bishop's Reg., Coventry.
[6] In the parish chest.
[7] Ibid.

ecclesiastical parish[1] for the purpose of uniting it with Beaudesert, but this did not actually take effect until 20 March 1915.[2] Meanwhile the Crown gave up the patronage of Beaudesert in exchange for that of Norton, Co. Kent, on 17 December 1914[3], and on 2 June 1915 the combined benefice of Beaudesert with Henley-in-Arden was put under the joint patronage of the Bishop of the Diocese and the High Bailiff of Henley.[4]

A detached portion of the parish of Wootton situated near Buckley Green, and that part of the same parish stretching from Blackford Bridge to the corner near Preston Bagot House and extending northwards to embrace Whitley ; also Impsley, James Farm, Brook Cottage, etc., in Ullenhall parish were transferred to the united benefice.[5]

The chapel of Ullenhall was built in the late 13th century and the vicars of Wootton from ' ancient time ' had to find a priest of their own proper charge ' to celebrate divine service there on Sundays and Holy Days and every Wednesday and Friday throughout the year.'[6] The terriers before mentioned also state that the vicar of Wootton was to supply a ' minister ' at his own expense, adding that all tithes, except those of corn and hay, were to be paid to him. The rents the vicar received in lieu of some of the vicarial tithe here under the Inclosure of 1776 amounted to £27 6s. 6d.[7] and under the 1840 Apportionment £17 12s. 6d.[8] When Ullenhall with Aspley[9] was constituted a separate ecclesiastical parish from Wootton on 27 June 1861 the advowson became vested in the Newton family of Barrells and descended with the manor of Ullenhall (q.v.). It is now held by the Church of England Trust.

The small tithes formerly paid to Wootton were then transferred to the vicar of Ullenhall. In 1256 Taurinus, prior of Wootton, granted the tithes of corn here to William de Romesty for eighteen marks.[10]

Henley and Ullenhall were in the diocese of Worcester until 4 September 1918, when the diocese of Coventry was formed out of the Archdeaconry of Coventry and that part of the Archdeaconry of Warwick within the county of Warwick, in which latter the two parishes are situated.

---

[1], [2], [3], [4] and [5] Bishop's Reg., Coventry.

[6]Dugdale, p. 818.

[7]In parish chest.

[8]Ibid.—From Aspley he received £64 4s. 9d. and from Wootton, £27 17s. 4d.

[9]Aspley was transferred *civilly* to Tanworth in 1895—Part of Tanworth village is still in the ecclesiastical parish of Ullenhall with Aspley including Aspley House, built c. 1808 by John Burman of Light Hall, an ancestor of the present writer.

[10]King's Coll. MSS., Camb.

THE GILD OF HOLY TRINITY AND ST. JOHN, HENLEY

THE Gild of Henley-in-Arden was of a social and religious order, its purpose being to render mutual assistance of various kinds between the brethren and to engage in works of charity, something the same as our modern benefit societies ; also the observance of ordered religious services, masses and prayers for the souls of departed members, the support of lights at the altars and before images. It was likewise concerned with the amusements of the people such as miracle plays which illustrated events in the lives of saints, and mystery plays which were connected with Scriptural history. Processions of members in coloured gowns and feasts in the Gild Hall were held periodically, after mass had been said in the Lady Chapel, with probably a special prayer asking God's blessing on the Gild. The members, who were drawn from all classes, included both men and women, the latter being generally their wives and other relations. It was under the control of a master who was elected annually when the accounts were audited, accompanied by ale-drinking. Expenses for attaining the objects of the Gild were provided by entrance fees, contributions, income from gifts of lands and houses and legacies.

The Gild may have been founded at the time the first parochial chapel was built in 1368,[1] but the first known reference to it is in 1408, when John Brome of Lapworth and Margery, his wife, granted the reversion of certain lands in the lordship of Henley and the town of Studley to ' the Gild of the Holy Trinity, St. John the Evangelist and St. John the Baptist.'[2] In 1428 the Pope granted an indult to choose confessors to the brethren and sisters of this confraternity.[3] A dispute having arisen between the master of the Gild and the Prior of Wootton, about certain matters, they, in 1430-31, agreed to refer them to arbitrators.[4] In 1434 John Stokes, then Master of the Gild, was one of those from whom the knights of the shire were commissioned to receive the oath.[5] Among the clergy taxed to a subsidy in 1475 is John Bonamy, Chaplain of the Gild, who was taxed a sum of 6s. 8d.,[6] and in 1513 Sir Thomas Bownel and Sir Thomas Webbe, chaplains, or as they are here called chantry priests, each paid a like sum in aid of the king.[7]

In 1534 the commissioners appointed by Henry VIII reported that there were two priests, Sir Robert Colyns, chaplain, who received by the hands of the Gild Master 106s. 8d., and Sir Thomas Bonell, already mentioned, who received 100s. annually.[8]

---

[1]It is not, however, among the returns of 1381 at P.R.O.   [2]*Cat. Anct. Deeds* A4262.   [3]*Cal. Papal Reg.*, viii, 42.   [4]King's Coll. Camb., MSS.   [5]*Cal. Pat. R.*, 1429-36, p. 385.   [6]Worc. Epis. Reg. Carpenter II, 67b, cited by Hamper.   [7]Dugdale, p. 808.   [8]*Valor Eccles.* (Rec. Com.), III, 93.

The same year the former and Henry Berdmor,[1] another chaplain of the Gild, signed the declaration renouncing papal supremacy, probably under compulsion, which reads in translation : ' The Roman bishop has not any greater jurisdiction conferred on him by God in this kingdom of England than any other foreign bishop.'[2]

Colyns died four years later and his will, which is preserved at Birmingham, reads :

' In die nomine Amen A° dni 1538° xij° die maij I Robart Colyns pryst off the Gyld off Hendley in Arden Order and make my testament and last wyll in this manner folowyng ffyrst I bequeth my sowle to God allmygty my body to be buryed in eccleastycall sepulture.[3] Itm. I bequethe to any moder x^s Itm to Syr Rychard my broder xx^s Itm to John Holmys my best dublett j syluer spone Itm to Kateryne my syster and her chylderne xx^s The Resydewe off all my other goodes with my dettes and all Thynges performyd I geve and bequethe to Syr Rychard my brother Chargyng hym to dyspose all thynges to Goddes plesure whom I order and make my sole executor Thees beyng wytness John Holmys Wyllyam Page with other more Oursear off this my last wyll John Hethe.'[4]

It will be noted that except for 10s. to his mother and his best doublet and a silver spoon to John Holmys, the testator leaves everything to his brother Sir Richard—Sir in this case signifying that he also was a priest, or as *Piers Plowman* has it, one of God's knights.

Notwithstanding the large revenues which came to the King from the dissolution of the monasteries further money was needed to carry on the wars with France and Scotland, and in 37 Henry VIII commissioners were sent round to enquire into the values of the lands and other possessions of the gilds and chantries.

Few of them were, however, disturbed until the first year of Edward VI, when an Act declared all these institutions to belong to the Crown and commissioners were again appointed to make ' Certificate into the Court of Augmentations ' of all lands, etc., belonging to them, and their revenues to be converted to the use of the King.

In the first-mentioned report of 1545[5] the commissioners state that ' the gild was founded by Ralph Boteler for four priests to synge dyvyne servyce within a chapell of Saynt John Baptiste and to pray for the ffounders soules,' and that its lands and tenements were

[1]He probably succeeded Bonell during 1534, and was still a chaplain eleven years later. See Henry Whelar's will at Birm. Reg., 4 Sep., 1545.
[2]P.R.O. E36/63, p. 121. It was also signed by Thomas Hartwell, vicar of Wootton, Thomas Penford, curate of Bearley and John Knyght, curate of Ullenhall.
[3]i.e., Burial according to the rites of the Church and in consecrated ground.
[4]Worc. Wills, 379.
[5]Chantry Certs. (P.R.O.), bundle 31, No. 44.

of the yearly value of £27 3s. 3d.   There were then three priests, one of whom, John Whatley,[1] received an annual stipend of £5 10s. and the other two, £5 each ; all probably resided on the foundation. Also an organist, Thomas Gosnell, deacon, who was paid £2 a year and allowed a dwelling with a garden at the rental of a red rose, the symbol of St. John the Baptist. A sum of 13s. 4d. was spent on obits and alms to the poor.

The rentals were received from properties in Henley, Beaudesert, Wootton Wawen, Lapworth, Tanworth, Beoley, Kinwarton, Warwick, Preston Bagot, Claverdon, Ullenhall and Whitley.

From another source we find that the other two gild priests besides Whatley were H. Berdsmore and Rich[d] Budworth.[2] In 1545, one Philip Stokes, who held a lease of Parkshuppon farm and Barrols farm, left to Budworth his ' ghostly father ' 6s. 8d. to pray for him,[3] and a like sum to the Gild.

The later report of 1 Edward VI[4] also says that Ralph Boteler was the founder and adds that ' he gave thereunto lands and possessions to the yearly value of £27 16s. 3d.   Nevertheless he could not have founded the Gild, for he was but a boy when we first hear of it and had not then succeeded to the manor (see p. 37).   He probably revived and re-established the Gild already existing, or he may have taken out a licence the application for which had been neglected at an earlier period, but no licence can be found on the Patent Rolls or elsewhere.

It seems probable that from his being such a liberal benefactor of the Gild at the time the chapel was built in the middle of the 15th century, Ralph afterwards came to be looked upon as the actual founder of this fraternity.   A founder no doubt he was in the sense that William Reynolds in 1507 wished to become one when he left a house in Henley ' to the interest that I may be prayed for in the bedroll as a founder.'[5]

The confiscated property was disposed of piecemeal during the early years of the young King Edward's reign, as is shown elsewhere,[6] ' The Gilde ' (presumably the Gild Hall) being purchased subsequently by Mr. More, a Bedfordshire man, who as we read ' lay every term in St. Giles's at the sign of the Sugar Loaf.'[7]   Whatever excuse there may have been in the case of the monasteries there was none for the wholesale plunder of the gilds, whose properties belonged to the people themselves, and their loss was felt severely.

After the Gild was dissolved Richard Budworth and Thomas Cosnel [? Gosnel] described as ' incumbents ' thereof, were, in 1553,

[1]R. and S. Gen[l]. (S.C.12) 26, No. 75, where he is described as ' clerk.'
[2]Ibid.
[3]*Beaudesert*. p. 11.
[4]Chantry Certs. (P.R.O.), bundle 53, No. 21.
[5]*Beaudesert*, p. 10.
[6]Ibid. p. lx.
[7]Hamper's notes to Dugdale's *Warwickshire* (B.M.).

stated to be each in receipt of a pension ; the former £4 and the latter £2.[1]

The following record[2] written some time between 1637 and 1647 shows the sums which were still being paid out of the former properties of the Gild in the reign of Charles I :

> The Kinge's rent out of the Gilde is £4 6s. 4d. the half yeare.
> To Mr. Baldene (Wm. Baldwin) Chefe Rente £2 4s. 10½d. the whole yeare.
> To Sir Charles Smith [of Wootton], 1s. 6d. the whole yeare.
> To the poore of Henley £1 every yeare.
> To the poore of Mansetter £1 every yeare.

Some Masters of the Gild.

William Barker, 1410-11.[3]
John Stokes, 1434.[4]
John Deyster, 1446-7 and 1456-7.[5]
Thomas Mason, 1472.[6]
John Pratte, 1507.[7]

The Catalogue of Seals in the British Museum contains this description of a 15th century seal belonging to Henley-in-Arden :

> ' The Trinity in a niche with trefoiled canopy, pinnacled and crocketed : on each side in a smaller niche a saint ; *left* St. John Baptist with Agnus Dei ; *right* St. John the Evangelist with book and eagle on the right hand, and in the left hand a palm branch. In the field on each side, a branch of foliage, SIGILLUM BURGEN [SIUM ?] DE HENLEYE.'

This device appears to have been originally the seal of the Gild and to have been used later with the inscription added as the town seal. As the borough was not incorporated it is probable the burgesses acted in their corporate capacity through the Gild.

[1]Dugdale, p. 808.
[2]Hamper's notes at B.M. quoting Sir Simon Archer's MSS.
[3]Archer Deeds, cited by Hamper (B.M.).
[4]*Cal. Pat. R.*, 1429-36, p. 385.
[5]Archer Deeds as above.
[6]Lapworth Deeds cited by R. Hudson.
[7]*Cat. Anct. Deeds*, 13228.

THE GILD HALL.

THE Gild Hall, the ancient home of the Gild, stands on the north side of St. John's Church and is an interesting specimen of old timber-frame work dating from the 15th century. It would be of no great age when in 1464 a croft is mentioned as lying between it and the stream running through the Little Park of Henley.[1]

In 1608 some sixty-one years after the Gild was dissolved it is described in a survey of the manor as a ' domus mansionale, called the Gildhouse,' of six bays and a garden and let to W^m. Smith at at yearly rent of 12s. 8d.[2] Fifteen years later (1623) we learn from a survey[3] that it was then ' very ruinous and decayed ' and would cost much in repairs to make it habitable. It further describes the property as :

> ' One Messuage or Tenement in Henley-in-Arden next adioyning to the chappell there called and knowne by the name of Guyld Hall contayning towards the streete and leaning thereunto five bayes of building And on the backside a kitchen and barne now converted into a Tannehouse contayning four bayes of building one garden or backside lately devided in twoe partes contayning by estimacion a quarter of an acre which tenement and backside extendeth in length from the street unto a Brooke called Belsore brooke And in breadth from the Chappell and lane leading to Belsore unto the Tenemente in the tenure of William Robins All which is nowe in the tenure of William Smyth Tanner and is of the yearely value of xs.'

The lease of it had been assigned to him eleven years earlier by John Parker of Henley, a yeoman.[4]

William Smyth died in 1637[5] when his heir, Richard Launder, became tenant and in 1647[6] he was presented at the Court ' for not tylinge and making handsome the little peece of buildinges adjoininge to the Church.'

In 1661 a lease of ' the Guildhall alias the Guildhouse ' was granted by the Crown to his son John Launder for thirty-one years at the old rent of 10s. a year without fine, but with covenant to repair ' the houses and mounds and fences.'[7]

From him it was purchased by Francis Baker, whose son, Christopher, a maltster, left it in 1716-17 to his brother Francis,

[1]*Cat. Anct. Deeds*, A8346.
[2]Land Rev. Misc. Books, 228 f. 61.
[3]Ibid. 258 ff 121-2.
[4]Anct. Deeds E908, 39 Eliz.
[5]Court Rolls.
[6]Ibid.
[7]Stowe MS. 498, p. 247.

also a maltster, at which time it (with its ' barns, stables and gardens '), was divided into two parts.[1]

For many years before it was restored in 1915 it had been used for a butcher's shop and one other shop. This restoration by Mr. W. J. Fieldhouse was very extensive but many of the ancient timbers remain though some were removed. All the doorways and windows are modern. The hall proper, which is in the upper storey, is reached by stone steps from the garden at the rear and a short modern staircase. This chamber has a roof of four bays and a modern fire-place at its south end, over which is blazoned Sir Ralph Boteler's arms ; and beyond it two small rooms. The view of the Gild Hall of 1821[2] shows the lower storey facing the street to have been mainly of stone, but it is now of timber framing filled in with modern bricks, and on stone foundations. In the hall there is a 17th century long table and other furniture. On this table in a case is the ancient mace,[3] which appears to be of brass and to have been formerly gilt, with a modern recessed base bearing the arms of Henry VI and the inscription : ' H. VI. R.' Nearby is the old wooden truncheon of the constable of the Court Leet, which is painted and has on it the letters 'H.R.' with a modern gilt crown at the base and the letter ' H.' At its side is a copy of the Rolls of the manor of Henley on vellum. There is also an old oak pitch pipe, for pitching the voice or tune, used in Beaudesert Church in 1820 and given by Mr. Joseph Godfrey in 1926. Hanging on the wall is the original Charter granted to Sir Ralph Boteler by King Henry VI in 1449 with the great seal attached, while nearby is a fine set of eleven pewter dishes inscribed on the margins ' Hen : Ley 1677 ' and four plates. Dugdale, writing in 1656,[4] says : ' Before the dissolution of this Gild it was a custome (as I have heard) that upon all publique occasions (as Weddings and the like) the Inhabitants of this town kept their Feast in the Gild House before specified ; in which they had most kind of Household stuff, as Pewter, Brasse, Spits, Andirons, Linnen, Tables, etc., and wood out of the Little Park at Beldesert, for fewell ; those which were at the charge of the Feast paying only vis viiid. for the use of them ; but now all is gone except the pewter, which being in the chapell warden's custody, they lend out for ivd. a dozen when any Feast is made.' It is probable that the pewter Dugdale mentions was recast or exchanged in 1677, also that its present inscription was marked or engraved at a distant place as the letters are divided in such a way as to indicate that it was assumed the dishes were personal rather than public property.

From the foregoing it seems likely that Church Ales, very popular with our ancestors, were held at the Gild Hall. It was the custom

---

[1] P.C.C. 108, Whitfield 1717.
[2] See facing p.
[3] At one time it was kept in the High Bailiff's seat in St. John's.
[4] *Warwickhsire*, p. 807.

several times a year for church- or chapel-wardens to buy, or more often receive presents of malt with which to brew a quantity of ale. Food too was usually given by the parishioners and the proceeds of the feast was devoted to the church or the relief of the poor. There is mention in 1563 of the Whitsun-lord of Henley, lord of the Whitsun Ale and revels, visiting Rowington where he with his fellows would probably entertain the inhabitants with 'pastoral' 'pastime' and 'morris,' for which he was paid 3s. 4d. by the churchwardens there.[1]

In the small front room at the end of the hall in a little window is reset a portion of 15th century coloured glass, representing St. Anthony, the patron saint of the Grocers' Company of London, whose arms were originally in the east window of the chancel, out of which it probably came. The arms below are those of John, Lord Dudley (1401-87), an ancestor of Ambrose Dudley, Earl of Warwick, lord of the manor of Henley-Beaudesert.

After the Gild Hall was restored, Mr. Fieldhouse revived the meetings of the ancient Court Leet and Court Baron which were then held in this hall.[2]

The photograph facing page 66 shows H.R.H. Edward, Prince of Wales,[3] in his car in front of the Gild Hall on 14 June 1923, while on his journey from Stratford to Birmingham. Members of the Court Leet in their robes of office are seen outside, Mr. H. Hawkes, afterwards high bailiff, and who acted as such on this occasion, being on the left.

---

[1] J. W. Ryland, *Records of Rowington*, II, 43.
[2] F. C. Wellstood, *Records of the Manor of Henley-in-Arden*, p. 141.
[3] Afterwards Edward VIII, who abdicated 11 Dec., 1936.

THE HOSPITAL

A HOSPITAL for the relief of poor people and travellers was built here in 1448, as is shown by the following Indulgence granted by John Carpenter, Bishop of Worcester :

'On the 28 day of the month of January 1448 the Reverend Father in his manor of Alvechurch granted forty days' indulgence to all his subjects and others, the diocesans . . . who [should contribute] any of their goods, etc., to the new building and support of the hospital or house of alms within the town of Henley-in-Ardern, for the refreshment of poor people and pilgrims there assembling, newly erected, etc., for three years from the date of these presents consecutively reckoned and so long to endure.'[1]

The pre-Reformation church put much reliance on good works, hence the doctrine of indulgences which allowed the ordinary sinner the benefit of the good deeds and prayers of the saints. An indulgence of forty days was equivalent to the remission of forty days' penance still due after the sin had been forgiven.

This hospital would be much more of an ecclesiastical than a medical institution affording such relief to the body as was possible in those days, but being concerned especially with the care of the soul.

Dugdale, writing in 1656, says 'some think that the Gild House, situate on the north side of the chapel is the hospital here spoken of.'[2] It may have been under the same roof as the two were sometimes associated, in which case it would no doubt be dissolved at the same time as the Gild.

Against this there is a tradition favoured by some that the house now known as The Gables was formerly the hospital.[3]

---

[1]Worc. Epis. Reg., Carpenter, I, 65b.
[2]*Warwickshire*, p. 807.
[3]Hannett, *Forest of Arden*, p. 44.

HENLEY MARKET CROSS

In the Market Place, just south of where stood the Market Hall, and near the spot once occupied by the stocks, are the remains of the 15th century Market Cross. It is one of the few still existing in this county and is of exceptional interest. Composed of local stone, the shaft and raised base of three steps are now all that is left, the head having gone into decay and fallen away. The head was four-sided with recessed niches under cinquefoil-headed canopies resting on a knop or ring, and borne up by four angel figures at the angles, each holding out a shield bearing a cross. The niches, so late as 1815, exhibited in relief first the Rood, second the Trinity, third St. Peter with his key, but the sculpture of the fourth was worn by the action of time and was not then distinguishable.[1] It is probable that it had contained the Virgin and Child. The canopies and finials were decorated with crockets of similar design to those at St. John's. The Trinity is rather unusual, representing as it does the Eternal Father holding out the Crucified Son for the adoration of the world. From the illustration made about 1863[2] it appeared that part of the head had then mouldered away and the figures were none of them discernible, but it did not fall off until about 1894. According to tradition the cross was saved from destruction in the 17th century by being covered by a shed. This shed may have been joined on to the Market Hall, which was taken down in 1793.

A market cross was, like all other similar crosses, a sermon in stone. Its message was of fair dealing between man and man. It became the centre of all public activities, and is mentioned in Shakespeare in this connection in *King Henry IV*, where the King replies to the Earl of Worcester, 'These things indeed you have articulate proclaim'd at market crosses, read in churches,' and so on. Even in Puritan times market crosses, or what then remained of them, were used for public purposes. Contracts of marriage between extreme Puritans were published by the 'register' of the parish at the market cross on three several Lord's Days, the contracting parties being subsequently married by a Justice of the Peace. The parish registers at Wootton Wawen contain entries relating to such publications at Henley Market Cross.

Proclamations of all sorts were made at the Cross, and on these occasions the bailiffs and burgesses would be assembled there in their gowns. It was the rallying point for religious and other processions, and has been so used even in our own time; in pre-Reformation days preaching would take place from its steps particularly by the Friars : So that for upwards of five centuries it has been the scene

[1] *Gentleman's Magazine*, Feb. 1815.
[2] *Forest of Arden*, p. 44.

of many interesting events.   Towards the end of last century a
heavy iron palisade was erected round it for protection, and, at a
later date, the shaft was secured with iron supports.   It is to be
hoped that this relic of bygone ages may continue to stand for many
years to come.   A stone seat was placed in front of the cross to the
memory of Dr. Nelson in 1933, inscribed : ' In gratitude to William
Ernest Nelson, O.B.E., J.P., High Bailiff, 1910-22, from the people
of Henley-in-Arden ' but this was run into by a motor car in 1937
and badly mutilated so that it had to be taken away.   New iron
railings had been set up in place of the palisade a little before the
seat was given.

*LEFT: The Market Cross with the Stone House behind and the Market
Hall on the left — that was demolished in 1793. (O'D) RIGHT: The shaft
and head of the Cross before the head crumbled away. (WI)*

THE MARKET HALL

THIS building is also referred to as the Market House, Townhall and Townhouse, and stood just north of the Market Cross. An early reference to it is in 1597, when it was agreed at the Court Leet that the Bayliff and his brethren should meet in the ' Haule ' once in every month. In 1609 under the influence of Puritanism it was laid down by the same Court ' that neither Master Bailiff nor any other inhabitant shall licence or give leave to any players to play within the Towenhale upon pain to forfeit 40s.[1] but this order was afterwards relaxed, for in 1615 a company of players visited the town and other places in the neighbourhood.[2] In 1727 the feoffees ordered the ' Town House ' to be repaired.

Hannett tells us it was taken down in 1793[3] and Capt. Saunders, writing not long after this date, describes it as having been ' an extensive Market House on pillars of wood open beneath, with a large room over appropriated to public meetings, Courts Leet, etc."[4] which building is partly shown in the illustration facing page 74. The open space beneath would afford shelter to traders.

He goes on to say that when it was pulled down ' the present insignificant shed was erected.'[5] This shed, as he calls it, is described in 1844 as a plain building of stone supported on pillars[6] and Hannett writes in 1863 that it was ' a small heavy open building, supported on eight pillars and being of no use has lately been removed.'[7] It was never replaced.

[1]Court Rolls, Transcribed by F. C. Wellstood.
[2]S. Timmins, *Hist. of Warwickshire*, p. 284.
[3]*Forest of Arden*, 1863, p. 45.
[4]The Free School was also held here.
[5]Saunders MSS., Shakespeare's Birthplace.
[6]Lewis, *Topographical Dict.*, 1844.
[7]*Forest of Arden*, 1863, p. 45.

THE RIVER ALNE

THE main stream rises near Aspley Heath, where the elevation is some five hundred feet. It takes an easterly course near Tanworth, by Tanworth Mill, the Bird-in-Hand, through Henley and Beaudesert to the grounds of Wootton Hall, where it is joined by a smaller stream which rises near Wroxall Abbey. The united stream then flows in a south-westerly direction until its confluence with the Arrow at Alcester. The name Alne appears to be of Celtic origin and identical with the Welsh Alwen which Welsh linguists translate ' very white.' This description would suit the Alne, which has rapids where foam forms on the surface.[1] It is a very small river now but in earlier times when the district was more thickly wooded it would carry a much larger volume of water. In 1673 John Hemynge and another were presented at the manor court for laying hemp in the river but were fined 6d. only, in consideration that the greater part of the hemp was carried away by the violence of the current. This offence seems to have been a common one in those days.

Henley, which lies in a valley, has been subject to severe floods during its long history. As may be seen on page 45 it is evident that the inhabitants suffered from them in the 16th century and had probably done so from much earlier times. In those days there were mill streams running through the middle of the town deep enough when in flood to drown children if they happened to fall in. The greatest flood in modern times was that of 18 June 1872,[2] when a horse and cart were washed away near the Bird-in-Hand. The horse was drowned but the driver luckily escaped. On 31 December 1899 there took place what is known locally as the ' century flood,' when the street was inundated to such a depth that one of the residents swam in it. The last great flood the town experienced was on 21 May 1932, when following torrential rain in the early morning a large volume of water collected near the mill and poured down the street in a stream a foot or more deep, causing traffic to be held up for some hours. On this occasion the water entered a number of houses in Henley and flowed through some of the cottages in Beaudesert, doing much damage as it had often done before.

At Barrells on 13 July 1889 there fell 3·64-ins. of rain in sixty-five minutes, which quantity is stated to have been unequalled at any station in the British Isles for ten years previously.[3]

---

[1] *Wootton Wawen*, p. 6.
[2] See illustration facing page.
[3] Symons, *British Rainfall* (1889), p. 70.

76

ABOVE: *The Parish Church of St John still had its pinnacles in this early 20th century picture, when the Gild Hall beyond had yet to be 'restored' and the Rectory was half-hidden behind shrubs and railings. LEFT: The second 1867 Baptist Chapel, demolished in 1936, with Billy Blackwell and Jim Taylor, plus two children from the White Horse — Edna Hawkes (now Thompson) and R. Goddard. (Both O'D) RIGHT: The White Swan before restoration. (WI)*

ABOVE: The Gild Hall in 1900. It was restored in 1915, two years before the annual Court Leet was reinstated there. BELOW: In 1921, the High Bailiff was W. J. Fieldhouse, restorer of both Gild Hall and Court Leet, here with the officers of the Court — behind: J. Harris: back row: F. Stinson, F. T. Cooper, J. Welch, A. Hawkes: front: R. Herring, E. J. Stephens, Mr Fieldhouse, M. Hawkes, J. Busby and R. Newcombe. H. Norman Welch is today the only Hon Burgess — elected Low Bailiff in 1945. Steward of the Manor is David Lodder and Joseph A. Hardy of Pennsylvania is the Lord of the Manor — which he acquired from the descendants of W. J. Fieldhouse in 1991. (WI)

Defence

Hopley. I don't know the
road very well. My speed was nearer
15 but I did not take much notice
as I was upset.
There is a "Halt" on the road but
I did not notice it.
I take it the road I was going to
cross over a main road but I did not
expect traffic so early in the morning.

ABOVE: The annual Mop Fair included an ox roast, here in 1921 outside the Three Tuns. (WI) BELOW: At Henley Petty Sessions on 13 April 1938 Mr Hopley was fined £3 and 12s 6d costs for 'driving motorvehicle in manner dangerous'. His defence: 'I don't know the road very well. My speed was nearer 15 but I didn't take much notice as I was upset. There is a "Halt" on the road but I didn't notice it . . . I was going to cross over a main road but I did not expect traffic so early in the morning.'

A satisfactory report having been made as
to the probable extent of the use that would be
made of a potato sprayer, it was proposed by
Cnellr H. Hawkes, Seconded by Cnellr R. Herring
and unanimously resolved, "That a potato
sprayer be purchased for use in the Parish"
Cheque for Mr I.E. Warden's Acct. was
duly drawn and signed. –   6. 8

                    Joseph Hawkes Chairman

*ABOVE: Proclamations were traditionally made from the Market Cross.
(JL) BELOW: On Thursday 14 June 1917, the Parish Council recorded
'A satisfactory report having been made as to the probable extent of the use
that would be made . . . resolved "That a potato sprayer be purchased for
use in the Parish" ' — cost 6s 8d. (WI)*

HENLEY MILL

As shown in a former chapter the mill of Henley with the dwelling before it was in *c.* 1185 granted by Thurstan de Montfort to the monks of Wootton. In 1372 it was called the Parkmill.[1] By letters patent of 6 February 1591 it was granted to Richard Carpenter ' for the heirs of himself, wife Margaret and daughter Alice,' and in 1608 the latter's husband, Thomas Gibbs, was the manor's tenant at £2 a year rent and a heriot of 20s. It was then described as a water mill and a horse mill under one roof with a dwelling-house adjoining of three bays, a garden and Millham meadow ; also a close called Quadge Meadow.[2] The above-mentioned Richard Carpenter was, in October 1597, ordered by the Court to ' remove his muck and cley hillock and kepe sufficient the mill end that men may passe, and his banckes that the water flowe not over the mill banck, betwene this and the feast of St. Luke upon for every default to forfeit 3s. 4d.'[3]

A survey[4] taken by the Parliament in 1650, the year after Charles I was beheaded at Whitehall, informs us that the property was then parcel of the late King's possessions and describes it as a small tenement or millhouse consisting of three rooms on the ground floor and two above, with two corn mills and a horse mill, all under one roof. It had a small piece of land adjoining called the Millham[5] and was in the occupation of Anne Peacocke, widow. To it belonged all multure, toll, suite, sucken (i.e., soke), customs, etc., which shows among other things that it had the usual privilege of grinding all corn used within the manor or township for which a toll had to be paid, usually in kind. It embraced 1 acre 3 roods and was valued at £5 10s. per annum. Three acres of land called the Quadge Meadow belonging to the mill is stated to be worth 60s. a year. The lessee was William Baldwin, then lord of the manor. In 1840 it was owned by the Hon. Ann Elizabeth Musgrave, lady of the manor, and the tenant was Henry Hoitt.[6]

The present mill was erected at the end of last century on the original site, and took the place of a smaller one of plain red brick, with a large water-wheel near the main road.

A picturesque scene met you as you entered the town from the north, with the old mill on your left, the toll gate house just beyond, and the still existing weighing-machine house opposite on the right.

[1]*Cat. Anct. Deeds*, A6402.
[2]Land Rev. Misc. Bks., 228, f. 62.
[3]Court Rolls.
[4]Parl. Surveys, Warw. No. 13.
[5]Plot of land near the mill pond.
[6]Tithe Apportionment.

PETTY SESSIONS

IN 1638 we find that the Justices were sitting at Henley, and at Easter 1654 they sat at the Bear Inn here. These were probably monthly meetings of the Justices of the Hundred out of which the Petty Sessions developed.

The first reference to Petty Sessions for Barlichway Hundred is in November 1795, when the Rev. Daniel Gaches, vicar of Wootton Wawen, was the chairman. In 1822 one of the sets of statutes allowed by the Home Office was ordered to be sent to the Rev. P. S. Ward at Henley, and at Midsummer 1831 a set of statutes was directed to the magistrates there ' care of the clerk of Petty Sessions.'[1] One of the Divisional Licensing Sessions was appointed to be held in the town in 1828, and there were special sessions there for the election of parish constables in 1846.[2] Henley Petty Sessional Division includes besides Henley itself, Beaudesert, Claverdon, Lapworth, Packwood, Preston Bagot, Rowington, Tanworth, Ullenhall and Wootton Wawen. The Sessions are now held in a hall, or court house, built in 1903, at the rear of the police station, before which the magistrates had sat at the White Swan since 1845[3] and probably from the beginning.

The police station was built in 1858 to accommodate a police inspector, and provide three cells and a yard.

There is mention in 1845 of an Association for the Prosecution of Felons at Henley,[4] which had probably come into being during the latter half of the previous century, for at that time it became necessary for the landowners, farmers and townsmen to unite in protecting themselves against the increase in crime. Such associations paid the expenses of searching for, apprehending and prosecuting those who committed offences against the person or property of subscribers, and served a good purpose in the days when there was only the local constable to deal with law breakers. We do not know when the Association at Henley came to an end, but the one at Tanworth still survives though the need for its existence no longer remains. The annual dinner, a happy social gathering, is still held there every year as in the past.

---

[1]Edward Cooper, Jr. (the writer's great uncle), is found to be Magistrates' Clerk in 1835 and had probably been appointed some years earlier [Records of Examinations to Settlements, 1835-46].
[2]All the foregoing from Quarter Sessions Minutes, Shire Hall, Warwick.
[3]Kelly's Directory, 1845.
[4]Ibid.

THE FREE SCHOOL AND OTHER SCHOOLS IN HENLEY

GEORGE Whateley, a native of Henley by deed of 28 September 1586, gave the house[1] now used as the Church of England School, also a yearly rent of 20s. out of Fordend in Ullenhall and two crofts called Ote Myles in Beaudesert, and 10s. out of a house in Bridge Street, Evesham,[2] all for the poor until such time as a school should be established in Henley, then the income to be divided equally between the school and the poor. If, however, ' the school should happen to be decayed and no schoolmaster there teaching,' then the whole of the income was again to be given to the poor. George Whateley was a woollen draper and alderman of Stratford-on-Avon, with a shop on the north side of Henley Street there and was thus a neighbour of the Shakespeares ; the Poet being then twenty-two years old. In the alderman's house were painted cloths for the walls, cushions, curtains, carpets (probably for the tables), chests, coffers, bedding for six beds, linen, brass, pewter, lead, silver spoons, a salt parcel gilt, basins of latten, a malt-quern, mustard-mill, and a candle-mould. He had two gowns, a camlet jacket (probably of camel's hair and silk), a cloak, and a doublet of Damask.[3]

We do not know how long it was after Whateley's death before the school was first held. In November 1776 the Trustees of Randall's Charity ordered that £10 by the year be allowed out of that charity to the Free School in Henley-in-Arden as soon as Lord Archer ' properly repairs the Market Hall and a proper master appointed.'[4] A little bell was removed in 1694 from St. John's Chapel to the Market Hall, the then lord of the manor, Andrew Archer, under his hand and seal certifying that he did not claim any right or title to it, and undertaking to return it at such time as the bishop should command.[5] Taken in conjunction with the resolution of the above mentioned trustees of eighty-two years later it seems reasonable to conclude that the bell was removed for the purpose of calling the children to the school there. The Market Hall of this period, a timber-framed building, supported on posts with an open space beneath, is partly shown in the illustration facing page 74.

[1]Report of the Charity Commissioners, 1826. Therein described as ' lying between the river of the High Street of Henley and another river called Floodgate Brook.'
[2]This house was bought under a bequest in Richard Whateley's will of 28 Nov., 1603.
[3]E. I. Fripp, *Shakespeare's Stratford*, p. 22.
[4]Charity Accounts.
[5]Now hanging in St. John's Church Belfry.

It was taken down in 1793 and the building erected on its site is described as an 'insignificant shed'[1] evidently with no room suitable for a school, so that it could not have been continued there.

In the Report on the Charities of 1826 it says that Whateley's house was at that time appropriated to the residence of the schoolmaster who enjoyed it rent free, and that a schoolroom had been added to the house on the land belonging to it. This new building and the repair of the schoolmaster's house was provided partly from the general charity fund and partly by subscription.[2]

The late John Hannett[3] in 1878 informed the Charity Commissioners that a schoolmaster had been in possession of the house since about 1820, but it appears that this should have been 1815, for he continues : ' Previous to the giving over of Whateley's house and premises for a school, the Master was paid up to 1815, £7 9s. and no house, then advanced to £20 with the residence, and since to £50 a year, which sum I have paid from 1872 like former Treasurers.'

It looks, therefore, as if the schoolroom was erected after 1815 and certainly before 1826.

Where the school was held after the Market Hall was pulled down in 1793 until this new room was built is not known.

At a meeting of the Trustees of the Charity Estates, held at the School on 22 May 1816, the following rules and orders were made : Those admitted to be the sons of ' poor, reputable ' persons of Henley who were unable to pay for their education ; that the number of boys should not exceed twenty in any one year who must have attained, or be within three months of, the age of eight years, and that none should remain longer than three years. Each boy to have attended the Sunday School of the Established Church for six months prior to admittance and all were required to attend the Sunday School regularly thereafter. The boys to be instructed in reading, writing and arithmetic, all the books and stationery being paid for by the parents. School to begin at 9-0 o'clock in the morning and 2-0 o'clock in the afternoon. Holidays to be three weeks at Christmas, one week at Easter, one week at Whitsuntide and reasonable absence during harvest at the discretion of the master.[4]

On the 10 July 1860 the Rev. Thomas Jones, perpetual curate[5] of Henley, conveyed to the archdeacon of Worcester for the time being, the house, schoolroom and outbuildings to be for ever appropriated and used as a school for the education of adults and children, or children only, of Henley and Beaudesert, and for the

---

[1] See page 75.
[2] Report of the Commissioners concerning Charities, 23 Jan., 1826.
[3] High Bailiff and Secretary and Treasurer to the Charities.
[4] Charity Accounts.
[5] Title abolished in 1868 when he became ' Vicar ' which he was so styled on his tombstone at Beaudesert in 1877.

residence of the schoolmaster and schoolmistress. Hitherto the Trustees of Whateley's Charity had, of course, been the persons legally entitled to act in all matters relating to the school and it does not appear by what authority the perpetual curate of Henley could convey the premises without their concurrence, which he seems to have done. By it the school was to be 'always in union with, and conducted according to the principles and in furtherance of the ends and designs of the National Society for promoting the education of the poor in the principles of the Established Church.' This meant that henceforth it was to be a church school under a National Society Trust, generally known as a National School.

The school was to be managed by a committee consisting of the principal ministers of Henley and Beaudesert, the churchwardens of both places, two of the Henley Charity Trustees, so long as the Charity Trustees contributed £30 annually, and three other persons, of whom the first were Dr. George Fayrer, Thomas Barnes Couchman and John Hannett, and such other persons as continued to be contributors of £1 yearly to the funds of the school. In the event of a vacancy by death such vacancy to be filled by subscribers of 10s. a year.[1]

For the next seventeen years the school managed to carry on with varying support though it was sometimes closed for lack of funds when the high bailiff and the incumbent both claimed the rent of the schoolhouse. In May 1877 an announcement was made in the Parish Magazine that ' it is impossible to carry on the National School without increased support ; it will, therefore, be closed at Midsummer unless sufficient funds for the payment of debts and suitable provision for the future working of the school are forthcoming.' In June as no response or promise of support had been made the school was closed accordingly.

Early in 1878 the Charity Trustees held a meeting, when it was decided to offer the school £30 from Randall's Charity, which, with the £30 from Whateley's Charity, would make £60 in all and enquiry was made whether ' a new scheme for the appropriation and management of the charities could be allowed.' The result was the Charity Commission Order of 8 July 1879 which put matters on a more satisfactory footing and acknowledged the Conveyance and Trust Deed of 1860 expressly excluding the school and schoolhouse from the control of the Charity Trustees, though in after years it seems to have been overlooked and disputes again took place between the high bailiff and the vicar about the rent of the schoolhouse.

As an elementary school, however, its years were numbered although its use as a Sunday School has been continued. On 9 April 1881 the first School Board was elected for the civil parish of

---

[1] Trust Deed in the safe at St. John's Church. For the greater part of the information about the Free School the writer is indebted to articles in the Parish Magazine in 1933 by the late Mr. A. C. Coldicott.

Wootton, its members being the Rev. G. E. Bell and Mr. H. G.
Hough (Henley), Mr. T. H. G. Newton (Ullenhall), Messrs. John
Smallwood and Joseph Hawkes (Wootton). The Board then began
negotiations with the managers of this church school and the British
School, respectively, for the use of their premises, but by 1884 the
present Central School had been built at a cost of £2,834 on the
site of some old cottages and a malthouse,[1] and was opened as the
Board School on 28 April of that year for all public elementary
pupils. The British School just mentioned was mainly for nonconformists and was built in 1863 at the cost of the late Mr. G. F.
Muntz. It is now used as the Baptist Sunday School.

In Henley Parish Registers John Parry, 'curate of Ullenhall
and schoolmaster of Henley-in-Arden,' is mentioned in 1707 when,
on 9 November of that year, his son, Charles, was baptised and again
on 29 October 1711 another son Henry was also baptised. It
would seem, therefore, that he was master of the Free School at
that time as there was then no other school in the town, so far as we
know, which would entitle him to the foregoing description. In
consequence it may be of interest to include this copy of a letter[2]
he wrote to someone unnamed at Worcester on 11 January 1711-12 :

'Revd. Sir,—It was not my fault yt Mr. Meors letter
subscribed by him, Mr. Jago and myself about Bewdesert and
Oldberrough, arrived not sooner; it lay by ye person who
faithfully promised speedily to deliver it three or four weekes
till I went for it, which was in the beginning of ye Holy days,
and soon after that I sent it with ye shell wherein it was inclosed
by our postwoman to Harry Hall, ye Worcester carrier from
Stratford. I hope he carefully delivered it. As for Moreton
Bagott, the chancel wall is visibly decayed, and as I find it
sunk very much, and ye timbre is not very good, and in the
body of the church ye timbre is much decayed. The rafters
and laces bend in ; in ye steeple there be two bells, and ye
timber is very old, but may be of service longer. As for the
parsonage house and outhouses, they are in very indifferent
repair, but as far as I can find or learn they are in as good
repair at this time as they have been known to be in for several
years past, and as I have been credibly informed they are in
better repair than they were when the tenant entered. My
family hath been visited, my child has had the feaver, and
myself had not my hea th since my scollers broke up. I have
been ery much employ'd in visiting the sick by reason many
o. neighbouring clergy are very much afraid of ye sickness and
small-pox. I have been sent for as far as Sambourn, though
it was five miles from Henley and myself not well. I thanke
God I walked so far with the greatest comfort and alacrity,

---

[1]Tithe Map.
[2]Printed copy formerly in the possession of the late F. C. Wellstood.

and administered ye sacrament to a man and his wife. The woman is since dead. I thanke God I am not afraid to visit the sick and bury ye dead, though ye persons be never so poor or the sickness never so dangerous. If this account of Moreton doth not give satisfaction, if you please to order two or three of the neighbouring clergy to visit I shall be oblidged to you.— I remain, Sir, with all imaginable submission, your most faithful and dutifull servant,

JOHN PARRY.'

The house George Whateley gave for the benefit of the town is a 15th century timber-framed building of a type fairly common to that period as will be seen from the illustration facing page 84. It consists of a hall in the centre originally open to the roof-timbers, with a block on either side each of two storeys, the upper ones projecting at the front. The hall would have an open hearth in the centre of the floor, the smoke escaping through a louvre in the roof. On the south side is the parlour, now divided into two, with a chamber over it, and on the north the former buttery and pantry with a chamber above similarly divided. The original four-centred doorway in the north wing opens into a passage which gives access to the old buttery and pantry on the left, and formerly gave access to the hall on the right through the screen, but now through a door-way in the later bricked wall. A floor has been inserted to provide a bedroom over the lower portion of the hall, partitions and ceilings have been added, but the original design of the house may easily be followed.

It would appear from the will of the Rev. Devereux Wilson, dated 19 May 1725 (see p. 177), that there was then a Latin or grammar school in Henley but no subsequent reference to it has come down to us.

On 22 December 1788 there appeared an advertisement in *Aris's Birmingham Gazette* which affords a good example of 18th century style in educational matters. It reads as follows :

'Beaudesert Grammar School, near Henley-in-Arden.

' The Rev. E. Jones respectfully informs his friends and the public that he has fitted up his house at Beaudesert in the most commodious manner for the reception of twelve boarders ; the number being thus limited, and his taking the classical part of the instructions upon himself, induces him to hope that by a regular plan of education, and a strict attention to the morals of his pupils, he shall be able to render the most perfect satisfaction to those parents, guardians and others, who commit their young gentlemen to his care.

' An assistant of approved abilities is engaged to teach the French language, the mathematics, geography, the use of the globes, writing, arithmetic, and the newest method of book-keeping. Music, dancing, and drawing by approved masters.

' A vacancy for a half-boarder : he must be at least fifteen years of age.

' The situation of Beaudesert is remarkably pleasant, and the playgrounds within the bounds are perhaps equal, if not superior, for its salubrious air, to any in the Kingdom. It is distant from Henley a quarter of a mile.'

The most likely house for a school of this kind would be Beaudesert Park, which since 1788 may have been rebuilt, but no other information about it has come to light.

During the first half of last century the Rev. S. H. Parker kept what is described as a Gentlemen's Boarding Academy at Henley.[1] Some years later, namely in 1850, we first read of Thomas Cooper's Classical and Commercial Academy,[2] which long continued to flourish. For the purpose of his school he built the house now occupied by the Midland Bank, with the schoolroom at the rear.

[1] *West's Directory*, 1830.
[2] *White's Directory*, 1850. He was great uncle of the present writer.

Henley-in-Arden Junior School, Class 6 of 1933 — back: Jim Watkins, John Weldon, Ron Cave, Eric Findon, Jack Hobbins, Chas Williams, Frank Marsh, Bernard O'Donnell, Henry Turvey, Michael Hawkes; standing: Barbara Fowler, Betty Wright, Dorothy Houghton, Harriet Salmons, Dot Neal, June Blackmore, Mina Ewins, Ivy Malins, Joyce Jilkes; sitting: Vera Reynolds, Sheila Foxhall, June Goldthorpe, Eileen Hereper, Betty Newman, May Ewins; front: Alfred Brinkworth, Tom Dipple and Ted Hobbins. (O'D)

THE NONCONFORMISTS AND THE ROMAN CATHOLICS

THE BAPTISTS.

As early as 1688[1] the year after the declaration of Indulgence, the Baptists established themselves in the town ' as a part or branch of the Alcester Church,' and it is recorded that Mary Bissel, Hannah Mullis and Mary Taylor (wife of Theophilus Taylor) were baptised in that year. Nine years later the Rev. John Beddome came to Henley from the Baptist Church Meeting in Horsley Down, Southwark, to assist the aged pastor Mr. John Willis, who died about 1703.[2] In 1711 permission was given by Quarter Sessions for meetings of the Anabaptists, as they were then called, to be held in the house of George Haynes and three years later at the house of Rev. John Beddome, formerly known by the name of ' Holmes's House.'[3] In this house was born, on 23 January 1717, his son, Benjamin Beddome, afterwards pastor of the Baptist Church at Bourton-on-the-Water, the celebrated writer of hymns, who is stated to have composed them to be sung after his sermons to illustrate the truths upon which he had been preaching.[4]

A chapel was built in 1822[5] which was replaced by another built in 1867 of Wilmcote stone at a cost of £1,732, the gift of the late G. F. Muntz of Umberslade.[6] Here a disastrous fire occurred on 1 February 1936, and the walls only were left standing. It was rebuilt on a somewhat smaller scale and reopened in September 1937. The present pastor is the Rev. F. J. Morris.

In the vestry there is a mural tablet inscribed :

' In memory of William Wheeler (many years deacon of this church) who died January 3 1826 aged 63 years. Also of Mary, wife of William Wheeler, who died March 16 1816, aged 64 years. Blessed are the dead which die in the Lord.'

There is a mural tablet in the chapel to the memory of the Rev. Wm. Radburn, pastor 1861-1884, who died in 1909, aged 91 years, and another tablet ' in grateful recognition of the Christian liberality of G. F. Muntz, Esq., J.P.' its great benefactor.

[1]In 1676 there were six Nonconformists over 16 years of age in Henley and Beaudesert but the denomination is not stated. Salt Lib. MS. 33.

[2]The foregoing from Minute Book, Henley Baptist Church, where 1688 is called the year of the ' Glorious Revolution.'

[3]Dissenting Houses, Shire Hall MSS., Warwick. It is stated in the Baptist Church Book, Alcester, 1712, that John Beddome purchased a large house, formerly an Inn at Henley, and fitted up one part of it for his residence and the other for a place of worship. Here he continued until 31 May, 1724.

[4]Dict. Nat. Biog.

[5]In 1821 there were 52 Baptists in Henley-Parish Register No. 4.

[6]Minute Book.

The Methodists.

There was a small congregation of Primitive Methodists in Henley when Hannett wrote in 1863,[1] but the later introduction of Methodism into the town dates from March 1891, when services were first held in an old building situated behind a house which stood on the site occupied by the present chapel. The first trustees[2] were elected in October of that year and they decided to buy the entire property, take down the house and build a chapel in its place, leaving the old Mission Room at the rear for use as a Sunday School. In May 1892 it was accordingly purchased from Mr. R. Newcombe and the building of the chapel was begun on 29 January 1894. It took six months only to complete and was opened for public worship on 26 July the same year. The architect was Mr. Allen of Stratford and the builder Mr. J. W. Lord of Henley. Ten years later the old mission room was pulled down and the present Sunday School built on its site. To Mr. T. R. Perkins, circuit steward and local preacher, the writer is indebted for the foregoing information.

The Quakers.

The first we hear of the Society of Friends, or Quakers as they are called, is in 1696, when one Joseph Beasley proposed to have a meeting at Henley and that a place be bought for a meeting-house and burial ground ; thereupon it was ordered that he and Francis Flower should enquire for such a place. It is not, however, until 1727 that there is definite evidence of a meeting-house being opened, though we have records of meetings taking place in the town as early as 1698, when we read : ' At a monthly meeting held at Fullford Heath [in the parish of Solihull] the 16th of the 10th month of 1698 it was then agreed that Fulford Heath and Hendley be from hence joyned in one monthly meeting and to be duly kept the third Sixth day in every month, that is one day at Fullford Heath and one day at Henley—that is a meeting of business both for men and women.' Three years later it is mentioned that the Henley meetings were held at the house of Richard Lucas.[3] In 1714 the small monthly meeting of Fulford Heath and Henley became part of that of North Warwickshire. At the first named place the meetings took place at the house of Joshua Sargent ' for a long series of years,' as there was no meeting-house there. It is mentioned in 1716 that the two places ' are willing and do join with Birmingham monthly meeting' but no further reference is made to it.

Eleven years later, in 1727, Fulford Heath was discontinued and we are informed that ' this being the year in which a meeting-

[1] *The Forest of Arden*, p. 46.
[2] They were : Messrs. James Evans, Joseph Fisher, John Harding, Thomas Harding, James Henson, George Hopkins, Thomas Pickering and Worthy Sly.
[3] Quarter Sessions Records, Mids, 1701.

house at Henley was opened it appears probable that the larger number of Friends then resided in that particular neighbourhood.' The following expenditure was incurred in 1735 ' for putting the meeting-house in order ' ;

	£	s.	d.
John London's bill for boards	0	14	2
For Nails	0	2	2½
For Calf's Skin	0	1	0
17 yards of Matting at 6d. and carriage ..	0	8	9
Lime and Glue to wash it	0	0	8
George Pool for doing it	0	1	4
	£1	8	1½

Towards the close of the 18th century the meeting at Henley experienced ' some sorrowful decline in numbers as all the country meetings of Warwickshire North.' It was finally discontinued not long after 1829[1] and the meeting-house which had been converted into a cottage was sold about 1866.[2] This building is the present No. 36 High Street and in 1826 it was inhabited by the Poor. Among the names of members of the two places are : Snape, Fowler, Allen, Lucas, Lort, Astley, Field, and Baker.

THE CONGREGATIONALISTS.

The Congregationalists introduced their teaching to Henley and district in 1837, when Mr. William Hood in his Journal writes : ' During the past year I have succeeded in commencing a new interest in Henley-in-Arden. The attendance on the Sabbath and also on a week evening is most gratifying, and a pleasing prospect presents itself of much good being done if a regular supply of preaching can be secured. This town is the centre of one of the most destitute districts in the county of Warwick ; including within a small circumference not less than twelve villages—all destitute of evangelical preaching.' With the help of friends Mr. Hood had then completed the first six months of services and the room occupied was regularly crowded and the number increasing. ' But,' he asks, ' what is now to be done ? Is this place to be relinquished ? Must a crowded congregation be left as sheep without a shepherd ? Shall so fine an opportunity of adopting an important station and of placing the population of twelve neglected villages under evangelical instruction be disregarded ? Will the friends of the Redeemer suffer this ? '

Means were found of establishing a station and in the following year, 1838, Mr. James Dann was appointed to it. In his Journal

[1]Quarter Sessions Records.
[2]This information is derived chiefly from *Friends in Warwickshire* by Wm. White, 1886, which is based mainly on old Minute books.

he says : ' We hope several are convinced of their sinful state and
are seeking reconciliation with God through Christ. The congregation, having been much increased and the people being unable to
erect a chapel, it was thought desirable to obtain larger premises.
A house has consequently been obtained on a lease for seven years
which has been altered into a chapel and was opened on 16
January last, 1839, when sermons were preached by Mr. Sibree,
and Mr. Pope of Leamington. I am happy to say the place is well
filled. Last Sabbath afternoon I commenced preaching at the
destitute hamlet of Lonsomford. I had the pleasure of meeting
about sixty persons to hear the word of life.'

Mr. David Prain[1] from Long Itchington was afterwards
appointed to the station of Henley, who writes in 1840 : ' The
attendance is greatly increased and sometimes in the evening the
gallery stairs are crowded and some retire for want of accommodation.' Mr. Prain continued here for about five years, after which
ministers were sent over for some time from neighbouring towns,
but owing to the difficulty of this and to lack of funds the station
was relinquished.[2]

In the Tithe Map of 1840 there are two buildings described as
' Meeting Houses,' one, the Baptist Chapel and the other situated
just north of Ashbury House. This latter building was afterwards
made into a cottage and in 1911 turned into a garage. It still
retains two old pointed windows and a pulpit built in the wall in
the form of an arched recess, reached by a semi-circular flight of
steps. As there were only two Nonconformist bodies in the town
in 1840 it would seem fairly conclusive that this meeting-house was
the chapel of the Congregationalists until we read the inscription
near the pulpit : ' J.H., 1749,' which is difficult to reconcile with
the statement mentioned above that they bought a house and turned
it into a chapel in 1839 ninety years later than the inscription.
In the absence of any further information on the subject it is
puzzling. Could it have been an early chapel but converted into a
house by the time the Congregationalists purchased it, the
inscription having been allowed to remain all through? If so it
might possibly have been in use at the earlier date by their fore-
runners, the Independents.

THE SALVATION ARMY.

The Salvation Army established itself in Henley in the latter
part of last century but was unable to carry on its work for long
owing to lack of support.

A somewhat amusing account of what happened at Whitsun
1889 is told by a correspondent in the *Stratford Herald* of the 14
June of that year. He writes :

[1]He resided at the present ' Freeman House.'
[2]These notes are taken from *Independency in Warwickshire* by John Sibree and
M. Caston, 1855.

' The announced Whitsuntide festivities at the Salvation Barracks came off on Monday with great *éclat*. A large number sat down to tea, after which several religious ' performances ' were entered into. This demonstration was, however, not without some opposition, for another tea, by ticket, at the next door, we are informed, was got up under the auspices of what is often denounced by the Liberal opposition as ' Beer and Orthodoxy.'

Their Barracks, which was closed about 1893, was a building in Beaudesert street formerly used as a malthouse, and now converted into two cottages—one at the front and one at the rear. It is situated almost in the centre of the row of cottages opposite the churchyard.

The Salvationists were probably drawn to this quarter because in those days the inhabitants of ' Belser ' were mainly poor people. There was much drinking among them and frequently violent quarrels, resulting sometimes in the shedding of blood.

THE ROMAN CATHOLICS.

Henley Roman Catholics attend the Church of Our Lady and St. Benedict at Wootton Wawen, which was opened on 29 November 1904 and replaced the chapel adjoining Wootton Hall, built 1813, which was then closed. A chaplaincy had long existed at the Hall owing to the residence of the old Roman Catholic family of Smythe and its predecessors, but when the property was sold to Mr. G. H. C. Hughes in 1904 it came to an end.[1] It is recorded in 1676 that there were only four ' Papists ' over sixteen years of age in Henley and six in Beaudesert.[2]

In the Quarter Sessions Records[3] for Michaelmas 1778 are the names of those local ' Romanists ' who took the Oath required by the Catholic Relief Act of that year, as follows : Jane Stratford, John Eberall, Joseph Luckett, all of Henley, and Edward Harcourt of Beaudesert. There are also nine names for Wootton. In 1821 the Roman Catholics in Henley numbered forty-nine, who occupied twelve houses.[4] Owing to the difficulties of transport to Wootton, caused by the war, Mass has been sung in the Gild Hall since early in 1943 by Father Collingwood of Wootton.

[1]For further information see *Wootton Wawen*, pp. 35 and 38.
[2]Salt Library, MS. 33. There were 17 at Wootton and 3 at Ullenhall.
[3]Shire Hall, Warwick.
[4]Henley Parish Register, No. 4.

THE TURNPIKE ROAD, COACHES AND RAILWAYS

THE main road from Birmingham to Stratford-on-Avon, which passes through Henley, is very ancient but the earliest reference we have found to it in the records is in 1282, when the 'high road' between Liveridge and Henley is mentioned.[1] In 1726 it was described as ' ruinous and bad ' and a turnpike trust was formed to look after it.[2] Toll gates with their houses were erected, and tolls collected in accordance with a fixed scale of charges.[3] The writer well remembers the toll gate house at the north end of the town in the early nineties of last century, though the gates had been done away with some thirty years before.[4] It was a small, low, red-brick building with a wooden porch, which may now be seen over the door of the cottage opposite the Manse, and was pulled down in 1894 to make a more convenient approach to the old railway station.   The weighing machine-house opposite to which it stood still remains as in former days, the roadway between the two buildings being just wide enough for coaches, wagons, etc., to pass through.   Wm. Taylor was the keeper of the toll gate in 1810, John Brant in 1840 and Wm. Leek was the last to hold the office.

The Industrial Revolution, which began early in the 18th century and the consequent necessity for easier communication and transport, made it imperative that the condition of the roads, then little better than rough tracks, should be improved.

The Turnpike Trusts took over the work which had formerly been done very imperfectly by the several parishes through which the road passed, and a marked improvement followed.   A further important advance took place at the end of the century, when Macadam and Telford began to make the road surface of sharp-edged pieces of stone broken to fairly uniform sizes and embedded in sand and earth.   Turnpike trusts were usually required to erect milestones on their roads, and the one built into a cottage a little below the Baptist Chapel on the opposite side of the road inscribed : ' From London cii miles ; From Stratford viii ; To Birmingham xiv—1748,' was no doubt put up by the above-mentioned trust.

The great coaching age, which did not really begin until the last half of the 18th century, helped to bring Henley into touch with

[1]*Cat. Anct. Deeds*, A4572.

[2]Turnpike Road Acts, Birm. Ref. Lib.   It is said the name ' turnpike ' was derived from the barrier first used to close the road which was originally a horizontal bar studded with spikes (or ' pikes ') and so hinged that it could be swung into a vertical position.

[3]See *Wootton Wawen*, p. 85.

[4]Miss R. Davis whose father kept the toll gate at the top of School Hill, Wootton Wawen, remembers the tolls being collected, and also dog carts being drawn by two dogs for which the toll was 2d.

the outer world, and in 1788 we read that the town was served by a mail coach and four post-coaches which passed through daily.[1]

In 1817 there seem to have been seven coaches passing through daily. The London Mail Coach was diverted, probably in 1821, and its loss would be felt here severely.[2] The arrival of the coaches was eagerly looked forward to by the inhabitants and welcome was the sound of the horn as the coach and four horses, driven by a coachman wearing a top-hat, cantered into the town to pull up at the Swan before proceeding on its way. Those calling at Henley in 1830[3] were :

Birmingham to London. Mornings : The Oxonian at 7-0 ; The Triumph at 7-30. Evenings : The Union at 5-0 ; The Prince at 8-30.

London to Birmingham. Mornings : The Union at 5-0 ; The Prince at 5-0. Afternoons : The Oxonian at 1-0. Evenings : The Triumph at 7-0.

All these went through Oxford and Uxbridge.

Birmingham and Oxford. The Oxford Day Coach : To Oxford at 12-0 ; To Birmingham at 4-0

Birmingham and Stratford-on-Avon. The Paul Pry : To Stratford, Thursday evenings at 8-0 ; To Birmingham, Thursday mornings at 8-0.

In addition there were coaches from Beaudesert (W. Johns') to Birmingham on Monday and Thursday mornings at 7-30 and to Warwick every morning at 8-0 ; in each case they were called ' The Shamrock.'

Horses for the coaches used to be changed at the Swan.[4] Stabling was provided at Liveridge for a number of horses to assist in drawing heavy coach loads up the hill, which was very steep before it was lowered at a later date, and accidents sometimes happened there   The writer's grandmother used to relate how early last century a coach was overturned when descending the hill and people living near hastened to the scene of the accident to succour the injured passengers.   On the coming of the railways the coaches were soon driven off the roads and Henley having no railway station anywhere near it in those days was left somewhat isolated.

A contemporary newspaper[5] at the end of 1838 is quoted as saying : ' A few months ago no fewer than twenty-two coaches left Birmingham daily for London.   Since the opening of the railway that number has been reduced to four and it is expected that these will be discontinued, though the fares by coach are only 20s. inside and 10s. outside, whilst the fares for corresponding places

[1] *Ariss's Birm. Gazette,* 22 Dec., 1788.
[2] *Cary's Road Book,* 1817 ; Stratford-on-Avon Council Book H. f. 118.
[3] *The History, Topography and Directory of Warwickshire* by Wm. West (1830).
[4] West, op. cit.
[5] Cited in Hayser's *Stage Coach and Mail in Days of Yore II,* 273.

on the railroad are 30s. and 20s.' As shown above only four of these twenty-two coaches passed through Henley but it may be seen how rapidly they all disappeared after the railway came.

In addition to the stage-coaches a good deal of travelling was done in private coaches by those who owned them, and by means of hired post-chaise and post-horses which were kept by some of the local innkeepers.

Stage-wagons were much used for conveyance of goods of all kinds and by passengers of the poorer class who could not afford the more expensive coach fares. The interesting illustration from a water-colour made between 1826 and 1838 facing page 94 shows a coach and horses outside the Swan and just beyond it is what appears to be one of the old stage-wagons.

Pleasure coaches brought people out from Birmingham in great numbers at the end of last century for a day or half-day in the country, and with the advent of the motor car soon afterwards the town began to lose much of its atmosphere of seclusion. Of late years the motor traffic has greatly increased and at certain times, particularly week-ends, there is a constant stream of cars passing through. The first motor car to be seen here was in about 1897, which threw up a cloud of dust as it progressed noisily through the High Street. The dust nuisance was, however, soon overcome by the introduction of the tarred roads and is now a thing of the past. The Midland 'Red' Bus service, connecting Henley with Birmingham and Stratford, was started on 6 June 1914.

In the Middle Ages and later horse-back was the chief mode of travel, and pack-horses were used for the transport of goods, but carts were common and wagons afterwards became so. In 1557 William Whately of Henley left to his son John a gelding with a pack-saddle and all furniture for a pack-horse.[1]

There was also a good service of carriers in 1830 as the following will show :[2]

To London : John Jolly calls at the Golden Cross on Sundays, Tuesdays and Thursdays ; and Pickford and Co. by canal.

To Birmingham : John Jolly, Mondays, Wednesdays and Fridays ; Wm. Turner, Wednesdays—both call at the above Inn ; John Howes, from his own house, Mondays and Thursdays ; Wm. Johns, from his house in Beaudesert on the same day.

To Bristol : Wm. Turner calls at the Golden Cross every Thursday.

To Warwick : John Howes, from his house, on Saturdays ; Wm. Johns, from his house in Beaudesert, the same day.

[1] Worc. Wills.
[2] West, op. cit.

In the last decade of the 19th century local carriers charged passengers 1s. each for the return journey to Birmingham.

As late as the second half of last century a sedan chair was kept in Henley by a family named Wells (butchers, of 83 High Street) for hiring out, and was used chiefly for taking ladies to parties and dances.

A private branch railway line to connect Henley with the main line at Rowington was begun in 1861 but abandoned after five years for lack of funds. The Great Western Railway, however, completed it more than thirty years later and it was opened on 6 June 1894. During the period between the last of the coaches and the coming of this railway Henley was a somewhat remote place, being four miles from the nearest station at Bearley (opened in 1860) and six miles from Knowle station (opened in 1852).

The writer remembers travelling on the first train to leave the old station for Birmingham. It was a stiff pull up until the first cutting was reached, and progress was slow, but normal speed was then attained. A few years later the driver of a train coming into Henley, being unaware of the steep declivity, was unable to pull it up at the platform and the engine and tender crashed through the stop-blocks into the field. Fortunately it was halted just short of the brook and no one was injured.

In 1908 the present North Warwickshire Line was opened for traffic and brought the town into closer touch with Birmingham to the north and Stratford-on-Avon to the south, resulting in an increase of residents from the former centre. During the Great War of 1914-18 the ' metals ' on the old branch line were taken up for shipping across the channel for use behind the fighting line, but it is said they never reached the other side. They have not been replaced and this line has ever since remained derelict.

Established] **E. GOULD,** [40 Years.

GENERAL CARRIER AND COAL MERCHANT,
HENLEY-IN-ARDEN.

Leaves Henley for Birmingham daily at 8 a.m., returning from the "Spread Eagle," Spiceal St., Bull Ring, at 4 p.m

COMMISSIONS PROMPTLY EXECUTED.

PLEASE ADDRESS:
"PER GOULD."

F. G. will be pleased to furnish Address Cards to his customers, gratis, on application.

E.G. will esteem it a favour if customers will notify to him any irregularities.

FURNITURE CAREFULLY REMOVED.   ESTIMATES FREE.
TRUCK-LOADS OF COAL TO ANY STATION.

In 1892 local carrier Gould advertised in the 'Forest of Arden Illustrated Almanack'.

THE SWAN AND OTHER INNS.

THE White Swan Hotel, which stands opposite the Gild Hall, had its plaster removed in 1935, revealing a charming building of the late 16th century, partly refronted a century later. It consists of a middle block with cross wings on either side, both gabled. The middle block has a gateway in its northern half with square timber framing above ; the southern half is of red brick with stone dressings and has a two-storied bay window with old moulded stone mullions. The upper storey and gabled top storey of the north wing are both iettied and have square framing with geometrical panels somewhat resembling mediæval foiling, similar to that of 'The Corner House.' The south wing has a timbered gable-head like the one on the north but the remainder of the wing is of brick and stone and both wings have modern bay windows.

In August 1608, it is described as 'An Inn called the Swan with barn, stables, etc., orchard and curtilage ' [that is a courtyard] covering one acre in all. The then tenant, Thomas Kirby, also held four acres of arable land in the common field called The Backfield and a small dwelling house and curtilage in the occupation of H. Clarke. For this property, which he held in right of Katherine, daughter and heir of George Whatley, he paid 4s. and suit of court to the lord of the manor.[1] Later in the same year Thomas Wheler ' of the Swane ' was presented at the Court Leet for ' syne or ronge '[2] and in 1613 as a victualler and tipler who broke the assize and suffered unlawful games in his house. In the Hearth Tax Returns of 1663 ' William Ingram in the Swane being a voyd house,' is stated to be liable for six hearths, the largest number in the town. He appears to have been followed by John Morrell (five hearths), who occupies the same place in the return for 1670.[3] In a letter[4] from Lady Luxborough to Shenstone, dated 27 July 1748, she writes : ' On Saturday two gentlemen set out separate roads for Oxford to get his [Mr. Dolman's] scholarship ; one of which brought this news to the Swan, and told it to Mr. Hall and Mr. Holyoak,' the parson and doctor, respectively. The Mr. Dolman here referred to was a cousin of Shenstone and brother of Miss Dolman whom he so much admired, as appears from some playful verses he addressed to her.

As shown in another chapter the Swan was in days gone by a well-known coaching inn and many a scene familiar to us in Dickens must have been enacted there. Thomas Chamberlain

[1]Land Rev. Msc. Bks., 228, f. 43.
[2]*Records of the Manor of Henley-in-Arden*, pp. 69 and 78.
[3]Shire Hall MSS, Warwick.
[4]Lady Luxborough's *Letters*, p. 43.

was its host in 1810. It seems likely that it took its name from the crest of the Staffords, overlords of Henley, which is, in the language of heraldry, a swan argent, meaning a swan, silver or white in colour.

This ancient hostelry last century was part of the Barrells property and in 1855 the inn premises and yard, the croft, the bowling green and bowling green close embraced 5a. 1r. 26p., and was valued at £931 19s. 10d.[1] The bowling green here mentioned was situated at the top of the Swan croft and was cut through by the railway, completed in 1908. It was a pleasant spot surrounded by some fine trees and was much favoured by local enthusiasts of this ancient game. The present bowling green was afterwards made at the lower end of the croft.

Formerly the North Warwickshire Hounds met at the Swan, making a picturesque scene in the street, but since motors came and traffic increased they have met at places like the Bird-in-Hand, which could be reached by way of by-lanes.

The Blue Bell is a late 15th century timber-framed building of L shaped plan, the northern part of which has an overhanging and gabled upper storey facing the street of close-set studding with tie beams and a collar beam. The south gable end of the south wing inside has close-set studding and a heavy tie beam, the room on the ground floor having cross beams in the ceiling. It has an interesting high gateway north of the gabled wing with an upper storey above it higher than the original part ; an addition probably of the 17th century.

The Three Tuns has a 17th century timber-framed wing at the back, but the Golden Cross, at the corner of Littleworth, was entirely rebuilt about forty years ago. The latter probably takes its name from one of the charges of the arms of Sir Ralph Boteler (see p. 58). These four inns with the Black Swan and Red Lion are the only survivors of some dozen which flourished at the beginning of this century. Of those which have gone the earliest we read of is the Bull's Head in a survey of 1810. Sixteen years later the house on the north side of the Swan is stated to have been known by the name of the Talbot Inn and then recently closed.[2]

This inn is of interest as having been the meeting place of St. John's Lodge of Freemasons from the time it was constituted in 1791 until 1795. William James, who kept it, was the first treasurer, and among the other original members Samuel Porter, a portrait painter, was worshipful master and another William James, the local attorney and railway projector, was the senior warden, afterwards becoming master. The Lodge was, in 1795, moved to the White Lion, Hockley Heath, but brought back to Henley, to the George Inn, two years later, soon after which it ceased working. In 1811 it was transferred to Birmingham and renamed the

---

[1]Survey of Barrells Estate, 1855, in the possession of Mrs. Willoughby Smallwood.

[2]William Chambers' Charity, Commissioners' Report, 1826.

Shakespeare Lodge.[1] The new De Montfort Lodge was constituted in 1929 and meets at the Gild Hall.

The house just south of the Almshouses was until about 1870 the Cross Keys, an ancient sign representing the arms of the Papal See. It has two gable ends towards the street and the upper storey retains its 17th century square framing. It was kept by Nathaniel Joiner in 1810.

Of those inns closed in comparatively recent years the Bear and Ragged Staff is partly timber-framed work of the early 17th century with later additions and alterations, now divided into two tenements belonging to Mr. R. L. Newcombe, who lives in the one at the corner of the Bear Lane. The sign of the bear and ragged staff which formerly swung before this inn represented the two badges of the Beauchamp Earls of Warwick conjoined, as they often were. They were so used by Richard Neville, Earl of Warwick, the ' Kingmaker ' (overlord of Henley) in right of his wife, and by John Dudley, Duke of Northumberland, as Earl of Warwick.

The George and Dragon, now an attractive private residence, known as ' The Old George,' which has been reconstructed, is probably of the 16th century but the old timbers in front are an addition from elsewhere. Its painted sign of St. George slaying the dragon could be seen hanging over the door until the beginning of this century and added to the old-world charm of the market place. The White Horse (No. 130 High Street) is of two stories and attics, the upper storey and two gables having close-set studdings of the 16th century. It had stabling at the rear for horses and four were kept in coaching days but its only means of access was through the front door ! In one of the front rooms at the King's Head, before it was converted into a private house, there were staples driven into the wall to which rogues and vagabonds used to be chained to await the magistrates. The last of the closed inns to be mentioned is the Coach and Horses, which as a public house probably dated from coaching days.

In conclusion it may be well to remember how marked has been the influence of inns on the social life of England, an influence not by any means wholly bad, for they have ministered to the comfort and well-being of large numbers of our countrymen through the ages, and many have sung their praises.

DR. SAMUEL JOHNSON AT HENLEY

DR. Johnson, when on his way to London in 1776, after his Scottish tour, stayed a night at one of the inns in Henley accompanied by Boswell. It has often been claimed that this was The White Swan, and it may well have been so, but Boswell merely records that

[1] *Trans. of Quatuor Coronati Lodge*, vol. xxxix. The Shakespeare Lodge at Stratford-on-Avon and the Lodge of Apollo at Alcester sprang from St. John's Lodge.

' we happened to lie this night at *the* Inn at Henley,' and he tells us that earlier in the day at an excellent inn at Chapel House, near Chipping Norton, Johnson had recited with great emotion Shenstone's well-known lines :

> Whoe'er has travell'd life's dull round,
> Where'er his stages may have been,
> May sigh to think he still has found
> The warmest welcome at an inn.

There were at least fifteen public houses in Henley and whichever it may have been we hope the choice was an equally happy one.[1]

It has been stated frequently that Shenstone wrote these lines at Henley, but they were written at The Sunrising on Edge Hill in 1751, then a famous hostelry. This is made quite clear in a book by Richard Graves entitled *Recollections of some particulars in the life of the late William Shenstone,* 1788, wherein we read that Shenstone had been on a visit to his college friend Whistler at Whitchurch, near Pangbourne, and being annoyed over two trivial incidents, ' took a cool leave' and came that night to the Sunrising, where he wrote the poem.

Shenstone's lines first appeared in Dodsley's *Collections of Poems by Several Hands,* in 1748, with the heading, ' Written at an inn on a particular occasion,' but when the poem was reprinted in 1764 ' Henley-in-Arden ' was wrongly substituted for ' an inn.'

Jack Blackwell, father and son, Henley's blacksmiths, here in 1914.

[1]Johnson's father, Michael Johnson, married his mother, Sarah Ford, at Packwood, 19 June, 1706.

MENTAL ASYLUMS

IT appears from the grants and annual renewal licences in the Quarter Sessions Records that up to 1805 all the private mental asylums in the county were at Henley and Wootton. In Henley William Roadnight's was the oldest, and was afterwards carried on by Mary Roadnight, who is mentioned in 1778 ; Thomas Burman was first licensed in 1797 ; Benjamin Gibbs in 1798 and Samuel Brown, The Stone House, in 1816. At Wootton, Mary Gibbs was granted a licence in 1818 and Edward Cooper,[1] of Henley, at midsummer, 1824, was licensed ' to keep a house belonging to Dame Catherine Maria Smythe opposite the paper mill at Wootton as a private asylum.' This would be the house now known as ' The Priory.' The only one to survive was that established by Thomas Burman at the present Burman House.[2] It was continued by his son, Dr. T. J. P. Burman (who built Arden House and died in 1840) and by his grandson, Dr. H. F. Burman, who died in 1850. The latter, at the time of his death, was assisted by Dr. W. B. Diamond, and in addition there were ten patients at Hurst House.[3] In 1854 the asylums are stated to be under the management of the same Dr. Diamond,[4] who died the following year. Ten years later we read that there were male and female patients at Burman House, females at Hurst House under Dr. Fayrer, and ' a small number of first-class patients 'under Mr. G. R. Dartnell at Arden House[5] where he remained until 1876, when it became a school (see p. 108). After Dr. Fayrer's death in 1868, Dr. Samuel Hollingsworth Agar acquired Burman House and in 1874 he bought Hurst House. In 1882, having built Glendossill, the patients from Burman House were transferred there. Dr. Agar died in 1905 and the mental home was carried on by his son, a doctor of the same name, until he retired in 1920, when it passed to his nephew, Dr. Willoughby Agar, the present high bailiff.

The Quarter Sessions records also contain the appointments of visitors to these asylums under the Act of 1774. Local visitors so appointed were the Rev. Thomas Hall, rector of Beaudesert and curate of Henley, in 1774 ; the Rev. Daniel Gaches, vicar of Wootton, in 1787 ; the Rev. P. S. Ward, perpetual curate of Henley, in 1805 ; and the Rev. John Ellis, vicar of Wootton, in 1826.

A notable name occurring is that of Dr. John Conolly of

---

[1] Of Ashbury House ; he married secondly, Martha, widow of Major C. Noble, of Hurst House. He was the writer's great-great uncle.

[2] The establishment included a house on the other side the lane, with which it was connected by a covered overhead bridge.

[3] *White's Directory*, 1850.

[4] *Kelly's Directory*, 1854.

[5] *Kelly's Directory*, 1864.

Stratford-on-Avon, who was appointed visiting physician of Henley mental asylums in 1823. This eminent man advocated a humane and rational treatment of the insane without chains and stripes which were then in common use. He remained at Stratford from 1822 to 1827 and then went to London, but returned to Warwick in 1830, when he again took up the work of inspecting physician to the asylums of Warwickshire. On his becoming resident physician to the Middlesex Asylum at Hanwell in 1839, he ordered all mechanical restraint to be discontinued.[1] The late Mr. James Wakefield (low bailiff) remembered as a boy joining other boys in watching and teasing the unfortunate patients who were shackled and confined in the basement of the Stone House, they being visible from the outside. Conolly may well have protested against this cruel mechanical restraint when he visited Henley.

The above-mentioned Mr. Dartnell, before he came to Arden House, was Inspector-General of Military Hospitals,[2] and in the well-known picture of Queen Victoria visiting wounded soldiers from the Crimea at Chatham Hospital, he is seen in uniform next but one to the Queen. His son, Major-General Sir John G. Dartnell, K.C.B., as a subaltern of the 86th Regiment fought in the Indian Mutiny. He was present at the capture of Chandaree, and led, with great bravery, the only escalade attack on the Fortress of Jhansi, when he was wounded five times, only escaping death by a miracle.

In 1874 he founded the Natal Mounted Police, which he commanded for nearly thirty years, doing fine service in South Africa, and he fought with distinction in the Boer War, 1899-1902, during which he held several important commands including that of the Imperial Light Horse. He is said to have had the courage of a lion and to have been much beloved by the men under him, to whom he was as faithful as they were to him. They would follow ' Hell-fire Jack,' as he was called, anywhere.[3] To his daughter, Mrs. Buckston Browne, who was born at Arden House, I am indebted for some of the foregoing information.

[1]*Dict. of Nat. Biog.*
[2]*Kelly's Directory,* 1864.
[3]*The Mounted Police of Natal,* 1913, by H. P. Holt.

THE LOCAL BANKS AND THE POST OFFICE

MESSRS. Tomes, Chattaway and Ford, bankers at Stratford-on-Avon from 1810 to 1834, had an agency at Henley which by a process of absorption became successively the Stourbridge and Kidderminster Bank, the Birmingham Banking Co., and the Metropolitan Bank, before being taken over by the Midland Bank in 1914.[1] The Bank Agent in the early days was Richard Burman, son of Richard Burman of Botley, who had set up as a draper in 1805 in the premises in Henley now known as 'Ye Olde Bank House' (opposite the Swan), which he had bought that year and where he combined successfully the two businesses. At his death in 1850 he was succeeded by his son John, who, however, failed in 1870 owing probably to his expensive tastes, particularly hunting.[2] The building was purchased by the Stourbridge and Kidderminster Bank about 1870 but since the late eighties the Bank has been carried on where it is to-day. Lloyds Bank was opened in 1914 as a sub-branch to Stratford-on-Avon in a portion of the restored Gild Hall, becoming a full branch in 1938, and when its present premises (long known as The Corner House) were purchased in 1943, the business was transferred there.

This building, which dates from the late 16th century, received drastic treatment in 1916, when the lower storey was rebuilt with brick and the upper storey was restored. The plan is L shaped with the main block facing north up the High Street and forms a prominent feature in the Market Place. West of it the street narrows considerably and on its east side is the Back Lane. The north front has a middle gable flush with the wall below but the gabled east and west ends are jettied. The timber-framing of these heads is in square panels each enriched with four thin quadrant braces which have a middle knop in each curve, thus forming a faint resemblance to mediæval foiling similar to that of the White Swan. The upper storey of all three sides is plastered. That of the east end is jettied and has an oriel window ; but the west end, which was probably also jettied, is now flush with the wall beneath. The lower storey is modern brickwork. The wing extending south is stuccoed and its west side has a gable in the middle similar to the others. East of the wing are modern additions.

THE POST OFFICE

In 1830 when Samuel Hoitt was postmaster[3] letters were carried by mail coach. They were despatched to London every

[1] *A Hundred Years of Joint Stock Banking* by Crick and Wadsworth, p. 59, and Appendix B.
[2] *The Burman Chronicle* by John Burman, F.R.Hist.S., p. 48, and *White's Directory*, 1850.
[3] In 1840 he owned and lived at the present Tudor House, Tithe Map.

afternoon at 4-0 and arrived there every morning at 9-0, and were despatched to Birmingham each morning at 9-0 and arrived from there each afternoon at 4-0.[1] John Hannett was appointed postmaster in 1844, when the post office was at the house just north of the Swan and he retired about 1869. It was afterwards moved to York House for ten years, then to No. 97, High Street, and subsequently about 1887 to its present home, the Stone House. In the nineties and in the early part of this century mails were carried between Wootton and Birmingham, calling at Henley, in a horse-drawn van by J. W. Green, whose son now conveys the mail by motor van.

The Stone House, as its name implies, is built of stone, and is in the ' Adam ' style of about 1770.[2]

Telegraphic communication was first established with the Leamington office about 1889 and messages were transmitted there on a single needle instrument ; this was replaced by a morse sounder in 1907.

Since the telephone was brought to Henley in 1909, telegrams have been telephoned to Birmingham for despatch from there.

To Mrs. S. G. Caswell, who retired from the position of sub-postmistress in 1941, the writer is indebted for some of the foregoing information.

At an exhibition held in the town in 1891 the complete arrangements of the telephone were shown to the inhabitants for the first time. Other new inventions then on view were electrical accumulators, a slot-meter for gas, and a typewriter.[3]

---

[1] *Hist., Topog. and Directory* by Wm. West (1830).
[2] In 1886 it was a boarding school, when H. E. **Bryant** was tenant. See illustration facing p. 74.
[3] *Stratford-on-Avon Herald*, 21 Feb., 1891.

THE PUBLIC SERVICES

HENLEY GAS WORKS

AT a meeting held on 20 November 1862 it was stated by Mr. Hedley, a civil engineer of Banbury, that an efficient works, including all expenses of laying down pipes, etc., could be provided at a cost of £1,600, and he was prepared to guarantee 5 per cent dividend for the first year, and 6 per cent. for seven, fourteen or twenty-one years. It was then resolved to form a company and issue 320 shares of £5 each, and that Mr. Charles East act as Secretary and canvass the town for shareholders. The following amounts in shares were subscribed at the meeting : Mr. W. C. Holmes of Huddersfield, who was to be the contractor, £800 ; Mr. Hedley, £100 ; Mr. Ford, £75 ; Dr. Fayrer, £100 ; Mr. T. B. Couchman, £100 ; Mr. Dartnell, £50.[1] The remainder of the capital was forthcoming, the gasworks was erected in Beaudesert and began supplying gas in 1864.

Electricity is supplied by the Leicestershire and Warwickshire Electric Power Company from their Avon Power Station, Warwick, and was first made available in May, 1930.

HENLEY WATER SUPPLY

It is mentioned in 1844 that all the water then came from local wells some of which had pumps,[2] and these conditions continued, except that more pumps were brought into use, until 1894, when a new scheme was introduced. A reservoir was then constructed at Ford Hall by Mr. J. E. Wilcox to hold 12,000 gallons. From it a cast-iron main was laid to the Ullenhall-Tanworth Road at Mockley, which was continued along Tanworth Lane to the Bird-in-Hand, thence to Henley with branches to Warwick Road and Ullenhall Road. In 1915, owing to the growth of Henley, the amount of water so obtained was found to be insufficient and a new reservoir was built at Liveridge Hill to hold 75,000 gallons. Into this certain springs gravitated from Lower Liveridge Hill Farm and a new main was laid from it to join up with the existing one at the Bird-in-Hand. These two schemes supplied the needs of Henley until 1936, when the Ministry of Health made some criticisms as to the purity of the Ford Hall water, and the Rural District Council decided to approach the Birmingham Corporation for a supply to be taken from their mains at Hockley Heath. Agreement having been reached, new case mains were laid to connect up with mains in Henley, and the scheme was enlarged to take in the parishes of Claverdon, Wootton Wawen and Bearley. The cost of this work, which was completed in 1939, was about £22,000.

---

[1]From an old prospectus.
[2]*Lewis, Topog. Dict.*, 1844.

The Liveridge Hill water was retained in case of emergency, and although Ford Hall was not cut off, no supply has since been taken from there except for about three weeks in 1941, when enemy action caused temporary damage to some of the Birmingham mains.

Sewerage

The sewerage of Henley was undertaken in 1894 and gravitated to works at the rear of Blackford Mill Farm. This proving insufficient, owing to the treatment being by land irrigation only, an extension was made in 1912 to new works near Pennyford Farm of the settlement tank type with filters designed by Mr. J. E. Wilcox. At the same time a small pumping plant was provided near the Bull's Head to raise the sewage from the low lying portion of Wootton which was then added to the sewer. This scheme has proved fully efficient. [1]

The Fire Station and Engine

The Fire Station in Station Road was built by Stratford-on-Avon Rural District Council in 1939 and contains engine room, men's room and storeroom. The motor turbine fire-engine now in use formerly belonged to Stratford Borough Fire Brigade and is under the control of a joint committee representing the town of Henley and the Rural District Council, but during the war was under the National Fire Service. An old horse-drawn manual fire engine, which had been used at Henley for over 100 years, was sold in 1934 to Mr. D. Copley of Sheldon, who kept it as an object of antiquarian interest until 1943, when he let it go for scrap. The pumping apparatus was worked by a vertical shaft on either side which moved up and down and the full crew was sixteen men, eight on each side. The jet, which is 8-ft. 6-ins. long, is preserved in the Gild Hall. It is a pity Henley did not retain this old relic of a bygone age, which would have been of interest to future generations. The Ambulance Garage, also in Station Road, was built in 1935, and a tablet inside reads: ' Owing to the incentive caused by a very generous donation towards the Jubilee Garage Fund by Mrs. K. L. Shewell, the remainder of the cost of the building was provided by the kindness of numerous donors from Henley-in-Arden and district, May 4 1935.'

---

[1] The writer is indebted to Mr. H. J. Weeks, **District** Surveyor, for information about the water and sewerage.

WILLIAM JAMES—PROJECTOR AND ENGINEER OF RAILWAYS.

WILLIAM James was the eldest son of William James, attorney and magistrate of Henley, by Mary, his wife, daughter of Simon Lucas of King's Norton. He was born here on 13 June 1771, baptised at St. John's Chapel on 6 July following, and educated at Warwick and Winson Green Schools. In due course he studied law in London and in 1796 when he was twenty-five he married the orphan daughter of William Tarleton of Henley and went to reside at the Yew Trees, then called Yew Tree Hall. He does not appear to have made much progress at Henley as a lawyer and a year or two after his marriage he moved to Wellesbourne on being appointed agent and solicitor to Lord Warwick and Deputy Recorder of Warwick, removing to St. John's in that town about 1801.

Although he had made several surveys for short private railways, he does not seem to have had in mind any scheme for the general use of railways as a means of transport until 1808, and it was some twelve years later before he actively advocated the establishment of railways for the public conveyance of goods and passengers. In 1820 Thomas Gray published his book, *Observations on a General Iron Railway* . . . and it is difficult to decide whether James or Gray was the actual pioneer of the railway system. It may safely be said, however, that by his many surveys and his writings, James did almost more than anyone else towards establishing public railways in this country, and it would seem that some of the credit hitherto accorded to George Stephenson is due to him.

But, whereas James was a visionary, Stephenson was the practical man who put his schemes into effect and achieved so much. In middle life James became an iron-master, colliery owner and landed proprietor on a large scale and in 1812 was stated to be worth £150,000, but owing to his having too many irons in the fire and to general misfortune, he became bankrupt in 1823. Thereafter he spent the remainder of his life at Bodmin, where he earned just enough to live upon by the management of agricultural estates and as a consulting engineer, dying there on 10 March 1837.[1]

On the aqueduct at Wootton, erected in 1813, it is recorded that James was then Deputy Chairman of the Birmingham and Stratford Canal, of which formerly he had been the engineer. As mentioned on page 95 he was an original member of St. John's Lodge of Freemasons at Henley in 1791.

[1]Sources : *The Locomotive*, 15 Mar., 1937; *The Two James's* by E.M.S.P., 1861 ; D.N.B., Local Records ; *Wootton Wawen*, p. 86.

THE YEW TREES, where James went to reside after marriage, though much altered and added to, is a charming old gabled house with a wealth of timber-framed work mainly late Elizabethan, but a gabled wing at the back is probably a century earlier. The house has been lengthened to the south by a brick addition, and on the north is an extension of the 16th century used as solicitors' offices for many years past, the present firm being Messrs. G. F. Lodder and Sons. The inner entrance of the porch has an ancient door studded with nails which admits to a lobby, on the north side of which is a room having a large stone fire-place with foliage ornament, while the small room on the south of it has a plainer stone fireplace dated 1651. The two rooms behind these have now been thrown into one which has an early 16th century stone fire-place with four-centred arch and carved overmantel of five bays. The room is lined with linen-fold panelling of the 16th century and at its north end is a 17th century staircase. The house is now a private residential hotel. The yew trees from which it takes its name are stated to have been planted by Simon Kempson[1] in 1730 during his residence here. The Rev. Poyntz Stewart Ward, Perpetual Curate of Henley, 1806-1842, owned and lived in the house.[2]

The Yew Trees in 1919. (O'D)

[1]He would be the son of Simon Kempson, 1642-1719 (see p. 60) who also probably lived here.

[2]Tithe apportionment, 1840—He was formerly assistant curate.

SOME HIGH BAILIFFS OF HENLEY

John Hannett,[1] High Bailiff, 1873-93, was born 25 October 1803 at Sleaford, Lincs., where his father of the same name, formerly Fleet Surgeon in the Royal Navy, practised as a surgeon until his death in February 1809, aged 42. John Hannett, who was first apprenticed to a printer and book-binder at Sleaford, entered the publishing house of Simpkin Marshall and Co., London, at the age of twenty-four. While with this firm he employed his leisure hours after business in collecting material which he afterwards used in his writings.

Hannett's first book, a practical treatise on the art and craft of bookbinding, of which he himself was a master, was entitled *Bibliopegia, or the Art of Bookbinding in all its branches.* It was published in the year 1835, under the pen name of John Andrews Arnett. The next book, published in 1837, was of a more ambitious nature, entitled, *An Inquiry into the Nature and Form of the Books of the Ancients with a History of Bookbinding from the Times of the Greeks and the Romans to the Present Day.* This book was well received, and in combination with ' *Bibliopegia* ' it passed through six editions between 1837 and 1865. In the same year (1837) appeared *The Bookbinders' School of Design as applied to the Combination of Tools in the Art of Finishing,* with eight plates by Joseph Morris. *Bibliopegia* was translated into German, and published at Stuttgart in 1837.

Long hours of work had overtaxed his strength and in consequence he left London in the year of Queen Victoria's accession to commence business on his own account as a printer and bookbinder at Market Rasen in his native county. On 10 November 1844 John Hannett removed to Henley and began business as a printer, bookbinder, stationer and postmaster, from which he retired about 1869. In 1848 he issued the fourth edition of *Bibliopegia* printed by himself but bearing the name of Simpkin Marshall and Co. At Henley he turned his attention to local history and wrote his valuable book on the towns and villages of the district which he named *The Forest of Arden,* published in 1863. A revised edition of this work was issued shortly before his death.

During the twenty years he was High Bailiff he took a very active part in all that concerned the welfare of the town and discharged his duties faithfully and well.

On 12 April 1893, in his ninetieth year, John Hannett passed peacefully to his rest. With his will was found a card on which he had written these lines :

> But late I saw him, still the same,
> Though years lay on him, mellow, ripe and kind,
> Age had but hardened, not subdued,
> Had but matured, not dimm'd his vigorous mind.

[1]The early information is from a memoir in *A History of the Art of Bookbinding* by W. S. Brassington, 1894.

After Hannett retired from business about 1869, be bought and went to reside at the picturesque house in High Street called 'The Gables,' where he ended his days. In 1687 this property was described as a cottage or tenement 'in two parts divided' with a hempleck adjoining, situated between land of Symon Kempson, gent. on the north and land of Robert Handy on the south, and extending from the High Street on the west to certain grounds called 'the Moores' on the east. It was then owned by Job Attwood, maltster, who occupied one part of it, and Wm. Harrison occupied the other.[1] In 1696 it was assigned to Benjamin Twitty of Cubbington in trust for Elizabeth Twitty, spinster, of Wawens Wootton.[2]

The house dates from the late 15th century but has been much altered. Its main existing portion is rectangular; the timber-framed and gabled end facing the street has an overhanging upper storey, the supporting beam of which is moulded and rests on curved brackets and projecting joists. It has a great stone chimney-stack, probably of the 16th century and the stone fireplace in the upper front room is square with a chamfered lintel.

An Elizabethan ceiling here hides the ancient roof. In a window in the room underneath is the figure of William de Senye, Prior of Wootton, also the arms of Wootton Priory and of Ralph Boteler, all apparently modern. Originally the house had another block on the north side similar in character to that existing on the south,[3] with the present projecting wing, then the hall and open to the roof, in the centre.[4] In 1863 the house was a butcher's shop.[5]

CHARLES COUCHMAN, J.P., High Bailiff, 1893-1910, was born in 1858, the eldest son of Thomas Barnes Couchman of Beaudesert Park, who had joined E. L. Gibbs in the firm of Henley Solicitors, the last-named having succeeded William Welch Lea. Charles Couchman was educated at Rugby and articled to his father, succeeding him in the practice about 1889. Some two years later he took into partnership Theodore Christophers and not long after that relinquished active participation in the work of the firm[6] and threw himself whole-heartedly into public life. He was an active county magistrate, sitting on the Bench at Henley from 1897 to 1919; a member of the Stratford-on-Avon Board of Guardians for twenty-five years, during which time he was vice-chairman for six years and chairman sixteen years; chairman of the Stratford Rural District Council for many years and the first chairman of

[1]Deed in possession of the present owner and occupier, Mr. C. E. Mercer, dated 14 June, 1687.
[2]Ibid., 1 Oct., 1696.
[3]Information from the late Mr. S. Wakefield, whose mother was born in the house.
[4] The bedroom in this wing dates from Elizabethan times, but the outside brickwork is modern.
[5]*Forest of Arden*, p. 44.
[6]Mr. G. F. Lodder joined the firm in 1902 and is still practising with his two sons as G. F. Lodder and Sons.

the Wootton Wawen Parish Council. To these offices, including that of High Bailiff, he brought exceptional ability and energy and was a wise and firm manager of public affairs who won the respect of all. For his outstanding services to the town and district he was made an honorary burgess of the ancient borough of Henley on 9 July 1919. He married, in 1884, Florence Catherine, eldest daughter of the Rev. Richard Thursfield, sometime vicar of Ullenhall, and while he was practising lived at the Yew Trees but upon his retirement went to reside at Ireland's Farm, and after some years returned to the town to live at The Elms. About 1910 he built a house known as ' Whitley ' on a fine site at Preston Bagot overlooking Wootton Wawen, but left in 1919 and lived at Weston-super-Mare until his death on 18 July 1932.

DR. WILLIAM ERNEST NELSON, O.B.E., M.A., Clare Coll., Camb., J.P., M.R.C.S., L.R.C.P., High Bailiff 1910-22, was the son of the Rev. William Nelson and was born at The Manor House, Feckenham, in 1871. As a boy he came to Henley when his father moved his preparatory school thence to Arden House in 1876, where it has since continued to prosper. On completing his hospital training at St. Thomas's Hospital he acquired Dr. James Arthur's medical practice at Henley and at the same time went into partnership of the school with his brother Oswald, who acted as the headmaster. In 1930 Dr. Nelson retired from general practice but retained his interest in the school until his lamented death in 1933 at the age of sixty-two. His son, Mr. J. P. Nelson, succeeded to the headmastership on the retirement of his uncle Oswald in 1927. Dr. Nelson's services and benefactions to the town are notable and some of them are recorded elsewhere in this book ; few have done more for the good of the town. From 1914 to 1919, during the Great War and after, he was medical director for Warwickshire in charge of hospitals.

WILLIAM THOMAS TAYLOR, J.P., High Bailiff, 1922-26, was born at Wootton Wawen in 1860 and educated at the British School, Henley. After being in a small way of business he began dealing in property in Birmingham and made such a success of it that he was able to retire in his early forties. Having erected a substantial residence for himself at the south end of the town, which he called Hollyhurst, and the row of villas adjoining, on the Ullenhall Road, he returned to Henley about 1905 and devoted his ability and energy to the work of local government, ultimately becoming High Bailiff and a county justice, sitting on the local Bench. For twenty-four years he represented Henley on the Stratford-on-Avon Rural District Council and Board of Guardians, and was chairman of the latter body for five years. He was also chairman of the School Managers. Mr. Taylor, who was held in high esteem for his sterling character and sound judgment, was a staunch churchman, and for many years churchwarden at St. John's Church. He died after a long illness in 1929.

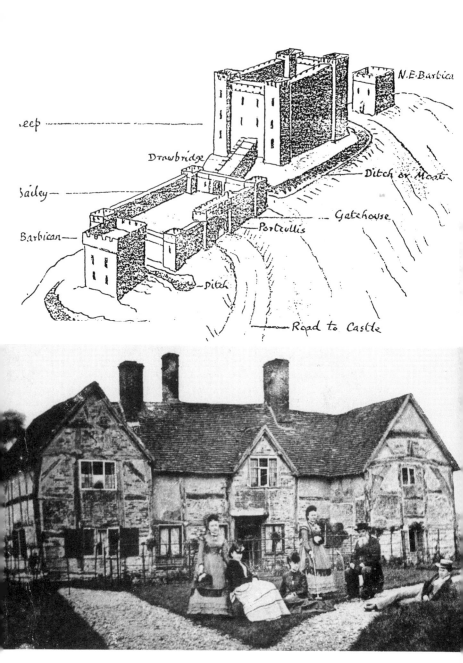

Keep

Drawbridge

Sally

Barbican

Ditch

N.E.Barbica

Ditch or Moat

Gatehouse

Portcullis

Road to Castle

ABOVE: A reconstruction of Beaudesert Castle (O'D) and BELOW:
Beaudesert Rectory in 1880. (WI

xix

GREAT WESTERN RAILWAY.

OPENING OF NEW LINE

BETWEEN

KINGSWOOD

AND

HENLEY-IN-ARDEN

On WEDNESDAY, JUNE 6th, 1894,

The NEW LINE between KINGSWOOD and HENLEY-IN-ARDEN will be Opened for PASSENGER and PARCELS TRAFFIC, and on and from that date,

A SERVICE OF PASSENGER TRAINS

Will run as under :—

		WEEK DAYS.												SUNDAYS.	
		T A.M.	A.M.	A.M.	P.M.	P.M.	P.M.	P.M.	P.M.	**T**	**T**	P.M.	A.M.	P.M.
Wolverhampton (Low Level)	dep.	—	7 45	9 52	12 10	1 5	3 32	3 40	4 23	5 25		6 10	8 35	4 25
Birmingham (Snow Hill)	,,	7 0	8 32	10 35	1 5	2 7	4 15	5 8	5 20	6 25		7 10	9 20	6 40
Kingswood	arr.	7 31	9 9	11 10	1 45	2 35	4 51	5 32	5 52	6 59		7 45	9 55	7 17
London (Paddington)	dep.	—	6 30	10 2	—	1 30	—	—	—	4 45		—	2 30	
Oxford	,,	—	8 45	11 54	—	2 53	3 15	—	6 9	7 25		5 27		
Leamington	,,	8 55	10 10	1 22	—	4 15	5 10	—	5 40	7 15		9 5	7 7	
Kingswood	arr.	9 21	10 39	1 51	—	4 42	5 33	—	6 7	7 42		9 30	7 32	
KINGSWOOD	dep.	7 34	9 25	11 15	1 58	2 40	4 55	5 37	5 53	7 0	7 50	10 0	7 37	
HENLEY-IN-ARDEN	arr.	7 45	9 36	11 26	2 9	2 51	5 6	5 48	6 4	7 11	8 1	10 11	7 48	

		T a.m.	a.m.	a.m.	p.m.	p.m.	p.m.	p.m.	p.m.	**T**	**T**	p.m.	a.m.	p.m.
HENLEY-IN-ARDEN	dep.	7 54	9 4	10 19	12 34	2 17	4 25	5 14	6 13	7 20		...	9 12	7 2
KINGSWOOD	arr.	8 5	9 15	10 30	12 45	2 28	4 36	5 25	6 24	7 31		...	9 23	7 13
Kingswood	dep.	9 9	—	11 10	1 45	2 35	4 51	5 32	6 32	7 45		...	9 55	7 17
Leamington	arr.	9 32	—	11 35	2 9	3 0	5 15	5 50	7 10	8 5		...	10 20	7 43
Oxford	,,	10 50	—	1 53	4 0	4 17	—	7 12	8 55	9 16		...	1 0	—
London (Paddington)	,,	12 15	—	3 20	—	5 45	—	8 40	—	10 45		...	3 35	—
Kingswood	dep.	8 8	9 21	10 39	12 51	2 59	4 42	5 34	6 25	7 32		...	9 30	7 32
Birmingham (Snow Hill)	arr.	8 50	9 48	11 20	1 25	3 37	5 18	6 12	7 3	8 8		...	10 10	8 13
Wolverhampton (Low Level)	arr.	10 3	10 45	12 7	2 1	4 28	6 14	6 59	7 52	8 57		...	10 55	9 3

T These are Through Trains between Birmingham and Henley-in-Arden.

ALTERATIONS OF PASSENGER TRAINS.

The 7.10 a.m. TRAIN BIRMINGHAM to KNOWLE will be TEN MINUTES EARLIER, make an extra stop at Small Heath at 7.8 a.m., and be extended from Knowle to Henley-in-Arden.

The 5.20 p.m. and 6.25 p.m. TRAINS BIRMINGHAM to SOLIHULL will be extended to Henley-in-Arden, calling at Kingswood at times shewn above.

The 6.35 p.m. and 7.40 p.m. TRAINS SOLIHULL to BIRMINGHAM will start from Henley-in-Arden and call at Kingswood at times shewn in above table, and at Knowle at 6.32 and 7.39 p.m., reaching Birmingham at 7.3 and 8.8 p.m. respectively.

PADDINGTON, May, 1894.   Hy. LAMBERT, General Manager.

Wyman & Sons, Ltd., Printers, 63, Carter Lane, Doctors' Commons, E.C.   [4099s]

The railway came to Henley on Wednesday, 6 June 1894. (WI)

XX

ABOVE: The Midland's Stratford service no 23 went to Henley, Wootton Wawen and Bearley, but horse drawn carriers still plied their trade. This was OA 4571, in service in 1914, and withdrawn in 1927 — known as 'Tommy'. BELOW: Cars have become the bane of places like Henley — here seen outside J. Welch, baker, after the Great War. (GW)

THE ARDEN NEWS AND ADVERTISER.

No. 4.   DECEMBER, 1890.   PRICE ONE HALF-PENNY.

'The Arden News & Advertiser' of December 1890 – No 4, price one halfpenny. (GW)

KEBLE HOWARD, AUTHOR AND PLAYWRIGHT

JOHN KEBLE BELL (' Keble Howard '), author and playwright, was born on 8 June 1875, being the third of twelve children of the Rev. G. E. Bell, vicar of Henley, by Mary Sophia, his wife, a daughter of Dr. Warren of Princes Risborough. After receiving education at private schools, including that kept by Thomas Cooper at Henley, he was sent to Worcester College, Oxford, in 1895, where as he says, he read a little and engaged in the usual sports. Going down from Oxford in 1897 he became a schoolmaster but gave it up in 1899 for journalism and secured a position as junior sub-editor at the Press Association. In July of that year he met Miss Marie Corelli, the novelist, when she opened a bazaar in Beaudesert Park in aid of St. John's Church restoration. The entertaining account he wrote of her speech and of his talk with her afterwards appeared in *The Sketch* and this led to his being appointed assistant editor of that weekly, of which he became editor from 1902 to 1904. His heart was, however, set upon writing books and plays and among his many works his most successful stories were *The Smiths of Surbiton*, *Love in a Cottage*, and *Lord London*, a sketch of the character of the late Lord Northcliffe.

He laid the scene of *The God in the Garden* in Henley, and caricatured therein the late Miss Annie Cooke, of Ashbury House, as ' Miss Carraway,' two of whose characteristics were her animosity to the local people and her devotion to her beautiful garden. In *My Motley Life* he drew some amusing pictures of life in the town during his early years towards the close of the Victorian age.

His first play, ' Compromising Martha,' proving a success, he wrote many others including ' Sweet William,' ' The Green Flag,' ' The Girl who Couldn't Lie' and ' The Embarrassed Butler,' which were produced in London. His dramatised version of ' The Smiths of Surbiton,' produced at the New Theatre in 1922, was very popular, and his farce, ' Lord Babs,' was in the middle of a successful run at the Vaudeville at the time of his death, which took place in a nursing home at Bournemouth on 29 March 1928. He was cremated, and the casket containing his ashes is buried in Henley Church (see p. 61). Keble Howard was one of the foremost humorous novelists of his time and enjoyed considerable fame.

PAUPERISM

It is sad to relate that pauperism here as elsewhere had become a formidable problem in the early 19th century and in 1820 we find that about one quarter of the population of Henley and Ullenhall were classed as paupers.[1] In that year the cost of maintaining the poor, including a proportion of the county rates and the upkeep of the local workhouse, had reached £817 at Henley and £397 at Ullenhall, having risen from £70 and £60 respectively since 1747. In addition to the workhouse some of the paupers lived in cottages belonging to the parish and others were boarded out among the poorer inhabitants. The Tudor system of relief, following the dissolution of the monasteries, had worked fairly well until the Industrial Revolution, with which difficult problem it was never intended to cope. Distress was caused by the inclosure of the common fields in the district and many were deprived of their livelihood, thus adding to the ranks of the poor, but the scheme introduced at the end of the 18th century of employing paupers at a very low wage and making up the remainder of the wage out of the poor rates was probably the cause of much of the large increased cost recorded above. A change for the better was, however, not far distant. By the Poor Law Amendment Act of 1834 out-door relief to the able-bodied was discontinued, with one or two exceptions such as medical attendance : but the aged and impotent were exempt from its operation. Willingness to enter a workhouse was now made the test of relief and resulted in a welcome lessening of out-door relief. The Act ordered that the county should be divided into administrative districts consisting of groups or unions of smaller parishes under Boards of Guardians. The civil parish of Wootton petitioned the Poor Law Commissioners that Henley should be the seat of such a board and the inhabitants endeavoured to strengthen their petition by citing the contents of a letter they had received from one Richard Philpson, who was proposing to establish a factory at Henley for heading pins. In it he says he is about to close with Mr. Burman for a house and premises for that purpose, but before concluding arrangements wishes to know whether the town is to be the seat of a Board of Guardians, as a workhouse at Henley would provide a greater number of hands. He promises to employ all the children from eight years of age upwards and all the old and infirm people to the number of 400 or more if he can get them, and concludes by saying that the process of heading pins is very simple and may be learnt in a few days. It was argued by the petitioners that the wages of 400 persons at say 6d. per day would mean £3,120 a year to the parish ; but evidently the authorities were not moved, for as we know the civil

[1]Overseers' Accounts.

parish of Wootton was placed under the Guardians established at Stratford-on-Avon and has so remained ever since. This step rendered the old workhouse at Wootton unnecessary and it became an ordinary dwelling-house.[1]

Every parish was responsible for its own poor, so that when a man lived in another parish and had no means of subsistence he was sent back to the place of his birth, or parish where he had gained a legal settlement. It may be of interest to add that among the documents at the Shire Hall is one dated 5 August 1790 relating to the examination of a vagrant named John Pearsall, born at Henley, who was apprehended as a 'rogue and vagabond' in the parish of Aston, Birmingham, 'wandering and begging there.' It states that Pearsall had gained a legal settlement at Wootton Wawen by serving a whole year as a hired servant with John Tarlton, farmer, and it was ordered that the constable of Aston should 'forthwith convey the said vagrant on horseback . . . to Wootton Wawen and deliver him there together with his pass and duplicate of examination . . . taking a receipt for the same, to some churchwarden, chapelwarden or overseer who is hereby required to receive the said rogue and vagabond and provide for him as the law directs.' Underneath is written : 'August 6, Received the pauper on foot, Jno Tidmas,' so it is evident that the unfortunate man did not get his horse for the journey but had to be content with Shank's pony.

Mrs Hewins delivered the milk in 1918. (O'D)

[1] *Wootton Wawen*, pp. 83, 84.

BEAUDESERT CASTLE

The castle with its courtyards stood on the oblong-shaped hill which extends from Beaudesert Church to within a short distance of the ancient trackway known as Edge Lane.[1] Being high up above the surrounding country,[2] it is by nature a commanding site for a fortress and an ideal situation for a castle.

It is possible that it was fortified by an early British tribe. Its position adjoining this ancient hill track was a favourable one, for in those days it was necessary to travel along the high ground to avoid the perils lurking in the densely wooded valleys. At a later date Teutonic settlers may have used it as an earth fort but when Thurstan de Montfort, the Norman, came early in the 12th century he built the castle which for many generations remained the home of his descendants, and the present earthworks are of the usual mound-and-bailey type of that period.

The old road to the castle begins at the end of Beaudesert Street and winds gradually up the south-eastern side of the first elevation to the entrance to what was the inner courtyard or bailey, where a gatehouse with its drawbridge and portcullis would stand. This courtyard was surrounded for defence by a palisade and a deep ditch running all round outside it. Further to the west there appears to have been an outer courtyard similarly defended by palisade and ditch. The original buildings within these court-yards were most likely of wood but they were probably replaced to some extent by stone at a later date. Here the retainers were housed and provisions stored. They contained the stables, granary and workshops, and the outer courtyard particularly would afford shelter for flocks and herds. In early days markets would most likely be held in one of these courtyards.

At the point where the raised bank of earth crosses the moat at the north-east there was probably another gateway with a barbicon and drawbridge, portcullis, etc., for this was the entrance to the keep. It will be noticed that the ground here has been raised artificially and is considerably higher than the courtyards. This is usual in Norman castles not only for reasons of defence, but to give the sentry who was on the look-out a better view of the surrounding country. The keep was always strongly fortified, for besides being the living quarters of the lord it was the final refuge of the garrison in case of attack. At this period the keep was usually a tower-house of timber surrounded by a palisade with the additional

[1]Probably ' the way which goes towards Lapworth ' mentioned in a deed of about 1360. *Beaudesert*, p. 3.
[2]It rises to some 300 feet above sea-level.

protection of a very deep moat[1] such as we find at Beaudesert.
Later on a wall probably superseded the palisade, and buildings
were erected of stone or timber on its inner face. Dugdale seems to
imply that there were loose stones lying about in his day and most
likely it was composed partly of stone and partly of timber.

In April 1262, when Peter de Montfort was beginning to take
definite sides with the Barons, the King gave orders to the Sheriff
of Warwickshire to prevent the fortification of the castle.[2]

John the porter of the Castle is mentioned in 1323, when a
messuage with a curtilage (i.e., a courtyard, or piece of land) in
Henley was granted to him and another by one, John Witchevet.[3]
In 1378 a cottage with a garden between a garden of the rector of
Beaudesert and land of the abbot of Bordesley is described as
extending from the road leading to the castle to the water called the
Holdebrok.[4]

The account roll of John Chamberlain,[5] constable of the castle
in 1411, contains an entry for repairs to the portico of the hall of the
castle as follows :

' In timber felled in the park for the repair of the portico of
the hall by John Tomes and Richard Redwyn for two days
each at 4d. per day, 16d. Likewise to John Wassell carpenter
brought for mending the said portico at the castle 18d.'

The hall was the main portion of the building, and in early
days served as the living and dining room of the whole household,
also the sleeping quarters for all except the lord and his family. It
would be of considerable size and open right up to the high-pitched
timbered roof. The same roll also informs us that the Castle Park
was inclosed with a hedge having pailings outside it and that the
door of the park was secured with a padlock, thus :

' In 31½ perches of hedge made and closed about the park
of Beaudesert at 2d. a perch and of the hedge, 5s. 3d. Likewise
in one man brought to fortify and amend the hedge of the park
aforesaid in divers weak places for 4½ days at 4½d. per day, 18d.
Likewise in one cart brought for carrying brushwood to the same
for 5 days at 12d. per day, 5s. Likewise in one man brought
to mend the palings of the said park made outside with the
same gross 20d. Likewise in one padlock bought for the door of
the said park 3d.'

John Chamberleyn received in wages 3d. a day for acting as
constable of the castle and collector of the rents and 1d. a day as
parker.[6] The sums recorded above would represent at least

---

[1]At Beaudesert the moats would be dry ones.
[2]Close R., 46, Hen. III, m. 10d.
[3]*Cat. Anct. Deeds*, A. 6916.
[4]Ibid, A630.
[5]Birm. Pub. Lib. MSS., Translation printed in *Beaudesert*, p. 3.
[6]i.e., of the Castle Park, known as the Little Park. See p. 19.

twenty-five times as much to-day owing to the difference in the value of money.

After Peter de Montfort was slain at the battle of Evesham in 1265, when the town of Henley was burnt, probably for the part its lord had taken against the King, it is said the castle was partly destroyed. If so it was rebuilt shortly afterwards, when Peter's son was restored to his inheritance. Its importance probably declined after 1369 when the de Montfort estates passed to the Earl of Warwick, and as no mention is made of it in the survey of 1547 we may presume that it had by then fallen into ruin.

Dugdale, writing in 1656, tells us that not one stone then remained on another, and that even the trenches were filled. At the present time not a single stone is visible, but about a hundred years ago a portion of a moulded capital of a doorway shaft, apparently of the 13th or 14th century, was dug up on the site of the castle by M. H. Bloxham of Rugby. [1]

It is said there was a well in the keep which would probably be very deep, and perhaps similar to that at Dover Castle, which descends a great distance into the earth. A visitor in 1855 has left it on record that there were wooden pipes then lying about which had been recently dug up. They had been made from tree trunks and appeared to be the remains of the old conduit. He was informed that the pipes having become rotten, the ground gave way under the feet of the cattle, some of which had broken their legs.

The mount in more recent times has been the scene of many popular rejoicings, and bonfires were lighted on its highest point to celebrate Queen Victoria's Jubilees of 1887 and 1897 respectively, and at the Coronation of King Edward VII. At the peace celebrations of Henley and Beaudesert on 10 July 1919 in order to avoid the wastage of fuel at that time, a rocket was fired from its height, followed by flares which illuminated the country brilliantly for miles round. Early last century it appears to have been the custom to celebrate the anniversary of Guy Fawkes' Day with a bonfire on the mount. Late in the same century steeplechases were held round the Mount, the Mount itself forming a natural grandstand. From its eminence on a clear day Edge Hill and the Malverns can be seen, and the view of the surrounding country nearer at hand is one of the most charming in Warwickshire.

---

[1] *Churches of Warwickshire*, 1847, p. 148.

BEAUDESERT CHURCH

THE church of St. Nicholas is a fine example of Norman architecture of about the year 1150, but the west tower is an addition of the 15th century. Thurstan de Montfort, who built the castle, was probably its founder and provided the fabric, but the work would be carried out by local masons. The original church consisted of the present rectangular chancel and nave, except that the north wall of the nave stood the same distance outwards from the chancel arch as the south wall. The nave was somewhat longer than now and the present south doorway probably stood in a thick wall at its west end with most likely a simple bell-cote above.

The walls of the nave were then higher and there was a range of windows high up all along the south side of the church but no lower ones as now. A portion of the westernmost one still survives near the door and there are indications of the easternmost one blocked up in the chancel. Both show that these windows were somewhat similar to the existing round-headed east window. On the north side all the windows were plain round-headed ones set high up in the walls the same as the two preserved in the chancel.

About the end of the 16th century the north wall of the nave was removed and the present one erected five or six feet nearer in, thus encroaching on the north respond of the chancel arch. The chancel probably then lost its vaulting, the nave was reduced in height and the present oak-timbered roof provided.

THE CHANCEL.—The 12th century east window is one of the finest Norman windows in any church in the county and appears never to have been restored. This round-headed window is decorated with zigzag and diaper ornament both inside and out and supported inside and out by plain round nook shafts, resting on plain bases. Internally the north shaft has its capital carved with primitive foliage, and that on the south is escalloped. On the interior and on the wall surrounding it there are traces of the mural paintings with which the church was decorated in pre-Reformation days. The two small round-headed windows of the same date in the north wall are quite plain and like the east window deeply splayed on the inside. On the south side one of the windows has been blocked up, the other is of the late 13th century with two lights trefoiled in the heads, and a quatrefoil above.

The present vaulted roof with square ribs was provided in 1865, when a plaster ceiling was removed. The shafts and capitals for the groining to spring from belong however to the Norman church. They consist of brackets in the two western angles in the form of escalloped capitals with square abaci ; of a semi-hexagonal shaft at each of the eastern angles, and two semicylindrical shafts one on each side of the middle of the north and south walls, all the capitals of which are sculptured.

In the east wall south of the Altar is a pointed recess with an edge-roll mould. It has now no basin but was probably an early piscina. At the east end of the north wall is an ambry, or locker, of uncertain date, with a modern door. Here the sacred vessels, altar linen and service books were kept. The square recess in the south wall near the east end is another locker used as a credence table, with rebates for a door. Outside on the east wall is a monument to the Rev. Richard Jago, who died 29 July 1741, a former rector and father of the poet of the same name.

THE 12TH CENTURY CHANCEL ARCH is semi-circular and is decorated with chevron and other enrichment, supported on three clustered cylindrical shafts having cushion-shaped escalloped capitals with massive square abaci and moulded bases, all much restored. It is plain on the eastern face. Above are two small blind windows re-set, each of two trefoiled lights with a quatrefoil above, probably late 13th century. The low oak screen separating the chancel from the nave contains on the north side a portion of the original rood-screen. It is in the form of flowing tracery of the decorated period and dates probably from the 14th century. The other portion is a modern copy of the old work. On either side of the chancel arch against the east wall before the Reformation there would most likely be an altar, in addition to the High Altar in the chancel.

THE NAVE has three north windows, two of which are high in the wall, and two south windows, all modern. The re-set north doorway has a plain round-head and is of the 12th century. Outside, above it, and just below the sills of the windows, is a sloping set-off in the wall. At the east end is a recess built in 1865 to clear the chancel-arch. The south doorway has four receding semi-circular arches ornamented with chevron and lozenge enrichment ; the three inner ones rising from circular shafts with escalloped capitals. It was almost entirely restored in 1865, when the porch, a poor and comparatively modern structure, was removed. On the door-jambs are what appear to be votive crosses.

The roof is probably of the 16th century and consists of four bays divided by trusses with tie beams, queen posts, collar beams and rafters. This roof most likely replaced a flat roof at the time the north wall was rebuilt in its present position. The original Norman roof would be a high pitched one.

Just inside the south door to the east is the interesting remnant of an ancient Norman stoup. It was originally in the form of a globe with an opening in the centre and scooped out in the base to contain the holy water, but it is now badly mutilated. Few stoups of this early period remain.

Near the door to the west stands the font, which is octagonal and of the 15th century.

The seats are modern and of plain oak, but four of the 16th century benches with shaped standards still remain. There is seating for 189 persons. A poor, mean gallery of deal at the west end and a comparatively modern plaster ceiling formerly disfigured the nave and chancel but they were removed at the restoration of 1865.

THE TOWER, which is perpendicular work of the 15th century, is separated from the nave by a lofty and pointed arch, and enclosed by an oak screen which was erected in 1902 ; the woodwork being a copy of the ancient rood-screen. The west window is of three cinquefoiled ogee-headed lights and below the transom the lights are cinquefoiled. The tower outside is embattled and divided into three stages by string courses on the south and west sides, in the lowermost of which on the south is a richly-carved canopied niche with a bracket at the foot from which the image has gone. This was probably a figure of the patron saint, St. Nicholas. The weathervane represents the legend of St. Nicholas and the children.

The internal dimensions of the church are as follows—the chancel : length 21-ft. 10-ins., width 17-ft. 3-ins. ; the nave, length 56-ft. 3-ins., width 18-ft. The tower, from east to west, 11-ft. 10-ins., and from north to south, 11-ft. The lack of alignment between the tower, nave and chancel is noticeable.

THE BELLS.—There are three bells, the treble, inscribed *Ave Maria Gratia Plena* and the second, *Ihesus Nazsarinus Rex Iudeorum,* both in Lombardic capitals and dating from about 1350 ; the third inscribed, *The Thenth Year of the Reign of Queen Anne,* 1711. The first and second are probably by a local founder and the third by Joseph Smith of Edgbaston.

THE PLATE includes an Elizabethan cup with fringed stem and dotted line ornament, and a cover paten.

THE REGISTERS begin in 1661, but there are transcripts at Worcester from 1607.[1]

THE CHURCHYARD, which is the burial place of the united parish, was enlarged in 1919.

A copy of the monumental inscriptions both inside the church and in the churchyard with some other information is given in *The Records of Beaudesert.*

THE REV. JOHN DOUGHTY, RECTOR FROM 1636 UNTIL DEPRIVED.[2]

This part of Warwickshire, indeed the greater portion of the county, was stronger on the side of the Parliament than of the King and Puritanism spread through the parishes. It seems to have been embraced by Henley and the district, though some opposed it. In 1640 a petition[3] was presented to the House of Lords by the

---

[1] The registers and transcripts, 1607-1837, are printed in *The Records of Beaudesert.*

[2] For list of rectors see *Beaudesert,* pp. xxxiv—xxxix.

[3] House of Lords MSS. Cited in *The Churches of Warwickshire,* p. 149.

parishioners of Lapworth against their then rector the Rev. John Doughty, who was also rector of Beaudesert.

The document accuses him of neglect of duty and other short-comings and concludes with these charges :

' The said John Doughty is a common resorter to the houses of Popish recusants, a favourite of them and their religion and a scoffer of goodness and good men [i.e., Puritans]. The said John Doughty preaching at Lapworth about Michs. last upon Matth. viii. 13, affirmed that it was not necessary for the minister to prove his doctrine by scripture, but the people ought to believe it on his authority ; and further said that there is now a generation of men sprung up that will believe nothing but what is proved by Scripture, insisting that turning and tossing over the leaves of the Bible is a disturbance to the congregation, with other words to that effect. The said John Doughty speaking of the new canons, said there was nothing in them to be disliked, and further that he did verily believe in his conscience, that if St. Paul had been there and made them, the Parliament would have condemned them, or words to that effect.'

The code of canons which had been passed by Convocation early that year was voted illegal by the Long Parliament soon afterwards and a committee was appointed which punished the Laudian Clergy for the way they conducted public worship.

Doughty was evidently a follower of Laud and the High Church party and we know he was deprived of the living of Beau-desert under the Commonwealth. After the Restoration he petitioned the House of Lords to obtain the benefit of the tithes and other profits of his sequestered rectory which were then in the hands of the churchwardens and overseers, who were waiting for the rightful owner to establish his claim.[1] For his Royalist sympathies he was rewarded with a canonry of Westminster and at his death in 1672 was given burial in the Abbey there.

[1]House of Lords MSS., 23 June, 1660.

RICHARD JAGO, THE POET

RICHARD JAGO, the poet, son of a former rector of Beaudesert of the same name,[1] by Margaret his wife, daughter of Wm. Parker, gentleman, of Henley, was born in the old rectory there on 1 October 1715. He was educated first at Solihull School, during the head mastership of the Rev. John Crompton, to whom he refers as a morose pedagogue, where ' most of the gentlemen's, and some noblemen's sons in that neighbourhood received the rudiments of their classical learning,' and here he met his life-long friend, Shenstone. Owing to his father's lack of means he was entered as a servitor at University College, Oxford, taking his M.A. degree from there on 9 July 1738. In his early life he was encouraged and helped by Shenstone and Somervile in his poetical efforts, but although he has a recognised place among English poets he cannot be considered to have reached high rank. His fame rests mainly on his elegies, ' The Blackbirds ' and ' The Goldfinches,' and on his longest poem, ' Edgehill,' though his fable ' Labour and Genius ' was popular in his own day. The following is a specimen of his blank verse in referring to the de Montforts' Castle :

> Reared aloft,
> And inaccessible the massy towers,
> And narrow circuit of embattled walls,
> Raised on the mountain-precipice ! Such thine
> O Beaudesert ! Old Montfort's lofty seat !
> Haunt of my youthful steps ! Where I was wont
> To range, chanting my rude notes to the wind.

Jago was appointed to the small livings of Harbury and Chesterton in 1746 and continued to hold them after being presented in 1754 to the vicarage of Snitterfield, where he afterwards resided for the remainder of his life. When Lord Willoughby de Broke gave him the living of Kimcote in Leicestershire in 1771 he resigned Harbury and Chesterton but retained Snitterfield. He published a sermon preached at Harbury on 4 May 1755 entitled ' The causes of impenitence considered,' on the occasion of a conversation said to have passed between one of the inhabitants and an apparition in the churchyard there. This incident he uses to enforce the necessity of repentance. He composed ' The Roundelay ' for David Garrick for the great Shakespeare Jubilee in September 1769, but from a letter to Garrick's brother George of the following month it is evident that he did not entirely approve of the great actor's part in it. He begins by indignantly denying George's accusation that he had ever said David was the author of some verses reflecting on a certain L.W. and continues that he looks upon this as

---

[1]There is a monumental tablet to the father's memory outside the East wall of the Church which states that he was a native of St. Mawes, in Cornwall.

only a pretence for his anger, the true ground of which, he suggests, is a report that he (Jago) had reflected on his brother's ' recital and other particulars ' at the Jubilee. This he admits he had done though not in public, ' reserving to myself (he says) the liberty of speaking my own sentiments in private.' He concludes by declaring that previous to the Jubilee he had taken every occasion to condemn the many severe and ungenerous things that were said against it. Among some letters of Jago's at the Bodleian (MS. Montagu d.2) to his publisher Dodsley, is one dated 17 November 1767 in which he tells him he has been corresponding with Richard Graves on the subject of some letters of Shenstone's with a view to their publication. Graves has about 150 of them but ' expresses many fears and difficulties concerning their appearance, some grounded on a point of delicacy about printing private correspondence, and others relating to the privacy of Shenstone's situation and the want of variety and uncommon events in the subject of the letters themselves.' Between them they could furnish about 200 letters with the addition of some others, and Jago considers ' there is the most reasonable prospect of a sale both from Mr. Shenstone's public character and from its being a kind of supplement to a work which is in almost every body's hands.' Apparently, however, nothing came of the project. In his later years Jago passed his leisure time in improving and ornamenting his grounds at Snitterfield as Shenstone had done at the Leasowes. The three silver birch trees on the lawn there were planted by his daughters. He died after a short illness on 8 May 1781 aged sixty-five and was buried four days later in a vault in Snitterfield Church. In his will (P.C.C., 248, Webster) proved 25 May 1781, after commending his soul to God through Jesus Christ, he desires his body to be privately buried ' in the middle isle ' there ' over against the reading desk.' Evidently his wish was carried out as there was formerly a flat stone in the centre of the nave to his memory which is now on the floor of the vestry. He left a leasehold estate at Spernall to Margaret (his second wife) and a freehold farm known as Crowleys in Ullenhall for the benefit of his children. We read that ' in person, Mr. Jago was about the middle stature. In his manner like most people of sensibility he appeared reserved among strangers ; amongst his friends he was free and easy ; and his conversation was sprightly and entertaining. In domestic life he was the affectionate husband, the tender parent, the kind master, the hospitable neighbour, the sincere friend ; and both by his doctrine and example, a faithful and worthy minister of the parish over which he presided.' His friend Shenstone kept him in remembrance by erecting a seat in his garden inscribed : *Amicitiae et meritis Richardi Jago.*

Sources : *The Worthies of Warwickshire* by F. L. Colvile ; *The Churches of Warwickshire* ; *William Shenstone* by M. Williams ; *Shakespeare's Land* by C. J. Ribton-Turner ; *The Records of Beaudesert* ; Local Records ; *The Private Correspondence of David Garrick*, I., 367.

ULLENHALL MANOR AND ITS LORDS

In 1083 William the Conqueror ordered that a survey, which was afterwards known as Domesday Book, should be made of all the land of England. He sent out commissioners for this purpose and it took them three years to complete their task. These men called before them the reeve and four of the leading villeins[1] of each manor and asked them certain questions : What was the extent of the manor ; how many men dwelt upon it ; how many ploughs, cattle, etc., there were ; whose was the manor in the reign of Edward the Confessor and whose was it now ; what was its value then and now.

A translation of the record then made relating to Ullenhall reads as follows :

> The same R(obert) [de Stafford] holds 1 hide in Holehale [Ullenhall]. There is land for 15 ploughs. There are 17 villeins and 11 bordars with 6 ploughs. Wood(land) half a league long and 1 furlong broad. It was and is worth 3 pounds. Waga held it.[2]

It will thus be seen that Waga, or Wagen, a Saxon Thane, held the manor in the Confessor's time, and that he was dispossessed of all his lands here, also at Wootton and elsewhere, by the Conqueror, who granted them to Robert de Tonei, alias de Stafford.

The hide therein mentioned was simply a unit of value and not a measurement as it became at a later date, when a hide was reckoned at 120 acres, more or less, according to the nature of the soil. Most likely the reason why land for the fifteen ploughs at Ullenhall was only assessed at a single hide was that the soil was poor. In those days the land was not divided into fields by hedges which form such a pleasant feature in the landscape to-day and such fences as were necessary to keep the cattle from the crops were temporary and artificial. The arable land was then split up into large open ' fields ' of which at first there were probably two, cropped and fallow in alternate years, each separated into long strips (see p. 21). Some centuries later the Three-Field system came in, when the crops were wheat or rye one year, barley or oats the next, and fallow the third ; roots were unknown. All the houses with farm buildings were clustered together along the small village street and there would be no outlying farmsteads. The common pasture and meadow land was nearby, and beyond the arable fields was the uncultivated waste, while further out still was the woodland where the tenants had rights of timber for repairs to their houses and for fuel, etc. The wood here was about $\frac{3}{4}$ of a mile long and one furlong wide.

[1] i.e., Men of the vill.
[2] V.C.H., Warw., I, 328b.

All the inhabitants of the manor, including the lord, had the right of grazing a certain number of animals on the pasture and waste and the meadow was so divided as to give each tenant some hay.

The villeins, who were the largest class in Domesday times, each held about thirty acres of arable land in acre or half-acre strips scattered in each of the open fields so that everyone should have his share of good and bad land. The villein thus supported himself and his family and in return he had to do ploughing and other agricultural work on the lords demesne[1] for two or three days a week, and special work on such occasions as seed-time and harvest. He was not a free tenant and could not acquire property, but his holdings were generally regranted to his son. His daughter could not be married or his son educated without licence or fine, but in the manor courts he could be sure of justice being done in matters which concerned him. There were certain ways in which he could obtain freedom and by degrees he became virtually a free tenant.

The bordars, who were an inferior class to the villeins, usually held five acres only in the common arable fields and a cottage. They also had to work on the lord's demesne two or three days a week and on special occasions.

A plough team usually consisted of eight oxen, of which each villein was expected to provide two but the bordars none.

It has been seen that the villeins and bordars together here numbered twenty-eight, which with their wives and families would give a probable total population of from 140 to 150.

Villeinage had disappeared to a great extent by the 15th century, though in some parts of the country it lingered on until the reign of Elizabeth.

The £3 which the manor is stated to be worth, both in the reign of Edward the Confessor and at the time of the survey, would be equivalent to probably about £120 of present-day money.

Robert de Stafford, to whom the manor was granted, was a near relation of the Conqueror and fought for him at Hastings. His descendants continued to hold Wootton for nearly 500 years but Ullenhall passed from him or his son Nicholas to Roger, Earl of Warwick, who granted it to one Roger, who hence assumed the name of Ulehale.[2] This Roger was followed by one William, whose son Robert held one quarter of a knight's fee of the Earl of Warwick in 1242.[3] Robert was probably succeeded by William, who died about 1284[4] and he by Robert de Ollenhal.[5]

The fee then went to Peter, son of John de Montfort of Beau-

---

[1]This included a compact portion of the village lands near the manor house and some of the strips in the three arable fields.
[2]Dugdale, p. 818, citing a MS. in possession of S. Archer.
[3]*Book of Fees*, 956.
[4]*Feet of F.* (Dugd. Soc. xv) No. 1016.
[5]Ibid.

desert, being held by him as a hamlet of Whitley in 1316[1] and as part of one quarter of a knight's fee in Honiley and elsewhere in 1326.[2] This Peter, as shown in the descent of Beaudesert manor, had two illegitimate sons by Laura, daughter of Richard Astley of Ullenhall. The elder one, Sir John de Montfort, married Joan, daughter of Sir John de Clinton of Coleshill, who brought him the manor there where he settled. He appears to have succeeded his father in the lordship of Ullenhall, for in 1453-54 his grandson, Sir William de Montfort of Coleshill, who had died the year before, is stated to have held it.[3] Sir William, by his marriage with Margaret, daughter and heir of Sir John Peche, became possessed of the manors of Hampton-in-Arden, Honiley and half-a-dozen others in Warwickshire, besides those of Coleshill and Ullenhall, all of which remained with his descendants until the attainder of Sir Simon Montfort,[4] whose wife was Anne, sister of Sir Richard Verney of Compton Murdak (now Compton Verney). He became involved in the rebellion of Perkin Warbeck, the pretender to the throne, who claimed to be the son of Edward IV, and was executed at Tyburn at Candlemas, 1495, when all his vast estates were confiscated. An interesting rental of his tenants here, made soon after the manor came into the hands of the Crown, is given on page 180. Henry VII, in 1496, granted it to Gerald, Earl of Kildare,[5] for the part he had taken against Warbeck. His son, Sir James Fitz-Gerald, however, being attainted in the 28th year of the reign of Henry VIII, it again reverted to the Crown.[6] In 1553 Queen Mary granted it together with the manors of Honiley, Blackwell, Packhurst, Winderton, and others, to Michael Throckmorton of Coughton.[7] This Michael, who was attainted by Henry VIII for trying to prevent his divorce of Catherine of Aragon, had only recently returned from Italy, where he had lived many years 'in good and great reputation with bountiful hospitality, entertaining the noblemen and gentlemen of England that had occasion to come that way.' He afterwards returned to Italy, where he died in 1558 and was buried in St. Martin's Church at Mantua, leaving Francis, his son, then aged seven, his heir.[8] Francis Throckmorton died in 1617 and was buried under the Renaissance Tomb in the chancel at Ullenhall, which is illustrated in Dugdale's *Warwickshire*. From him it descended to his son John, who obtained livery of the manor in 1636.[9] It had, however, already been conveyed in 1630 by his father, probably on mortgage, to William Bolton of St. Leonard's,

[1] *Feudal Aids*, V, 178.
[2] Feet of F., Mich, 20 Edw. II.
[3] Dugdale, p. 818.
[4] Ibid.
[5] *Cal. Pat. R.*, 1494-1509, p. 84 ; L. and P., Hen. VIII, 1, 1299.
[6] Dugdale, p. 818.
[7] *Cal. Pat. R.*, 1553-59, pp. 400-1.
[8] Chan. Inq., p.m. (Ser. 2), 131 (195).
[9] Fine R., 12 Chas. I, pt. 1, No. 20.

Shoreditch,[1] and he was in possession of the manor at the time of his death in 1648.

In his will, proved on 21 December of the same year, he states that he leaves to his son William the lease of his dwelling-house in ' Hoggesden ' in the parish of St. Leonard's, Shoreditch, having at his marriage settled the manor of Ullenhall upon him and also money.[2]   This son, who is found to be dealing with the manor in 1650,[3] died in 1651 and is described as a mercer and freeman of London in his will.   He left half of ' his goods and personal estate ' to his three daughters, Elizabeth, Dorothy and Mary, equally.[4] Elizabeth, daughter of William Bolton of Ullenhall, married on 13 July 1661 Edward Bullock of Falkbourne Hall, Co. Essex,[5] and she and her husband were dealing with one third of the manor in 1665.[6]   In 1696 Edward Bullock, Mary his wife, and John Bullock transferred ' the manor ' to Wm. Parker and John Hopkins.[7] A lease of the manor was in 1712 granted by John Parker of Henley-in-Arden and four daughters of Wm. Parker to Wm. Somervile of Edstone, the poet and hunting squire, and Henry Neal of Allesley.[8] It then came into the possession of the Smiths of Wootton Wawen and in 1724 Charles Smith, then of Ludlow, was lord.[9]   It descended with the manor of Wootton Wawen, as is shown in the writer's book on that place, and Sir Edward Joseph Smythe, Bart., who married Catherine Maria Holford, a descendant of the Smiths of Wootton, was holding it in 1832.[10]   From him it went to Robert Knight of Barrells, who in 1837 is stated to be lord of it.[11]   He was a natural son of Robert Knight, Earl of Catherlough (son of Robert Knight, Cashier of the South Sea Company), by Jane Davies, a farmer's daughter of the Moat Farm, Ullenhall.   Robert, who in 1797 was High Sheriff of Warwickshire, married Frances, daughter of Charles, eighth Lord Dormer of Grove Park, Warwick, by whom he had two sons and two daughters.   The elder son died young and the younger one, the Rev. Henry Charles Knight, inherited the manor and estates on the death of his father in 1855, but sold them in the following year to William Newton of Whateley Hall, Castle Bromwich, a Birmingham merchant, who is named as lord in 1859.[12] He died at Barrells on 24 November 1862 and was succeeded by his

[1]Feet of F., Trin., 6 Chas I.
[2]*Misc. Gen. et. Her.*, viii, pt. x, p. 287.
[3]Recovery R., Mich. 1650.
[4]*Misc. Gen. et. Her.*, viii, pt. x, p. 287.
[5]Ibid.
[6]Feet of F. Div. Co. East, 17, Chas. II.
[7]Feet of F. Trin. 7, Will. III.
[8]Moulton's Catalogue of Deeds for Sale, p. 31.
[9]Gamekeepers' Deputations, County Records, Warwick.
[10]Ibid.
[11]Ibid.   He owned the great titles of Ullenhall : £383 2s., of which £317 9s. was on his own land—Tithe Award, 1840.
[12]Ibid.   Henry Charles Knight shared the proceeds of the sale with Charles Raleigh Knight.   See p. 000.

son Thomas Henry Goodwin Newton, Barrister-at-Law, who was High Sheriff of Warwickshire in 1887.

At his death in 1907 his son, Hugh Goodwin Newton, B.A., Oxon, Barrister-at-Law, of the Inner Temple, inherited it but when he died in 1924 the manor and the advowson of Ullenhall were sold to the Martyrs' Memorial Trust, now known as the Church of England Trust, who still hold them.[1]

William Newton and his son are buried in the family vault in the chapel yard east of the old chancel, but no inscription marks their last resting place. The grandson, Hugh Goodwin Newton, lies in a separate grave near by and a stone records that he was born 14 March 1873 and died 27 June 1924.

The arms of Newton of Barrells Park are : *Argent a saltire azure, surmounted by another of the first ; thereon five leopards' faces of the second, the whole between four battle-axes proper.* Crest : *On a wreath of the colours in front of a cubit arm erect grasping a battle-axe in bend sinister a sun rising in splendour, all proper.*

The reputed manor of BARRELLS is first mentioned in 1681 (see p. 182) and again in 1730, when Robert Knight, son of the Cashier of the South Sea Company, purchased the ' manor and estate' from his second cousin Raleigh Knight.[2] In 1769 this Robert, then Earl of Catherlough, was still holding it,[3] and at his death in 1772 it passed to his elder natural son, Robert Knight,[4] after which it descended with the manor of Ullenhall.

The MONASTERY OF BORDESLEY, Co. Worcester, is stated, in 1535, to be holding a manor in Ullenhall Henley as follows :[5]

> Manor of Ulnall Henley with Denseyes[6] Yende, Co. Warw. Value in rents of assize there 9s. 7½d.
>
> In farm of demesne lands there 62s. 2d.
>
> In fines heriots reliefs and other perquisites of the court there is one year with another 20d. [Total] 73s. 5½d.

No other reference to this manor has been found and in 1547 the Bordesley Abbey estate in Ullenhall is called a grange.[7] It is evident from the catalogues of Ancient Deeds for the 14th and 15th centuries that this religious house held a fair amount of land in Ullenhall and some messuages, etc., in Henley.

The descents of the manors of Aspley, Forde Hall, Botley and Mockley are dealt with in *Victoria County History*, Warwickshire, Vol. III, by the present writer.

[1]Information from the late A. C. Coldicott, for many years agent for the Barrells Estates.

[2]Heralds' Coll. MSS.

[3]Gamekeepers' Deputations, Shire Hall, Warwick.

[4]Ibid.

[5]*Valor Eccles* (Rec. Com.), III, 272.

[6]Danzey.

[7]Dugdale Soc., Vol. II, p. 116.

ULLENHALL CHAPEL

BEFORE the Reformation Baldwin Heath of Forde Hall, who made his will on 4 April 1526,[1] bequeathed his ' sowle to Almyghty God to his blessed modre Synt Marie and to all ye Wholy Cumpany of hevyn,' thus recognising our Blessed Lord as ' Very God ' and implying the doctrine of the Holy Trinity. Among other bequests he left to the chapel of Ullenhall two torches[2] price 4s.

He directed that a priest should sing masses for his soul for the souls of others named and for all Christian souls, in the Chapel of St. George in the church of Tanworth for a year after his death.

When Henry VIII broke with Rome John Knyght, curate of Ullenhall, was one of the clergy who in 1534 signed the declaration renouncing Papal supremacy.[3]

In the first year of the reign of Edward VI (1547-48), when an account was taken of all the lands, rents, cattle and money which had been given to the maintenance of obits and lights in churches, it is recorded of Ullenhall that ' there is landes to the yearely value of xs. putt in feoffment but to what use it is not known till the deedes thereof may be seene.'[4] In the Wootton survey made at the same time it is found that 1s. 0½d. a year from land had been left to maintain a lamp there, so an annual sum of 10s. (about £10 in present-day money) would apparently be sufficient to provide both lamps and obits at Ullenhall. The former, which would burn before altars and images, and the latter being masses for the dead, would then all be done away with and the yearly income seized by the King.

Five years later in 1552, when Edward VI had need of a ' masse of mooney,' commissioners were sent out all over England to take into the King's hands such plate, etc., as then remained ' to be emploied unto his highnes use.' When they came to Ullenhall they found the following :[5]

> j chalice and j bell.
> one vestment dornix[6]
> one cope dornix
> ij towells
> one altarclothe

As it was usual to leave a chalice, at least one bell and an altar cloth, it does not appear that the King's coffers can have been swollen very much from what was pillaged here.

[1] Worc. Wills.
[2] Torches were used in processions ; they were also carried at obits, and large standing torches on such occasions and at funerals were placed round the hearse on the floor of the church.
[3] P.R.O., E.36/63, p. 121.
[4] Hamper's notes to Dugdale (B.M.).
[5] Hannett, *Forest of Arden*, p. 99.
[6] A fabric composed of worsted, silk, wool or thread.

The chapel of St. Mary, pleasantly situated on high ground a little distance from the village, consisted originally of a nave and chancel without aisles dating probably from the late 13th century. When the Newton family built the new church near the village in 1875-6 the nave was pulled down and the chancel only allowed to remain to serve as a mortuary chapel.

The view of the exterior, facing page 126, shows us the old building as it was in 1800. The chapel has an east window of the late 13th century of three lights within a plain pointed arch, the mullions of which cross in the head, with an external hood-mould. In the south wall are two windows the western one of which is probably of the 14th century and was formerly in the south wall of the nave before it was pulled down. It consists of three separate ogee-headed lights, the middle one being higher than the other two ; each light is trefoiled in the head. The other south window to the east has two separate trefoiled lights in pointed heads ; the cusps have sunk spandrels except over the mullion inside. There is a similar window in the north wall.

The east wall has a foiled and pierced gable cross, and at its angles are plain diagonal buttresses. On one of the stones a cross has been cut with three dots at the ends of the arms, probably a votive cross. The buttress in the middle of the north wall is of the 15th century but that in the south wall is modern. The west wall bellcote, west doorway, porch and diagonal buttresses are modern but the gable cross which is carved on a lozenge shaped piece of stone was retained from the demolished south porch. There is a sundial on the south side of the bellcote which was put up in 1835 at a cost of £2 8s. 6d.[1]

In the south wall in the usual position for the piscina is a rectangular locker.

The fine wrought iron altar rails bear the inscription : 'J. Ward, T. Williams, donors, 1735.' Hannett, writing in 1863, informs us that these rails were at that time used as a balustrade to the stairs of the gallery at the west end, and that the communion rails then in use were modern ones dated 1820.[2] The late Mr. A. C. Coldicott told the writer that when he went to live at Ullenhall in 1890 there were no rails and this continued until he, having discovered those of 1735, in the wood yard at Barrells, the late Mr. H. G. Newton replaced them in their original position in 1919.

The seats, which are placed sideways, are of the first half of the 18th century. The panelling between the south windows and the carved high-back chair are probably of the 17th century. There is a good candelabra.

On the floor in front of the altar step are some beautiful mediæval patterned tiles. They are of various designs, some with

[1] St. Mark's Charity Accounts.
[2] In 1821 a sum of £14 16s. was paid to Wm. Price for stonework at the Communion Table.

the arms of Westminster Abbey (which are those assigned to Edward the Confessor) and date probably from the 15th century.[1]

The 15th century font has an octagonal bowl, the lower edge being moulded, and it rests on a plain shaft. One of the two staples remains in the bowl, a relic of pre-Reformation days, when the lid was fastened down to prevent superstitious uses of the christening water which always remained in it. The font stood out in the chapel-yard in the centre of the iron palisade surrounding the Newton vault until Mr. H. G. Newton moved it back at the same time as the altar rails in 1919. It had probably been there ever since the nave was pulled down.

Towards the middle of last century we read that the nave and chancel then had an unsightly gallery and high box pews,[2] those in the nave being 4-ft 4½-ins. high and the ones in the chancel 7-ins. higher, while the altar consisted of a small common deal table. The chancel had a coved ceiling of 1755 and the nave a similar one but of later date. Modern dormer windows disfigured the nave on the south side.[3] Some of the panel work of the lower part of the ancient rood screen then remained,[4] a relic of pre-Reformation days when, the chapel must have been a fair specimen of its kind. During the reign of George III, in 1793-94, the King's arms which were put up in the church cost £13 11s. 1d. In 1796 boarding for 'the backs of the Commandments' and sawing it cost 6s.[5] These would probably be hung on either side of the Holy Table.

There is an interesting cup with cover paten of late 16th century type, but with only the maker's mark upon it. This, which is now at the old chapel, was in the safe at Barrells when in 1884 Archdeacon Wm. Lea wrote his book on Church Plate, the Newtons having provided modern plate instead, and he apparently never saw it. He mentions only the following : Two cups, one large salver paten, one small paten, and one flagon, all of modern mediæval pattern in plated ware. The flagon is no longer fit for use, its place being taken by a glass bottle, and the small paten is missing. The remainder is still in use at the new Church and no additions have since been made.

The old chapel had two bells : one of about the latter half of the 14th century (probably by John Kingston of Warwick) with a cross, and inscribed : *Ave Maria gracia plena*, which is now in the open bellcote at the west end ; the other, a very ancient

[1]*Birm. Arch. Soc.*, Vol LX, 1936, Article by P. B. Chatwin, F.S.A., with illustrations.

[2]The Knights' pew, however, was probably of good craftsmanship, for a fine oak pew door with painted shield of arms of Knight was found by the late Mr. A. C. Coldicott at Dean's Green, where it was in use as the top of a pig-killing bench. Mr. Coldicott gave it to the late Miss Henrietta Knight of Brook End, Henley.

[3]*Churches of Warwickshire*, pp. 142, 143. In 1856 the ceiling was whitewashed and the walls coloured (St. Mark's Chty. Accts.).

[4]*Churches of Warwickshire*, p. 143.

[5]St. Mark's Charity Accounts.

cylindrical bell, with no inscription was given by the late T. H. G. Newton to Emmanuel Mission Church, Sparkbrook.[1]

There is a local tradition that the old bells were brought from Studley by a Mr. Knight and it is said that this can be verified, but in view of the date of the Studley ring it must have been over 200 years ago.[2] It seems most unlikely.

The new church has eight bells all cast by J. Warner and Sons, London, 1874. Numbers one to seven reading from the last, i.e., backwards, are inscribed ' Come let us make a joyful noise,' one word on each bell. The eighth, the tenor, bell bears the initials E.N. and M.R.N. : Elizabeth and Mary Rose Newton, the donors, and on a lozenge-shaped shield their arms, three battle axes.

THE CEMETERY, formerly known as the chapel-yard, was consecrated by the Bishop of Worcester, 9 November 1835, and the expenses in connection with it are recorded in St. Mark's Charity Accounts for that year, as follows :

	£	s.	d.
Received of Robt. Knight, Esq., by payment of Mr. Edward Cooper [estate agent] the fees for consecration of the Burial ground at Ullenhall—Henry Clifton	16	17	6
Thoˢ. Cooper [Impsley], Bill for Journey and expenses to Worcester Post-Chaises, &c.......	4	18	0
Joseph Pettifer, Bill for sawing Pails, &c., for Chapel yard Fence	2	13	0
Thoˢ. Jordan Bricks	4	10	0
Henry Taylor, paling, &c., to consecrated ground for Chapel yard.........................	3	8	2
Edwᵈ. Cooper, Jr., Plans of Chapel and yard for Mr. Clifton, &c. .·.....................	4	3	0

In one of the cottages on the west side of the cemetery lives the sexton, Mr. Benjamin Franklin. Adjoining is a building which was formerly the Parson's stable, first mentioned in the same accounts in 1743 and again in 1829, for use, probably when he rode, or drove, over from Wootton. In 1748 a sum of 8s. 4d. was paid for stone for the horse block, for mounting horses, which would stand near by.

MONUMENTS

Against the north wall, near the Altar, is a fine monument in the Renaissance style to the memory of Francis Throckmorton, which is illustrated in Dugdale's *Warwickshire*. The inscription, now almost illegible, formerly ran : ' Here lieth the body of Francis Throckmorton, esquire, borne in the Citie of Mantua in Italy, son and heir unto Michael Throckmorton, esquire, and of Agnes Hide of Southamptonshire, which Michael was born at Coughton Court in the Countie of Warwick, and youngest brother

---

[1] *Church Bells of Warwickshire*, by H. T. Tilley and H. B. Walters.
[2] Ibid.

to Sir George Throkmorton of Coughton aforesaid, knight.   And after that the said Michaell had lived many years in Italy, in good and great reputation with bountifull Hospitalitie, entertaining most of the Noblemen and gents of England that had occasion to come that way, and did returne into England in the beginning of the reigne of Q. Mary, and received of her gift the manors of Honily, Blackwell, Packhurst, Winderton, Ullenhall in Ullenhall and others as appeareth in her Majesties Letters Patent bearing date in the first year of her reigne : and after went into Italy againe, where he departed this life and lieth buried in S. Martin's Church in the said Citie of Mantua under a fair Tombe.   The said Michael married Judith Tracie, daughter of Richard Tracie of Stanway in the Countie of Gloucester esquire, and of Barbara Lucy of Charlecote in the County of Warwick, and sister to Sir Paul Tracie Baronet, and had by her six children, whereof three, that is to say Francis, Michael, and Judith here departed this life without issue, and the other three are living ; that is to say John Michael and Judith. Anno Dom. 1617, and in the fifteenth year of the reign of our Lord James the 1st King of England.

> Mors mihi lucrum, portus & refugium
>   sic transit gloria Mundi
> Omnia vana vidi, solo mea XPo repono.
> Mors tua, Mors XPi, fraus Mundi, gloria Coeli,
>   Et dolor inferni, sunt meditanda tibi.

Above the east window is a moulded stone panel with the arms of Knight impaling St. John : Ar. 3 bendlets gu. on a canton of the second a spur or impaling ar. on a chief gu. 2 mullets or.

On the north side of the east window is a plain tablet bearing the arms of Knight, Earl of Catherlough, surmounted by a coronet and inscribed : ' In the vault under this chapel lie the remains of Robert Knight, Earl of Catherlough, Viscount Barrells, Baron Luxborough and Knight of the Bath.   Born 17 December 1702. Married 10 June 1727 Henrietta St. John, sister[1] to Viscount Bolingbroke, Secretary of State to Queen Anne, by whom he had one son, Henry, and one daughter, Henrietta.   Died 30th March, 1772.'

On the south side of the east window is a similar tablet bearing the arms of Knight impaling St. John and inscribed :

> In the vault of this chancel lie the remains of
> Viscountess St. John, B. 25 February, 1723, D. 6 March
>   1752.
> Josiah Russell, B. 1674, D. 7 May 1755.
> Baroness Luxborough, B. 15 July 1699, D. 26 March 1756.
> Honble. Henry Knight, B. 25 December 1728, D. 15 August
>   1762. S.P.

[1]She was half-sister.

Countess Duroure, B. 21 November 1729, D. 1 March
1763.

Elizabeth Powell, B. 7 January 1692, D. 11 March 1765.

Caroline Knight, B. 20 July 1772, D. 22 August 1772.

Henry Knight, B. 24 May 1795, D. 14 November 1800.

Count Duroure, B. 6 February 1763, D. 24 September
1822. S.P.

[Some details of the bill for building this vault are as follows :
Robert Knight, Esq. to George Coppage 1830.

Oct. 15—Myself 1 day, 3s. 4d., Labourer, 1 day, 1s. 8d.

Oct. 23—Myself, 6½ days at 3s. 8d., £1 3s. 10d. ; brick-
layer, ½ day at 3s. 4d.=1s. 8d. ; labourer, 6¾ days at
2s.=13s. 6d. ; boy, 3½ days at 1s. 2d.=4s. 1d.

Oct. 30 to Nov. 3—Other similar items amounting to
£8 7s. 3d.

Total, £10 15s. 4d.

Soon after this work was done the bodies were translated from
the Mausoleum in Barrells Park which was then pulled down.[1]]

Against the south wall near the altar is a tablet inscribed :

To the dear memory of the Rev. Henry Charles Knight,
second son of Robert and the Hon. Frances Knight of Barrels,
born October the 7th 1813, died December the 1st 1887 ; and
of Katherine Paterson his wife who died May the 9th 1884.

Frances Knight died June 15th 1916.

Lucy C. E. Marshall died June 22nd 1932.

Henrietta Knight died August 28th 1914.

Katherine Knight died April 21st 1922.

Make them to be numbered with thy Saints in glory
everlasting.

Underneath the above monument :

In memory of Henrietta Knight who died August
28th 1914 and is buried in this churchyard. By her will she
bequeathed one thousand pounds to found the Knight
Charity for the benefit of the old and poor people of the parish
of Ullenhall and in memory of her father Henry Charles
Knight, born October 7th 1813.

A tablet on the north wall :

R.I.P.—In loving memory of Capt. J. E. Marshall,
D.C.L.I., killed in action March 30 1915.—Faithful unto death.

A tablet on the south wall :

The noble army of martyrs praise thee.

In loving memory of Capt. Evelyn Marshall of the Royal
Warwickshire Regt., son of Canon Edward and Lucy Marshall
of Sutton near Ely, and grandson of the late Henry Charles
and Katherine Knight who after serving through the operations
in Gallipoli (being one of the last to leave Sulva Bay) was

[1]See *Wootton Wawen*, p. 65.

mortally wounded at El Hanneh on the Tigris and died on April 6th 1916 in his 30th year.

'Qui procul hinc' the legend's writ
—The Eastern Grove is far away—
'Qui ante diem periit
Sed miles, sed pro patria.'

In the porch. An iron plate inscribed : J. Tarlton and R. Burman Chapel Wardens 1820.

Outside on the west wall is a stone with an oval-framed inscription so much worn that it cannot be read though the small head of a child is still fairly clear. It was to the memory of William Mortiboyes of Studley who, by his will of 18 January 1733-34, left money for teaching poor children to read.

Ullenhall Church

Between the village and the entrance gates to Barrells is the modern parish church of St. Mary which has an apsidal chancel, transepts, and nave with aisles. An inscription at the east end records that 'This church was built to the Glory of God and in memory of William and Mary Newton late of Barrells by their sons T.H.G., W., and H. and daughters E. and M. R., Anno Dni., 1875.'

There is no burial ground and all burials take place at the old chapel.

The Parish Register entries begin in 1855 and prior to that year were kept at Wootton Wawen.

An early view of Beaudesert Church. (O'D)

VICARS OF ULLENHALL

RICHARD THURSFIELD, 1862-72, Caius Coll., Cambridge, B.A., 1854, M.A. 1875, Deacon 1854 by the Bishop of Chester, Priest 1860 by the Archbishop of Canterbury [Crockford]. He died at Worcester on 20 July 1906.[1]

JOHN GEORGE, 1873-78, St. John's Coll., Cambridge, B.A. (Sen. Opt. and 3rd cl. Theo. Trip.) 1866, M.A. 1869, Deacon 1867, Priest 1868, Gloucester and Bristol [Crockford].

MELBOURNE RUSSELL WEST, 1879-99, Queen's Coll. Oxford, B.A. (4th Cl. Lit. Hum) 1865, M.A. 1868, Deacon 1865, Priest 1866, by Bishop of Lichfield [Crockford]. He died at Leamington Spa on 25 December 1901.[2]

LOTON PARRY, 1899-1901, Deacon 1894, Priest 1895, Worcester [Crockford].

WILLIAM FREDERICK PELTON, 1901-32, Late scholar of Gonville and Caius Coll., Cambridge, B.A. (Sen. Opt.) 1882, M.A. 1886, Ridley Hall 1888, Deacon 1889, Priest 1890, London. Cambridge University Extension Lecturer, 1897, Author of *The Master Key to the Apocalypse*, 1926 ; *The Rest that remaineth*, 1929 [Crockford].

FRANK RIDLEY WHITTAKER, 1932-42, Bishop Wilson Coll., Isle of Man, 1908, Univ. of Durham, L. Th. 1910, Deacon 1910, Priest 1911, Sodor and Man [Crockford].

WILLIAM GODFREY COOPER, 1943, Deacon 1938, Priest 1939, London, Lately Curate of Bucknall with Bagnall, Staffs., Instituted 3 February 1943.

[1]From a brass plate in the Church.
[2]Ibid.

CHAPELWARDENS' AND CONSTABLE'S ACCOUNTS OF ULLENHALL

THE meetings of ratepayers took place at Easter and prior to the year 1819 they were held at one of the local inns including the Catherlough Arms,[1] which was then kept by John Greaves and afterwards by his widow. After that date they were held in the vestry which was the blocked up south porch of the old chapel. At these meetings the accounts were passed and the levy fixed. The new chapelwardens and the constable for the ensuing year were chosen, also the new overseers. They received no pay and they were legally bound to serve for the year of their election unless specially privileged. It was usual for the chapelwardens to be sworn in at Wootton but the constable had to attend the Court at Pathlow[2] for this purpose, and owing to the distance or for some other reason he sometimes failed to make the journey there, when fines were imposed. In 1799 ' Five years arrears of fine to the Lords of the Hundred and Liberty of Partloe ' came to 13s. 4d. and ' an amercement for the third borough not attending ' 5s. The accounts contain recurring items for administrative expenses besides the usual outlay on matters pertaining to the Church and parish. Bread and wine at ' Easter, Whison, St. Michael, and Christmas,' amounted to 14s. 8d. in 1779. Here, as elsewhere, at that time it was evidently considered sufficient for Holy Communion to be celebrated four times a year only and things remained very much the same until what is known as the Catholic Revival about the middle of last century. The communion table in 1810 was covered with a velvet cloth and there is a mention twenty years earlier of table linen which had been stained very badly with wine, so that as in early Puritan days the communicants appear to have continued to partake of the Bread and Wine sitting round the table, which would probably be moved into the centre of the chancel for the purpose.

The various purchases of books include a Bible £3 10s., a new prayer-book for the clerk £1, a ' form of prayer ' 7s. 6d., and ' 6 books for the coier ' £2 0s. 6d. So the choir then probably consisted of six in number and was accompanied by musicians playing on old-time instruments, for a basoon was purchased in 1766 costing £2 12s. 6d.,[3] a hautboy in 1792 at 19s. 6d., and two basoon reeds in 1822 at 3s. The clerk, Wm. Smith, received a salary of £4 4s. a year in 1823 and this worthy would sit in the lowest seat of the ' three decker ' pulpit. At matins and evensong he led the responses and said ' Amen,' and recited the alternate verses of the Psalms.

[1]Now ' The Spur ' from one of the charges of these arms.
[2]The Liberty of Pathlow, its Court Leet and Court Baron was granted to Sir Francis Smith of Wootton in 1617. *Wootton Wawen*, p. 27.
[3]St. Mark's Charity Accounts.

Collections for the Briefs are frequently mentioned. These were for the benefit of communities and individuals who had suffered misfortune or for the repair of churches, etc., but no interesting details are given such as those to be found at Beaudesert.

Bell-ringing was very popular with our ancestors and new bell-ropes seemed often to be needed, but as disused ropes became the chapelwardens' property, it is said they were sometimes replaced earlier than they otherwise would have been.

The surplice belonged to the parish and was looked after and washed at the parish expense.

' Parsons half-year's salary,' which was gathered from the inhabitants, is entered at £7 10s. in 1775, and a stipend of £15 a year seems very small, but at that time the chapel was served from the mother church of Wootton.

The constable's duties included matters relating to the defence of the realm. On 16 December 1745 a sum of 5s. was paid to Sam¹. Sandols for a sword. It was the time of the unsuccessful insurrection of Charles Edward Stuart, the young Pretender, who with his Highlanders had reached as far south as Derby twelve days earlier. In 1751 repairing the armour cost £1 2s. ¹

During the war of American Independence, in 1779, when we were also fighting France and Spain, the constable spent 6d. searching with a press warrant and 1s. while searching ' the ale houses,' probably in drink.

Defence matters are barely mentioned again until Napoleon began to plan the downfall of England and from thence active preparations were made here as elsewhere to meet the danger. In 1797 occur these entries :

	s.	d.
For writing the Cavalry ' Apart ' Notices and delivery	2	6
A journey to Stratford to draw Cavalry.............	2	6
For serving a summons R. Knight Esq. for the Cavalry	1	0
Journey to Stratford to enroll yᵉ Cavalry..........	2	6
Journey to Stratford when the Militia were to appear to be enrolled	2	6
Journey to Warwick to hire a supplementary Militiaman and have him sworn and expenses........	5	0
Later items for the same purpose are :		
1803 Journey to Stratford with the men to serve in the Army of Reserve and expenses............	4	6
1804 Giving notices to householders to be sworn in Special Constables	2	6
Paid Special Constable's expenses	11	8
1805 Horse and self going round the hamlet to take account of the Volunteers and Militia	6	6
Making 2 lists under General Defence Act......	6	0

¹These two items are from St. Mark's Charity Accounts, see p. 184.

It is said that 300,000 volunteers mustered in England early in 1805 to meet Napoleon's threatened invasion of our shores, which however, he never attempted. After his final overthrow at Waterloo in 1815 no further expenditure on these forces is recorded in the accounts.

The constable also looked after local taxation. In 1792 for assessing the windows, wagons and horses and delivering the notices 5s. was charged. The first-named was, in effect, a tax on light and air and tended to impair the health of the people. Nevertheless it was not repealed until 1851. Payment was often evaded by bricking up the windows, and even to-day some of these remain blocked up in old houses. In the same year as the entry was written the tax on wagons was taken off, but horses continued to be taxed until 1874. During the war with France owners of horses used for agricultural or trade purposes had to pay 2s. on each horse rising by degrees to as high as 14s. in 1808. In 1797 for delivering notices and assessing the clocks and watches, 5s. was charged. A new tax was imposed on clocks and watches in that year ; for each clock, 5s., gold watch, 10s., and silver or metal watch, 2s. 6d. As a consequence the demand for these decreased to such an extent that the industry was nearly ruined and the tax was repealed in the following year.

The chapelwardens were responsible for the collection and distribution of the charity money. Mention is made in 1823 of Francis Brittain's charity amounting to £3 a year for providing gowns for poor widows of the parish and of a sum of £2 yearly received from lands at Aspley for the charity school There are small payments for relief given to travellers passing through such as : 1794 'Relieving a sick man on his travel,' 2s. ; 1797 'Paid a sailor on his pass,' 6d. Sailors were frequently left in a deplorable state, often with wounds, and with no state aid or pension in those days. It is recorded in 1826 that the chapelwardens journeyed to Hockley House to be examined by the Charity Commissioners and that their travelling expenses amounted to 10s. 6d.

The free school stood at the north-east corner of the chapel,[1] and it is mentioned that six boys and two girls were put into it in 1798. Thomas Astley, who was the schoolmaster in 1823, received a salary of £4 a year.

Another duty which fell to their lot was to keep down the vermin for which they paid so much a head—for a fox, 1s. ; sparrows, 4d. a dozen ; urchins (i.e., hedgehogs), 4d. each ; a marten (i.e., weasel), 6d. Hedgehogs sucked eggs and were supposed to suck the milk from cows.

Ale-drinking at the parish expense seems to have been a recognised practice. At 'Gunpowder Plot,' in 1777, the powder cost 1s. 4d., but the ale no less than 5s. which in those days would

[1]Illustration in Aylesford Collection, Birm. Pub. Lib.

purchase a large quantity. The expenses of the funeral of Wm. Hopkins (probably a pauper) in 1791 were 3s. 9d., while the outlay on ale, bread and cheese amounted to 8s. 8d.

In 1777 the constable's meeting was held at The Spaw in Beaudesert and in 1781 at The Talbot in Ullenhall, both inns having long ago ceased to exist.

The levy made by the chapelwardens varied from ½d. to 3d. in the £, according to the expenditure. In 1773 the amount paid out was £7 8s. 3d., and each succeeding year until the turn of the century it remained about the same. In 1801 it rose to £11 6s. 9d. and from that date there was a slight increase until 1819 when an exceptionally large proportion was paid to Wootton, namely £21— 10¾d. which swelled the total outlay to £34 4s. 1¾d. For the last year of the accounts, 1828, the money spent amounted to £20 17s. 5d. A highway levy in 1802 at 6d. in the £ came to £35 19s. 10d. The constables' accounts, which began in 1773, with a total of £2 14s. 2d., had increased to £7—10d. by 1807 when they ceased altogether. These sums for the first eight years are stated to have been paid out of town land.

The power of the vestry was supreme in those days and managed all local affairs without the aid of parish, district, or county councils.

ST. MARK'S CHARITY, which has been referred to in footnotes was founded originally to help in the repairs to the old chapel and to contribute towards levies, wars, musters, etc. (see p. 184).

The feoffees of this charity in 1828 ordered that a pound and stocks be made forthwith at their expense. They paid Richard London 15s. 9d. for an estimate and plan of the pound, but the cost of building it is not given. It stood on the site of the present Ullenhall church day school and was, of course, used for straying cattle. Thomas Dolphin's bill for the stocks amounted to £2 3s. 4d. and these were situated on the spot now occupied by the war memorial cross, opposite the blacksmith's shop. In them petty offenders against the law paid the penalty of their misdeeds, and were often pelted with stones, rotten eggs and other missiles.

In conclusion it may be of interest to mention a sum of £1 4s. 8d., spent in 1775-76 by this charity on straw and ' wottlins.' The latter appears to be a corruption of the word wattles, or hurdles, for in the old days in Warwickshire some of the building was done with ' close hurdle-work plastered over with a mixture of clay and chopped straw.'

Some other items are :[1]

	£	s.	d.
1743 Joseph Greaves for 7 thrave of straw for yᵉ Chappel Stable	0	10	6
1753 For 7 quarts of Ale for yᵉ Raring[2]	0	1	9

[1]The first four entries are from St. Mark's Charity Accounts ; the remainder from the Chapelwardens Accounts.

[2]?Rearing-feast which took place when a roof was put on or a building finished.

1755	Chamberlain for 5 bunches of Stakes and Ethrings[1]	0	1	8
1765	Pd. Pears for Tile and Creas[2]	1	6	0
1783	A footnote : Malt was 7s. 6d. a strike and ' measure small '			
1797	Paid for militia cockades	0	1	0
1817	Mr. Gilbert for 100 suffen Tiles[3]	0	6	6
1821	Mr. Jones for iron pallicading in the chappel	9	13	6

Right Honᵘ Henrietta Lady Luxborough.

Lady Luxborough, 1699-1756.

[1]Etherings, flexible twigs for bindings hedges.
[2]Crease, a curved tile.
[3]?Draining tiles (Suff, a drain.).

THE HON. HENRIETTA KNIGHT, LADY LUXBOROUGH

LADY Luxborough was Henrietta, daughter of Henry, Viscount St. John, by his second wife, Angelica Magdalena, a daughter of Georges Pellisary, treasurer-general of the marines and super-intendent of the ships and galleys of France. The French blood in her veins perhaps accounted for her poetic and artistic temperament, a contrast to that of her more materalistic husband ; she was generous and impulsive, romantic, sentimental and talented. She was half-sister of that eminent statesman Henry, First Viscount Bolingbroke, between whom there existed a lively affection and, true understanding. ' I have always observed in you,' he wrote, ' the symptoms of a good heart, and have always loved you, for sentiment in my opinion is preferable to wit, and you have both.'

Her marriage to Robert Knight, which proved anything but happy, took place on 10 June 1727, her husband being the son of Robert Knight, Cashier of the South Sea Company, who after the collapse of the ' Bubble,' fled to the continent with a reward of £2,000 on his head, but afterwards obtained a pardon and returned to England.[1] Three years after the marriage her husband pur-chased Barrells from his second cousin Raleigh Knight. We first hear of the Knight family at Beoley in 1484, and in 1554 they settled at Barrells. Originally yeomen they rose to ' gentlehood ' and Robert was raised to the Irish peerage in 1745 as Baron Luxborough of Shannon and (after his wife's death) was, in 1763, advanced to the dignity of an earldom by the title of Earl of Catherlough.

Lady Luxborough is described by Horace Walpole as ' high coloured ' and ' lusty ' with a ' great black bush of hair ' in which at first she wore the portrait of her husband from whom she soon ' was parted . . . upon a gallantry she had with Dalton,[2] the reviver of Comus and a divine,' and ' retired to a hermitage on Parnassus,'[3] by which is meant Barrells. At another time he implies that not only was she in love with Dalton but that both she and her friend Lady Hertford, Duchess of Somerset (in whose home he resided as tutor to Lord Beauchamp), had been guilty of improper conduct with him.[4] Walpole was, however, prejudiced and his malice was perpetually manifested against her family, particularly Bolingbroke ; his words should, therefore, not be accepted without reserve.

---

[1] There is a cenotaph to his memory in Wootton Church erected by his son.
[2] John Dalton, Poet and Divine, 1709-1763.
[3] *Dict. Nat. Biog.*
[4] *Letters*, Cunningham, vi, 233, Cited in *D.N.B.*

New light is thrown on Lady Luxborough's separation from her husband by an interesting series of letters which have recently come into the possession of one of her husband's descendants, Mrs. C. O. Higgon, M.B.E., to whom the writer is indebted for the copies of them appearing on pages 145 to 158. They leave little room for doubt that Henrietta was in love with Dalton but in the letters to her husband she vehemently denies that it was anything more than platonic. The affair caused a great scandal in society, the immediate occasion of which appears to have been the finding of a letter from Henrietta to her lover which was allowed to ' lye loose about.' This is the letter which so stunned her half brother, Lord Bolingbroke, with surprise and caused him to write to her husband thus : ' I should not tell what to think that a lady of quality should prostitute herself to such a low fellow and y^t ye dullest poet in Christendom should turn her head or warm her heart seemed to me incredible,' and he, who always loved her to the day of his death, was forced to admit that such a letter could not be excused by any pretence whatever, though he found it so difficult to believe. All her piteous appeals failed to move her husband who could not be persuaded to forgive her or live with her again, and he never did. It is difficult from the evidence of the letters to pass judgment, but, as she herself admits, her conduct was to say the least ' more than prudence or decency allows,' though it probably went no further. A contemporary writer,[1] on the cause of the separation observes that : ' Lord Luxborough was unquestionably a man devoid of morals who roved from fair to fair and was perhaps glad of an excuse to quiet his wife.'[2] Be that as it may, there is no doubt his pride was wounded by the talk which went on and it probably had something to do with his unforgiving attitude.

With the full approbation of her parents Henrietta was established at Barrells in 1736 and lived there separated from her husband for the remainder of her life. By the terms of the separation she was forbidden to travel out of England, or within twenty miles of London, or on the Bath road where her friend Lady Hertford lived at Colnbrook. Apart from this Lord Luxborough seems to have done what he could to make his wife comfortable at Barrells, but in later years his treatment of her was somewhat cruel.

In spite of all that had befallen her she seems to have been happy enough on her own at Barrells which she made the centre of a well-known eighteenth century Literary Coterie including the poets Shenstone, Somervile, Jago and Richard Graves. Moreover, she had an abiding interest in her garden which was fostered by Shenstone, one of the most original and successful of early landscape gardeners.

She, however, appears to have been constantly short of money and to have lived far beyond the allowance of £500 a year made by

[1] MS. Notes at B.M.
[2] See also her brother John's callous letter on page 149.

her husband which was not nearly enough for her tastes, even allowing for the greater value of money in those days when for instance her men servants' wages were only £8 to £10 a year each. As will be seen her husband's admonitions to keep within her income went unheeded and even in his last recorded letter to her he was constrained to write thus : ' Can it be said for the credit of any Person to drive with a coach and six horses when the wages of the servants who attend the equipage are unpaid ? Can it be for the credit of any Person to entertain their neighbours with an elegant dinner, and the Butcher's Bill unpaid ? When this is so, the Butchers and the Servants give the entertainment, not the Lady at the upper end of the table, who assumes the false credit of it.'

It is her published letters to Shenstone[1] which give her a place in literature, though not a high one. As a picture of contemporary events of the district they are, however, of great interest and possess much charm, Her verses never reached high merit and four little poems ' By a Lady of Quality,' attributed to her by Horace Walpole, are only of moderate worth.

On the first page of the collection Shenstone has written these words, ' Letters from the Hon. Lady Luxborough written with abundant ease, politeness and vivacity in which she was scarce equalled by any woman of her time.'

They reveal a charming personality and a nature which gave itself up to friendship, which indeed was the characteristic note of the coterie.

It may be seen from the letters how close was the relationship, indeed one of affection, which existed between Lady Luxborough and Shenstone. 'I propose,' she writes, 'with your leave to take a night's lodging [at the Leasowes] as you were so kind to desire, by which means I shall have more of your company and shall see your improvements more at leisure and your woods will afford a different scenery when they are embrowned by the shade of evening or when the moon glimmers through their leaves, whereas I have never yet seen them but in full sunshine and when walking (had it been any other place) had been a toil. If you do not write me a line to the contrary by Thursday's post, you will see me next Monday the 7th inst., at your Ferme ornée, and I hope to bring you on the 8th to my Ferme negligée, for that you will find it. Having had so much company in my house and the hay harvest having employed my servants the gardens were neglected just when they ought to have been put in order, and the dry time has prevented the new turf from joining and my pavilion when almost finished was pulled down again in part to add to it a shrine for Venus so that it is still uncovered, and the roses, etc., are all faded, and give an ugly aspect to my shrubberies, which wait your directions to be new modelled.'

In another letter to Shenstone she says : ' It is the conversation

[1] She did not meet Shenstone until she had been some three years at Barrells.

of a chosen few that smooths the rugged road of life, such as yours
strews it with flowers, but as they soon fade so did you vanish and
all the company that surrounded my hearth.'

After Shenstone had visited her in August 1748 she writes :
' I am certain the rugged walk to Ullenhall Chapel, however
conducive to health according to the Physician or to happiness
according to the Divine, would never have inclined me to undertake
it had not the company I was with smoothed the road and levelled
the ruts ; for such was the effect it had, at least upon my imagination.
But the roads are as rough as ever, and I as lazy, which shows that
we hermits are to blame, droning our time away in our cells.'

But another time she advises Shenstone to marry a rich
heiress with whom his name has been associated, so that money
troubles might no longer hinder his poetical work, unless he had
made up his mind to celibacy, which does not look as if their
intimacy could have been other than platonic.

We read of Lord Luxborough often staying at his neighbouring
estate of Edstone and of her son and daughter also being there.
In one place she remarks that ' my daughter is now nineteen and I
never lay under the same roof with her since she was six.' Her
son, she says, bore a good character and behaved well to her, but
later on her husband prejudiced him against her.

Some idea of Barrells at that time may be gathered from these
letters in one of which she writes that ' Good carving is too fine
for my humble roof. The room is only hung with sixpenny paper
and is so low that I have but five inches between Pope's head and the
little motto over it as you thought was too good to reject. I have
employed Williams [of Birmingham] to paint the ornaments you
would have had carved, in stone colours, pretty strongly shaded to
appear to rise like carving. Mr. Moore of Warwick has mended my
figure of Milton so well though it was broke in a thousand pieces
and a hand and arm lost, that I shall employ him further.' Shenstone, writing in 1750-51, about the alteration of a room, makes
this suggestion : ' If your ladyship does not choose to go to the
expense of a carved frame what think you of a white oval frame to
your glass in the middle and a festoon on each side. This, with
the stucco, need amount to no more than £3 3s.'

The upper storeys are referred to thus : ' The yellow room,
which Miss Dolman[1] lay in when you were last here, is empty.
I should rejoice to see you.' In 1752 she talks of ' the ceiling of my
bedroom, which I would have adorned a little with papier-maché,
and the ground painted of a colour, but I do not know where to
get the paper ornaments.' ' My dressing-room looks just as I would
have it, and the festoons over the windows are not the least elegant
ornaments of the room ; the doors seem to envy the windows and
are in as plain a dress as that of the Quakers.'

[1]A cousin of Shenstone's to whom he was warmly attached.

Ascending still higher a letter of October 24, 1752 reads : ' My old servant, Price, is struck with a palsy and one half of his body is dead. As his weight and size do not agree with the narrowness of my garret stairs, there was not a possibility of carrying him higher than the first storey.'

Speaking of the grounds she says : ' My hermitage has been dry all this wet season by the alteration I made when I thatched it. I am just come in from the summer-house where I drank tea with Mrs. Bartlet, Mrs. Davies [of Stratford-on-Avon], Mr. Holyoak [Vicar of Oldberrow] and Mr. John Reynolds [Vicar of Wootton]. The two latter we have left at bowls by moonlight.'

She mentions that ' the ha ! ha ! is digging,' and that a sundial is set in the middle of the court and refers to the serpentine, upper garden and lower garden, coppice wood, hermitage pit, lime walk, shrubs and aviary ; also the Piping Faun in the oak tree and the erection of statues and urns in the grounds.

She tells of ' planting twenty-seven good straight elms in lines parallel in the lower part of long walk,' and of ' planting the lane that joins the coppice.'

A visitor agrees with Shenstone 'by admiring the amphi-theatre of wooded hills that we see from the windows and the situa-tion of the Hermitage which he thinks preferable to any in England.' ' He was against my planting the service walk with flowers also against my painting the niche where Venus is as she is supposed to have been bathing and to crouch herself in that manner upon the approach of somebody by way of hiding herself, and would have the niche adorned with moss, etc., like some bathing place.'

The grounds now have a neglected appearance but the large double oak tree under which she had sat with Somervile, and where she wished for the company of Shenstone and Whistler[1] in the Springtime still continues to thrive. One can still trace the ' Service walk ' and the Hermitage which she loved best of all her garden and admire the vista to Oldberrow Church. The ' ha ! ha !' too remains—this being a sunk ditch to keep out the cattle without an obstruction to the view caused by a wall or fence.

The difficulties of travel in those days are brought home very forcibly as we read that ' The Birmingham coach could carry Mr. Outing [her secretary and factotum] any Monday from Henley to London by Oxford.'

This coach, which had not long been established, left Birming-ham early in the morning and pulled up for breakfast at the Swan in Henley and stopped for the night at Chipping Norton, going on next day to Oxford where the second night was spent, arriving in London via Uxbridge the third day. It took the same time on the return journey.

In 1751 a journey to Stratford-on-Avon calls forth this

[1]Anthony Whistler, a friend of Shenstone's at Pembroke Coll., Oxford.

comment : ' I did indeed, yesterday dine with Mrs. Kendal but the roads, the weather and everything so bad, except her company that I never was so fatigued in going forty or fifty miles in a day.'

She complains of the ruts of the Portway, and of four of her horses being sent for to join two of Mrs. Meredith's horses to bring her from Wolsely Bridge to Barrells ; and mentions Mrs. Kendall's coach and six and the sending of her own coach to Warwick with the High Sheriff.

The roads at that time must have been in a deplorable condition. There appears to have been no regular post and letters were sent by messengers, farmers or tradesmen between Barrells and Shenstone's residence, The Leasowes. On one occasion Lady Luxborough says : ' I write to-day to Mr. Outing by the Evesham gardeners to say I hope to see you next week. Johnson[1] of Northfield put my postillion in that lucky road to carry you the letter. I wrote you a letter of great length which I sent to Henley to be conveyed to Birmingham Post Office, directed to you, to be left there. I have heard of giving one guinea to musicians to play, and ten to leave off. Thus are you, I believe, inclinable to reward old Emma and to dismiss her from the office of postwoman.' Another time she writes : ' I dare not trust my servant and horse to the weather and still less to the curious post office at Birmingham, so changed the cover put it in a frank and sent it to go through London.'

She had agreeable neighbours in Lord and Lady Archer of Umberslade, Lord and Lady Plymouth of Hewell, William Somervile of Edstone and other neighbouring gentry and clergy among whom were Richard Jago of Beaudesert, Parson Allen of Spernall, W[m]. Holyoake, Rector of Oldberrow, and curate of Ullenhall, and Thomas Hall, Curate of Henley—the little fat, oily man of God as she calls him. Amidst her domestic troubles she seems to have lived a life of comparative enjoyment in the company of educated and literary people of the day and her house was often full. She is called a female Bolingbroke and is said to have inclined to her brother's way of thinking in religious matters : that of a free thinker. We know, however, that she attended the Church services and that she died in the Christian Religion. She breathed her last at Barrells on 26 March 1756, aged fifty-seven, and her end is related to Shenstone by Parson Holyoake whose brother, Dr. Holyoake, of Henley, attended her professionally.

' The night before she died I read the Recommendatory Prayer to her ; and I hope she is perfectly happy though she had so great troubles and afflictions in this life . . . Mrs. Davies and [Mrs.] Outing have been with Lady Luxborough all her illness, which I am glad of, Lord Luxborough is expected to-morrow to give orders about the funeral.' Not long before her death she had

---

[1]He supplied her with coal.

received the Sacrament ' with great devotion.' Lady Luxborough was buried first in the chapel at Wootton and later removed to a mausoleum in Barrells Park. In 1830 when the mausoleum was taken down her body was again removed to a new vault under the chancel of Ullenhall Chapel where we may hope it will now rest in peace. Lady Luxborough bore her husband a son, Henry, and a daughter, Henrietta, who both survived her but died before their father. The Earl by his second wife, Mary le Quesne, had no issue, but during her lifetime he had at least four natural children by Miss Jane Davies of the Moat Farm, Ullenhall, the eldest of whom, Robert Knight, succeeded to Barrells and his father's other estates.

Sources : *Lady Luxborough's Letters to William Shenstone, Esq.*, pub. by Dodsley, Lond. 1775. Letters on p. 145 *et seq. Dict. Nat. Biog.* F. L. Colvile, *Worthies of Warwickshire.* J. Hannett, *The Forest of Arden.* M. Williams, *William Shenstone.* W. Cooper, *Wootton Wawen.* Local records.

Letters Relating to Lady Luxborough's Separation from Her Husband

From the Hon. Henrietta Knight,[1] *to her husband, Robert Knight. No date, but before April* 1736.

' My dearest Life for god sake consider what effect this parting will have, and try to bring yourself to be under ye same roof as me for ye sake of yr Dear Children and what Mr. Knight and his Wife will say ; Mama is so good as to wish it you know how terrible ye world's censures are, if you could pass over this you'd ever find me behave as you can desire or direct. I take my solemn oath that this silly but Platonick passion is ye only one I have ever had, & yet I now despise my self and ye object of it whose face I will never see more nor write to him—Try me for a little while & then if you have ye least complaint I'll not so much as endeavour to excuse myself. I am in ye most terrible affliction, incapable as yet of shedding tears, if you can be molified for god's sake endeavour to hide what has passed to ye world. If this affair is made publick as you intend think what tryumph it will be to Mrs. Knight and what an affliction to my poor pappa. Do for Heaven's Sake don't speak of this & come home again to yr. unfortunate but ever affectionate H.K.

' I love you better than ever indeed I do I told Mama why I never would consent to what you suspect me guilty of.'

From the Hon. Henrietta Knight to her husband, Robert Knight. Dated 1736.

' My dearest Life, whom I love beyond anything notwith-standing appearances against me, for God's Sake let me see you &

---

[1]Afterwards Lady Luxborough.

ask your pardon on my knees for as much as I have been guilty of, which I own is more than prudence or Decency allows, but yet I swear the passion was Platonick & is no more : Punish me in what way you please but there is nothing yt I can feel except that of not living with you it would be ye death of yr unfortunate wife

H. Knight.   1736.'

Can you not forgive ?

' I have read this over which in my first surprise I did not do, & I am now sure more than ever, that I never wrote it as ye dictates of my own heart, & little thinking that I should be thus accused, I was so imprudent as to translate & coppy out a large Bundle of such foolish letters 13 of wh. I burn'd last week, to make room for things I was placing, & before God I swear not one was other than coppys & translations, I yet flatter myself I shall find the original of this which I wd have kept had I known it could ever be of consequence.   I again repeat that ye most I ever granted to ye person I am suspected of was Compassion, which I have often accused my self of as a crime, tho' I'm now accused of worse.'

[The above letter, with postscript, is written on the back of the following which appears to be Henrietta's letter to her lover referred to on p. 152, and to have been sent to her by her husband when he accused her.]

' As soon as you were gone I employ'd myself (as it must ever be in something that suggests you) in reading over yr letters, which I have resolved to burn, but could not bring my heart or hand to execute what my reason told me was proper for I found after having made a large bonfire, that all remained which spoke your passion, & none were consumed but those which necessity had made cool and indifferent, these innocent victims are sacrificed whilst the guilty ones remain as cherished proofs of what were better to forget at least if not punished.   But what do I say ? They are perhaps already forgot by you or repented of.   How different is your stile already even when security permit you to speak the dictates of your heart ! pardon this reproach—perhaps my fears belie you, but I can't help remembering the time when one hour or two brought me some publick or private letter of your passionate tender sentiments wrote in your own hand, in one of the latter I find these words which I will repeat & answer.

' *I love you still nay more, & must ever do so unless you pour into my wounded soul the dear balm of your Compassion & teach me by gentle means to conquer it.*

' Pardon the present answer those words suggest to me. I have poured that balm & it has worked its effect for your passion is conquered.   I expect at least thanks for the cure & might in vain ask the same Remedy in return for my self for alas tis not in your power to give it since Vertue has not prevailed.   Time alone can work the Cure.'

From the Hon. Henrietta Knight, to her husband, Robert Knight.   No date.

' The alternative given me is severe that it is very difficult to chuse. The being deprived not only of Mr. Knight's affection, but also of his conversation is what makes me suffer so much that ye rest is as nothing : Liberty is so sweet that it is more natural for me to chuse to be in a remote cottage Free, than at home a Prisoner. But as it appears to my Friends that ye latter will be best for my family & as to ye world, I will consent to it, provided that it is allow'd me if after days or weeks or months I should find my Confinement insupportable or ye air necessary, that I may then go to some Lodging in ye Country 20 miles off or more, or to any other place more distant from London. The being confined to one Floor & ye being deprived of so small a comfort as that of pen and ink and paper wh I wd never employ but to write to my dear Friends and Relations & even that by permission of Mr. Knight is very hard, but I must submitt. Though I am innocent of anything more than an imprudence, & not guilty of injuring him as he supposes; I think I might be allow'd to write or hear from my aunt and Cosin Seymour Cholmondeley, & Mr. Knight in France & my Br. Bolingbroke but if Not I must submit : the receiving no visits is a small misfortune since I am allow'd to see my Dear Father Mother & Brothers & Miss Soame, ye loosing my Daughter is made up to me by her being in her grandmamma's care & my being allow'd to see her & her Brother.

' If Mr. Knight had trusted to my promise and ye behaviour his generosity would have engaged me to He would never had reason to repent & we should neither of us have been exposed to ye remarks of ye malicious words, but He chuses it, and I am doomed to misery. May he however enjoy all happiness in this world & ye next. Mine can only be there where probably my affliction & confinement will soon send me his affectionate & injured Wife, my Tears allow me to say no more.

' I forgot to mention that before I had resol'd & declared that I would never see ye person he is jealous of any more, because I was sencible it must cause a strong suspicion of what I am charged with, & because that ye compassion I had had for ye violent passion He had for me was entirely ceas'd, And as I was resolved never to consent to have an Intrigue with him I had brought my self even to dislike & hate him by persuading my self to have him be indifferent to me, so that nothing need have been fear'd, But I am too unhappy to expect to be either believed or trusted.

' As to what Mr. Knight designs to allow me is matter of great indifference to me, but whatever my Pappa thinks proper must ever be approved of by his Dutiful daughter & yr unhappy wife.'

H. Knight.

' P.S. I have not asked nor do not design it, whether it is not in my power to force you to live with me ; Nor whether it is in yrs to lock me up upon a base suspicion because I think nothing worth contending for, when one has lost ye Heart & Esteem of ye Person that one still loves better than anyone in ye world.

' I am very sorry upon your own account as well as mine—that you will not consent to conceal your unjust suspicions to ye world as well as yr just reasons of complaint. Think how much that procedure would be approved by your best & wisest Friends, & what tears it would save your wretched wife If I did not love you should I desire to live on with you after you had such suspicions as would ever make you jealous of me, & make me consequently yr obsequious slave which I yet could be if you let me see you. Adieu.'

From the Hon. Henrietta Knight, to her husband, Robert Knight.

' 14 April 1736.

' You seem'd displeased yesterday that I did not answer ye question you ask'd me instantly. You must excuse me if you consider that was what my happiness (if any there be left for me) depends on, therefore I might expect a moment or two to recollect my thoughts ; but I was just going to answer you when you left me hastilly, and ye apprehension that you may do ye same again makes me write rather than speak on a subject which its natural to avoid. You asked me I think whether I was resolved to continue at Barrels green in case I went thither ? To which I have nothing to answer but what I have already given under my hand, which is that I will go thither & endeavour to live there as you desire meaning to stick to my written consent as you do by your written resolution— But if your severe reproaches when there, or the air of the place disagreeing or any other unforeseen accident should make it intollerable to me, I should then depend on the promise you have made of 500 pr anm to live elsewhere. Your own advice to me a fortnight ago was to try it for one Winter, & this I agreed to & am not gone back from ; I can add no more because ye place is so unknown to me yt I can not judge how it may suit or agree with me, but this I am certain of, that I will do my best to bear with it since it is a place you have so long chose to fit up ; as to your additional Building you know I wrote to Mr. Knight to pay for it, wh. request is granted, and no time is limited in ye paper I signed for my staying at Barrells or quitting it. So as that is uncertain I think it reasonable that you should not begin it 'till I have try'd ye place in winter in ye mean-time what ye do propose to do is but what I daresay you would do if I was dead, it being yr house & yr son's & since that in Town is to be sold so small a part of ye money can not be regretted when laid out at Barrells. Since we are upon a topick I generally shun, give me leave to ask whether it might not be better for ye sake of avoiding future misunderstandings to settle ye 500 you propose on me now yt we are both in Town to have it done regularly ; so yt in case I should be obliged to quit Barrells there may be no more dispute ? This I only mention to avoid any future discourse on so dreadfull a subject since you remain inexorable—any mark of tenderness or forgiveness from you would throw me at yr feet, but ye contrary gives me what degree of courage I have.   May all happiness attend you !   Were you to restore me to yr heart there is nothing besides that I would not sacrifice.   Think what a punishment it is for my crime to be deprived of your esteem & of my children's company :   The rest is not worth naming.   But if your cruel reproaches or fresh suspicions are not too aggravating to bear, & yr place agrees with me I will submit to yr resolution we agreed upon since it appears best to you and Pappa ;   and at all events I'm ready to try it by going with you to Barrells.   Adieu most tenderly

'from yr unfortunate wife—H.K.'

From the Hon. Henrietta Knight, to her husband, Robert Knight.

' My Dearest

' permit me to tell you I was in no anger, tho' you seem'd to think me so But you must consider what it must cost me to come to so melancholy a resolution, & I thought it was no ways improper to give my oppinion before hand of what relates to ye settlement proposed, because I never intend afterwards to disturb you with it. if you please To fix whether you will agree to it I'm ready now & am

yr ever affectionate wife

H. Knight.

' To Robert Knight, Esq.'   Tuesday.

From Mr. St. John to his brother-in-law, Robert Knight, Esq., 1736.

' Tuesday 29 June.

' Dr. Sir

' You'll receive two letters from me this post one of them I wish the familly at Battersea saw, this I wd not have you say is from me. Tis only to renew my solicitations for ye visit you promised us I'll say nothing in praise of ye Country or place but use a more persuasive argument which is to assure you of a most hearty welcome its a very long journey you lye at Tetworth or Islip ye first night and ye next day at Noon you are here I'll meet you at Dyne.   Ye very latter end of July or beginning of August will suit me but, will it you ?   if it wont say when it will for you Must Come—as to yr unlucky affair, Entre Nous, I must tell you my notion ;   which is yt if I had been her husband, by God I wd have dated my Ease & happiness from ye hour she gave me justifiable cause to part with her for I know yt my temper & hers wd have hitt so ill yt I should literally have hanged myself if she wd not have play'd ye whore and given me ye occasion of Separation she has done to you.

' You ll think me mad for this Notion, but by ye Eternal god I think you now a happy man I've never thought you so before.

' Adieu pray Come.   We insist upon it.

' yrs J. St. John.'

From Mr. St. John to his sister, Hon. Henrietta Knight. Dated 6th July,
1736.
' Chipping Wardon.

' Dr. Sister

' I received two letters from you the last dated came first to
hand as it came by the Cross Post in the latter you relate yr
melancholy Story & desire me to pitty you & to believe you
guiltless, For the first I do most heartily and sincerely, not do I
ever think of you but in that light, for the latter Dr. Sister, dont be
angry if at least I suspend my judgement & fr these reasons.
Because tho' Mr. Knight has but very lately communicated this
unhappy affair to me & with an account of what you've consented
to before me, & note yr Terms you've agreed to for ye Future yett
I've known it these 4 or 5 months by all my friends and acquaintance
tho' it has been but a matter of speculation ever since yr Birthday,
yett of late ye whole World has agreed (I mean before Mr. Kn.
spoke of it) on ye same story as to person and circumstance. Now
Dr. Sister I can assure you yt neither Mrs. St. John nor I have ever
listened willingly to reports till they came so thick so well authorised
& so exactly agreeing yt indeed they left no room for doubt
even for the most partial of wh. I was one. However I've yt
opinion of yr parts & good sense, & of Mr. K's reasonable
temper & I'm persuaded you'll make yr innocence appear tis a
good friend in adversity & often confutes ye grossest Malice. The
manner in wh. you account for ye Resolution Mr. Kt has taken of
returning no more to Barrells I fancy is not a right one, you say tis
ye effect of being Blamed & censured in town for selling his house
& sending you in the Country, indeed his doing it without a
declared Cause was Wrong, but I dare say if he declares & proves
his reasons he will not be blamed I must ingenuously own to you I
can't agree because I should do ye same in ye like case with this
difference yt I would have declared it immediately, there should be
no delay in those cases when true & I should not have been at
all ashamed for I think tis a mans own actions not those nearly
allyd to him, yt can bring him to shame or dishonour : since ye most
upright & best men have been unfortunate in seeing ye imprudence
of their friends and relations. To Conclude Dr. Sister, should I
say there is not a foundation in reason to give credit to it I should
say false yt I shall not blame you but to myself is as certain How to
Blame Mr. K. for doing what Honr. & his own Character required
I don't know.

' Tis most Unhappy and I feel for you, but what's Blamable
will be so, what is not need fear no Reflection, I flatter myself still
ye latter will be yr Lott, that it may be is ye most sincere & hearty
wish of yr affect Brother & true friend.

' J. St. John.

' Mrs. St. John desires her best wishes for yr health &
happiness may be acceptable to you.'

From Robert Knight to his Wife, Hon. Henrietta Knight.
                                                    ' Kingsclere.
                                                    ' 13 July 1736.

' I came here last night & found two Letters from you, all
the things you mention having done in regard to the House,
furniture, etc., I approve of and indeed the Style of your letters I
will not now say anything by way of Reproach for what is past the
Power of Human Nature to remedy, but this much I will say in
justice to my self, that had you always thought as you now seem to
think, we might both have been happy—As to your wishing to see
me at Barrells, I can give you no other reason but that not only
your unfortunate Conduct in General is the publick discourse of
town & Country, but even particular Circumstances & the poor
Wretch's name is spoke of as the Cause of our unhappy Separation,
& sometimes the other . . . is named. I mention not this to aggra-
vate your afflictions but to convince you that it would never be
proper that We should ever meet again in this World, but be assured
that I sincerely wish you happyness in the next and that I shall
willingly pay for any conveniences you are desirous of to make
Barrells a comfortable habitation to you—Deschamps I know is
naturally dilatory therefore I agreed in your hurrying him & the
Cabinet Maker all you can.

' I approve of the disposition you mention for the Green
Mohair Room and I will order when I get to London or perhaps
sooner one Guilt table and a pair of Stands to be send down—
as to the Sconces I think it will crowd the Room too much & one
of these will be too near the door, but if you think otherwise they
shall be sent. I think you have disposed of the Green Mohair
window seat very well—and you may do the same with the Yellow
damask stuff ones—viz two at Wooton Church and two at Ullenhall
Chapple, this may be done as you please hereafter.

' I think the alteration of the Wainscot in the Great Parlor may
be deferred till another year, for these reasons that till the farm yard
is laid out into a Kitchen Garden it will not be pleasant to look out
upon it & likewise it may be done at any time there are so many
other things to be done. As you require my advice with
regard to the number of Servants I shall give it to you readily to
the best of my judgement. It appears to me that Smith, the
Cook, the Laundry Maid and the Country House Maid will be
necessary, I mention her because she will serve in the House & to
milk one, two, or even three cows, which is the most you can want,
the others of them you may spare, they may be sent to Stratford
on the Chaise & from thence go up in Necombs Waggons who has
convenient Place for Passengers. James I take it for granted you will
keep & also John who is able to drive a Coach and the Chaise in
the french manner very well which will be useful to you—The
Coachman will not stay but till Winter, therefore you may discharge
him on or before Michaelmas and I will endeavour to get him into

a Place—As to Pherry his wages are ten pounds a year & the feeding one cow, but not to eat in the house, you may discharge him if you think fit but consult with my cousin Knight. I should think you might find a servant who would be Gardener & take care of the grounds about the House, then your family wd consist of 4 Women Servants, James & John, and this gardener, in all seven which will be necessary and I believe as far as I can judge sufficient. I write to you with the freedome you desire, but with no thoughts of restraining you.   Perhaps John may expect something more wages if he drives.   He has now 7 pounds—if you made it up to 8 pounds which is equal to James I fancy all will be pleased but say nothing of that till the Coachman be gon.   I would write more but the post will not wait.   You undervalue the land about the House, the whole farm was 56—of which for two years past 27 has to let say the Great Meadow at 18, and ye Long Meadow at 9.'

This letter is addressed to Honble Mrs. Knight, Barrels, near Henley-in-Arden, and signed R. Knight, Warwickshire.

From Lord Bolingbroke to his brother-in-law, Robert Knight.
'Argeville Aug. ye 30 1736.
' Dear Sir,
' Your letter of ye 2nd and 5th instant both came to this place in due time, and I received them att my return from a journey I took to visit a friend in ye neighbouring Province. it is with difficulty I write att this time, having been disabled in my hand by a severe cut I got about three weeks ago, but ye contents of yrs are of so great importance yt I must not be silent upon them. I own to you that ye First intimation of ye unfortunate affair you mention stunned me with Surprise. I was willing to hope a mistake on one side, and an indiscretion on ye other, had given occasion to it, yt it might be made up, or that it might be so conducted as to make no noise, nor cause any Shocking Reflections in ye world, even when I received further and more particular accounts, and had a copy of ye letter in my hands.   I should not tell what to think, that a woman of quality should prostitute herself to such a low fellow, and yt ye dullest Poet in Christendom should turn her head, or warm her heart, seemed to me incredible.   I thought it was no less so, yt any woman engaged in such a criminal commexe, should suffer a letter of this kind to lye loose about, for so I was informed it did.   Such letters may be, and have been intercepted, but I never heard before of any yt were layed about in ye way to be found, as this was most regretfully, according to ye information I have had.   This circumstance weighs with me on one side.   On ye other, the letter has not ye air of what it has been called, a jeu d'esprit.   I confess it seems writ in good earnest, and on a particular occasion.   But, however all this may be—such a letter under a woman's own hand cannot be excused by any pretence.   I should not excuse it myself.   I cannot therefore plead yt you should.   I could only have wished that some way had

been found, and some I think might have been found, to bring ye Separation about in ye five months time, and a little more gradually and plausibly. But those Reflexions are no longer in Season and therefore I shut up the subject by assuring you that this event has given me as sensible an affliction as I ever felt, of which you cannot doubt if you call to mind that I was at ye time concerting with yr Father. The death of my Lady St. John is not an event of ye same kind, it gives me neither joy nor sorrow. Silly as she was, she had not enough to be ye cause, during a long course of years, of much mischief. a wise woman would have found her account better in a contrary conduct. I write to both her sons on the occasion, but I cannot be hypocrit enough to condole. My Lord St. John broke with me in such manner, and after many repeated acts of injustice and therefore unnatural Enmity, that I think my writing to him att this time would gall with him, who never knew either himself or me, for a desire of Reconsilement and on ye prospect of advantage, or for a confession of former wrongs on my part, advantage I expect none, as I never received any in point of fortune from him, and from his gift, in ye whole course of my life. Wrong I never did him and he has done me wrong, ye catalogue of which would appear enormous if I was to draw it up. he may reckon it wrong perhaps yt I was not insensible, as well as silent, under paternal Tyranny, but I could never brook any Tyranny. let me hear from you, how he takes ye woman's death, what his turn, and yt of ye Family is likely to be upon this occasion. You may convey yr letters safely to Alexander and he will convey them to me with no sample of writing this mark of yr Friendship, because I have always depended on yr friendship, as I must believe that you have, and am sure yt you may on mine. Adieu, sincerely yr most affec. Brother and most humble servant,

'B.'

From Lord Bolingbroke to his sister, The Hon. Henrietta Knight. Dated Argeville. Dec. ye 7th 1736.

'A Journey made to Bourbon, and the expectation I had of seeing Mr. Knight here for several weeks together hindered me from writing to you, Dear Sister, as soone as I should have done otherwise—he has been here for about a week, and we have had a good deal of discussion concerning you and yr present situation. He appears extremely moderate in his judgement on what has happened, speaks very civilly of you and pitys yr condition. We spoke of yr desire to see yr daughter and he entered very clearly into yr reasonableness of ye thing, but he seemed to think, rightly enough, yt it could only be for a night, whilst you continued so far out of ye world, and in a place where yr child could not have ye necessary improvements of education. We both agree in the opinion yt you mention in yr letter to me to be on yr own, and that is that to ye best Service which can be done you att present, is for you and your friends to be quiet. Time will deaden reports, assuage resentment, and whatever measures may be thought best for yr future ease and happiness you will have ye better grace and ye more strength in taking those herafter, for having submitted now. it is hard indeed that even yr submission should be turned against you and the maxim that Innocence will not submit, is often false. I am sure I know it to be false. As to ye noise, that burst out immediately, I am not at all surprised at it, for yr late mother talked ye whole matter over to servants, besides whispering it in ye ears of twenty other persons. in short, child, you all conducted yourselves like people who wanted commonsense. But what is passed cannot be recalled, th sole use ye can make of it, is for protect yr future behaviour. Now as to that, there is a point that I ought to mention to you. I know it has been said tho' not to me ; and I know that those that wish you well, believe, that yr Husband would not have taken yt sudden violent resolution which he took when he went to yr Father and Mother, if he had not been worked into a fit of passion by other provocation that you gave him. I touch this, ye truth of which you can best tell, because I have a reason to think that he complains that since all thys Eclat, you have insulted him more than ever : tho' innocence will and must ofter submit in ye course of human affairs yet innocence will preserve a dignity in distress yt guilt cannot assume. but then thys dignity will not break out into injurious and insulting expressions, and especially towards those who think themselves wronged by us, and therefore justified in ye hardship of their proceedings. that of yr Father, in turning ye Daughter out of doors, is such as no man, I hope for ye honour of humanity, but he, would have been guilty of. Adieu. My Wife embraces you, and I am what you shall ever find me, yr most affectionate Brother, Friend, and Servant.

'B.'

Addressed :
  'For Mrs. Knight, at Barrels Green
  To be delivered by Mr. Brinsden[1]
  to father.'

From Lord Bolingbroke to his Sister, Hon. Henrietta Knight. London.
August the 10 1738.
  'it is not ye multiplicity of business yt would have kept me from writing to you so long Dear Sister, but I was desirous to have something positive, and at ye same time comfortable to say to you. I wish I had ye latter now, I think I have ye former, yr Husband is got into new measures of conduct, & under a new influence since I left England, so yt I do not flatter myself to be able to incline him any way, and he is I find, determined not to consent to any change

---
[1]Bolingbroke's Secretary

in ye present situation but under such conditions & by such measures, it would revive all the rumours yt have been said about yr past conduct, and perhaps cause new ones to be advanced, in a manner still more publick. this shocks me and stops me. the only expedient yt presents itself to my thoughts is this. I will have ye best advice of chancery lawyers taken and when I have yt in my pocket will begin by determining your father-in-law, who is a good natured man, in yr favour, if I can, after which I shall be able jointly with him to determine yr Husband to somewhat more reasonable than seems to be promised by his present disposition. One thing I assure you of, yt all I can do shall be done to mend the unfortunate circumstances in which yr own family has helped to pin you down, for I am Dear Sister most affectionately and sincerely yours.

'B.'

From Robert Knight to his wife Hon. Henrietta Knight.
'Golden Square 22 April 1742.
'Madam,
'The great change in your circumstances, since our separation (the unhappy cause whereof I shall not now mention) gives me this occasion of writing to you ; You was then wholly unprovided for, and future was but £210, I was willing to allow you £500 a year, which considerably exceeded what your Father at first asked for you ; You know this allowance has ever since been regularly paid, but comparing your present circumstances with mine, I think and persuade myself you will think too that the future payment of it since it is by no means necessary would be unreasonable.
'You have nobody to provide for but yourself. I must maintain and give portions to my Son and Daughter, and if proper opportunities offer, of promoting their happiness by advancing them during my life, I should be sorry to want or be straitened in the power of doing it. Out of regard therefore to their Interest only (for you must see, that mine personally is not concerned in it) I must make you the following proposal ; That Articles of Separation be executed with such provisions for securing me against debts of your contracting as are usual in such Cases, and that you relinquish the jointure or rent charge which by the Marriage Articles you will be entitled to for your Life in case you survive me ; if you agree to this, I will agree that you shall have at present, the interest of £8,000 part of the Settlement, the income of your brother Hollis St. John's Estate, and of his share of the Theatre, secured for your life, which 3 Articles depend upon my consent, and make together £407 a year, which I take it to be a full equivalent for the jointure, as it depends upon your surviving me, and I likewise confirm what your Father has settled upon or given you by his Will, in such manner as shall be reasonably desired. I compute your annual income supposing you accept the proposal, will be as follows :

of the £8,000 at 3½ per cent.	£280
of Mr. Hollis St. John's Estate	100
of the share of the Theatre	17
of the £10,000 by your Father's Will	280
of the Residue of his Estate estimated but at £5,000. .	175
of the House in [Illegible] Street	100

£1,082

My Income including the Int. of the £8,000 which you are to have if this proposal is accepted you know is barely £1,800
excluding the 280

£1,520

'I think upon a Comparasson of your and my Income (supposing this proposal to be complyed with) and our circumstances and obligations before observed, you must be convinced, that you will be better provided for than myself.

'Having this occasion to write to you, I shall mention one thing more for your consideration, which concerns my Son's Interest only, that is, to secure to him at your death £5,000 out of the Residue of your Father's Estate, in which case I will agree to secure him the like sum at mine, and for that purpose will charge it on my Estate in Somersetshire not settled. If your regard for him is equal to mine, I think you will not refuse this, since it will no way lessen your income for life.' [Remainder of letter omitted.]

'R. Knight.'

From Hon. Henrietta Knight to her husband, Robert Knight. (*Feb.* 1750-1)

'You'll pardon I hope the trouble of this letter it being only a Proposal which can no ways injure you nor my Dear Children and I am induced to make by no other motive than ye Fear of being in Debt my Self, or of incumbring You or Them with any Demand yt might hereafter be made on my account, rather than which I chuse to reduce my income ; I need not tell you that I expected to have more at command after my Father's Death than I have by agreement, wch I came into willingly, as I thought it for ye advantage of our children, I mean to keep to it, and am ready to perform ye part of giving up my jointure by a proper Form whenever you and your Lawyers judge it can be done. I no ways complain of my income, but as yr money is settled out of my power, and as before I knew how that would be, I laid out a great deal of money upon Barrells, I find it necessary in order to owe no money, nor injure any one, that I should lessen my income an hundred pr annm by selling ye value of my life in it for a present Sum. It is a thing done so often that it will be easily computed, and perhaps several persons would be glad of ye offer, but I thought that as you

by agreement pay me half yearly £200 per ann^m in money it would
be more worth yr purchase than a stranger, I therefore make you
ye first offer, and am willing to live so for ye future as not to fear
running into Debt, w^h will be better for us all ; and I do not see
that by this proposal of mine I injure any body, but my self ; who
might to be sure spare by living in a Town and by not laying out
anything on a Place, which is to be my sons, and therefore draws
on ye expences of a gentlemans Seat, but I regard my self less than
justice to all, and ye advantage of my children, which makes me
propose this, and if it proves agreeable to you, it will be doubly so
to yrs Sc H. Knight.

' Mr. Outing, ye Bearer of this is joint Trustee with Mr. Osborne
for £2,000 I secured to my Children. He is an honest gentleman
in whom you may confide and I have given him Power to treat
with you abt this having an opportunity of letting him know my
thoughts without writing by ye post.

' H.K.'

Addressed :
    ' To Robert Knight, Jun. Esq. in Golden Square.'

Letter from Lord Luxborough to his wife, 19 *Feb.* 1750-1.
' As Lady Luxborough desires an answer soon Lord L. sends
it directly being very Clear in his opinion, which is that since she
is desirous to come into the Proposal made to her by Mr. Outing,
the first step to be taken is to propose to Mrs Wymondfold who can
if she pleases influence her Husband Thier Consent, Lord L's
and his son's are necessary but Wymondfold's is not. & it might
be done without his knowledge. This proposal must be made to
Mrs Wymondfold, as Lady L's own thought, but if this scheme
should not take place, Lord L. is of opinion that Lady L. could not
raise the sum of money that would produce, without parting with
twice as much for her income. And this leads him to lay before
her the great sum of money she has expended in the nine last
years, in order to illustrate his former observation, that there is not
within his knowledge an instance of any Person retrieving their
circumstances as long as they continued to live in the same place
where they had contracted debts by a proper manner of living, nor
does he find Lady L. knows an instance. The residue of her Father's
estate, as Mr Osborne assured Lord L. amounted to £1,700 It is
to be presumed that sum fully paid her debts & in reason should
have been a warning to her to have taken care to contract no more.
But it was far from having this salutary effect, that tho from April
1742 to ditto 1745, being three years her income was £1,000 per
annum, amounting in 3 years to £3,000. Yet she contracted debts
in that small space of time, which obliged her to sell £200 per
annum in her life estate to raise £1,600. By which it appears she spent
more than after the rate of £1,500 per annum during those 3 years.
This one would reasonably imagine might have been a second

warning, but it has not proved so, for from 1745 to the present time it does not appear that she has paid any servants wages, unless to those who have been discharged, and yet from Lady Day 1745 to ditto 1751 her income has been £800 per annum which in the gross amounts to £4,800.

'The jewels left to her by Mr. Hollis St. John, which she promised to keep to give to one of her children at her death, Lord L. has been informed are sold, as also her silver Plate and Dishes (but this he is unwilling to believe) were it true, it would add to what she has expended at least £1,000 ditto remaining unpaid at least £1,000. By this account it appears that £11,400 has been expended in nine years deduct from thence £1,500 the sum Lady L. says she has expended for her diversion in improvements on Barrels, then the remaining Sum amounts to exactly £1,000 per annum for the current expenses. Now upon a supposition of Mrs. W. & her Husband coming into the scheme proposed, it would reduce Lady L's income under £700 per annum, which is £400 less than she has expended for nine years past—If they should not come into it, then the debts must remain unpaid till she can pay them off by savings out of her yearly income, or raise enough by reducing her income £200 per annum & then her income would reduce under £600 per annum, which would be £500 less than her annual expenses have been for some years past. If therefore she seriously reflects on her past conduct, & on her present circumstances, she has too good an Understanding to believe herself, or to think Lord. L. can be brought to believe, that a few expensive dinners in a year can make the difference of £400 or £500 per annum or even more than the difference of £50 at the end of the year—

'From these considerations, which are most weighty, Lord L. recommends to Lady L. to reduce immediately the number of her Servants & Horses one half.

'Can it be said for the Credit of any Person to drive with a Coach & six Horses, when the wages of the Servants who attend that Equipage are unpaid ! Can it be for the credit of any Person to entertain their neighbours with an elegant dinner, and the Butchers Bill unpaid !

'When this is so, the Butchers and the Servants give the entertainment, not the Lady at the upper end of the table, who assumes the false credit of it—Lord L. would enlarge on this subject but that he wishes to avoid saying any more than what may induce Lady L. to suffer her own judgement to govern her future, as her Passions have too evidently governed her past conduct.'

BARRELLS HALL, ULLENHALL

BARRELLS HALL, situated at what was formerly known as Barrells[1] Green, stands in a beautifully wooded park and is a plain and dignified building but with no claim to architectural excellence. From the list of contents recorded in the inventory[2] of Nicholas Knight in 1652 it appears to have then been merely a farm house of the ordinary Warwickshire type. At the death of John Knight in 1681 it was called the Manor House and the residence, orchards and gardens covered a little more than one-and-a-half acres, the whole estate including the waste being 400 acres.[3] At the time Robert Knight, afterwards Lord Luxborough and Earl of Catherlough, purchased it in 1730 from his second cousin Raleigh Knight,[4] it was of no great pretensions but had become a small country residence, nevertheless the farmyard was not converted into a kitchen garden until about 1736 when we read the Great Parlour looked out upon it (see p. 151). The south front ' with lofty portico supported on fluted columns with Corinthian capitals'[5] was designed by Bonomi and erected either in the later days of the Earl of Catherlough[6] or by his trustees for the occupation of his natural son, Robert Knight, who succeeded to Barrells about 1772. The east wing was added in 1883.

It is said that Robert Knight was not on good terms with his son, the Rev. Henry Charles Knight, never acknowledging his paternity, and that he did everything he could to depreciate the value of the Barrells estates which the son would one day inherit. This is borne out by the report and valuation made in 1855[7] the year of the father's death, wherein it is stated that the mansion deserves a better fate than the rapid decay which has resulted from inattention to those common observances which preserve buildings in a ' wind and water-tight condition.' It was estimated that it would cost about £2,000 to put the house in a tenantable condition without ornamental finish and £1,000 to repair the stabling and

---

[1]In the Lay Sub. Rolls for 1327 and 1332, one, William Barel, paid 12d. in respect of land held in Aspley in Wootton Wawen and in 1413 Richard Barell of Ullenhall occurs in Ancient Deeds. The name Barrells, applied to an estate, is first found in a P.C.C. will of 1581, and it is probable that a descendant of the above-mentioned William acquired the estate now called Barrells about that time and gave his name to it.

[2]In the possession of Mr. A. Marshall, Stratford-on-Avon (see p. 181).

[3]A survey of Barrells taken 1681 in possession of Mr. A. Marshall (see p. 182).

[4]Heralds' Coll. MSS.

[5]*Forest of Arden*, 1863, p. 104.

[6]His arms are over a wing to the left of the doorway.

[7]In the possession of Mrs. Willoughby Smallwood, Stratford-on-Avon.

coachhouses. The disclosure is made that the house cost £6,250 but that in its then condition it was worth as materials only £590.

The whole estate was at that time suffering from excessive wetness and the estimated cost of necessary drainage was £14,500. The farm houses and buildings were for the most part ' in a state verging on complete dilapidation,' and would cost £7,400 in repairs. With the exception of some trees in the park and a few scattered trees on Crowleys Farm, Impsley Farm, Oldberrow Court Farm, and on the lands near Henley the trees on the estate were ' hardly worthy of the name of timber.' The trees which numbered 28,829, were valued at £6,037, whereas the timber in Mockley Wood alone had cost £3,779 in 1816.

The total area of the estate was 2846 a. 3r. 2p.; gross rents, £3,290 3s. 7d.; rents, including impropriate rent-charge, £3,618 17s. 10d.; net rents less fixed outgoings, £3,327 7s. 6d.; total value, £109,473 16s. 6d.

Henry Charles Knight had some years earlier decided to let the estates be sold on his father's death because Charles Raleigh Knight, the next to him in the entail, had threatened to contest his claim to them, when the time came, on the score of his illegitimacy, and rather than face the heavy cost of litigation with uncertain results, had agreed that the proceeds of the property should be shared between them. This was accordingly done, and when Mr. Wm. Newton, a Birmingham Merchant, purchased it in 1856, he found it in a very neglected state and that some of the stables had been pulled down. He removed the portico, built a lofty hall extending to a lighted cupola and new kitchens and stables. His son, Mr. T. H. G. Newton, who succeeded him, made many alterations and improvements to the house and grounds. After his father's death in 1907, Mr. H. G. Newton lived there for a short time but since then it has been unfurnished and unoccupied. It is now (1941) the property of Mr. J. W. Marsh who was contemplating residence there but in the early part of 1933 a disastrous fire took place which destroyed the servants' quarters. It is at present in a desolate condition.[1] The avenue of trees from Barrells to a point on the Ullenhall road nearest to Henley still remains, and it is said the Knights had intended to continue it to the opening at the Green Gates in Henley and so make a private drive into the town that way, but it was never carried out.

[1]Some of this information from Mr. A. C. Coldicott, sometime agent for the Barrells Estate.

OLD HOUSES IN ULLENHALL

Botley Hill is a late 16th century timber-framed house with a projecting upper storey and porch wing, Near the house are considerable remains of a rectangular moat with water. It was the home of one of the branches of the Burman family for a period of more than 130 years ending in 1864, of which Dr. Thomas Burman, of Burman House, Henley, was a member.

Impsley is a timber-framed house probably of the 16th century with later additions. John Whateley was living there in 1616, and John Tarlton, Yeoman, in 1768. Thomas Cooper[1] resided there from 1815 until his death in 1847 and was succeeded by his son, William.[2]

Hall End Farm is an L-shaped timber-framed building of the 17th century and as mentioned in another chapter was the birthplace in 1776 of William Booth the forger.

Six small houses scattered about the parish show remains of timber-framing of the 17th century.

Crowleys in Ullenhall village has been modernised but it stands on a moated site.

The Mansion House, Barrells Park, which went for auction at the Grand Hotel, Birmingham on Thursday, 23 October 1924. (GW)

[1]Chapelwarden of Ullenhall, 1822-8.
[2]The writer's grandfather.

NICHOLAS HEATH, ARCHBISHOP OF YORK

Nicholas Heath (1501-79) was descended from the Heaths of Forde Hall, Aspley, where his brother held certain lands.[1]   The family died out in the reign of Henry VIII when Baldwin Heath of Forde Hall,[2] left two daughters : Joan, who married John Fullwood, second son of Robert Fullwood of Clay Hall, and Phillipa who married Ralph Sheldon of Beoley.   According to Wood,[3] Nicholas Heath was ' a most wise and learned man of great policy and of as great integrity.'

He received his early education at St. Anthony's School, London, and afterwards went up to Christ Church, Oxford, but before he took his degree he removed to Christ's College,Cambridge, from which he graduated B.A., in 1519-20.   He became Bishop of Rochester in 1539 and succeeded Hugh Latimer as Bishop of Worcester in 1543.   Four years after Edward VI came to the throne he was deprived of his See for refusing to subscribe to the Prayer Book, but was restored at the accession of Queen Mary and in 1555 was elevated to the Archbishopric of York becoming also Lord Chancellor in the following year. The year after Elizabeth succeeded to the throne he was deprived of his Archbishopric and he died at Cobham in 1579.[4]

---

[1]*Dict. Nat. Biog.*, Wood, *Athenae Oxonienses*, 1721, II, 704.   *Warw. Antiq. Mag.*, p. 187.
[2]See p. 126.
[3]Wood, op. cit.
[4]Ibid. and *Dict. Nat. Biog.*

WILLIAM BOOTH THE FORGER

WILLIAM Booth was the son of John Booth of Hall End Farm and
Mary, his wife, and was baptized at Beaudesert on 21 February
1776.[1] His father, who had at least seven other children, was a
respectable farmer, and held the office of churchwarden of Beaudesert for a number of years, being so mentioned in 1772 and 1784,[2]
and chapelwarden of Ullenhall in 1796.[3] About 1799[4] William
Booth, then some twenty-three years old, moved to Perry Barr
where he rented a farmhouse and 200 acres of land. There he is
said to have been kind to his neighbours and the poor and they
could not believe him guilty when he was arrested on suspicion of
murdering his brother John while on a visit to Hall End on 19
February 1808. John was found in a stable with severe head
wounds from which he died.[5] At the trial at Warwick Assizes on
8 April following, the prosecution alleged that these were caused by
a spade which was found near the body with blood upon it, but
the Defence pleaded that they were caused by a vicious horse which
was in the stable at the time and that the blood had dripped from
the hands of a labourer who had cleared the dying man's mouth to
help him to breathe. The judge summed up against conviction
emphasising that is it better for twenty men who are guilty to escape
than for one innocent man to be hanged, and William Booth was
acquitted.[6] In an old Account Book of St. Mark's Charity,
Ullenhall, occur these entries : ' Paid the fourth of John Booth's
Inquest, £4 16s. 2d.' and the surgeons to the inquest, Mr. Burman
and Mr. Jones, £2 2s. each. Paid Mr. Hunt for the prosecution of
William Booth for murdering his brother, £30 3s. 4d.'

One day in February 1812 the inhabitants of Perry Barr were
startled by the news that a servant of Booth's, named Job Jones, had
been arrested and charged with uttering to a Walsall saddler a
forged £2 Bank of England note and being in 'possession of forty-
seven other similar forged notes.[7] Suspicion now fell upon Booth
himself but a whole month went by before the constables obtained
a warrant to search his house and then they experienced some
difficulty in carrying it out for he had taken great precautions not
to be disturbed in his criminal activities. On entering the house

[1] *Records of Beaudesert*, p. 112.
[2] Ibid, p. 26.
[3] Chapelwardens Accounts.
[4] In this year he was evidently liable for service in the militia for the parish paid
over to Birmingham Overseers £3 2s. 6d., being the amount due to the wife of his
substitute from 4 May to 26 Oct.—Vestry Accounts.
[5] He was buried at Beaudesert, 26 Feb., 1808.—Parish Reg.
[6] *The Trial of William Booth of Perry Barr*, 1812, printed by J. Drewery.
[7] *The Staffordshire Advertiser*, 15 Feb., 1812.

there was a lobby communicating with the parlour and the kitchen but access to the former was barred by three strong doors. Over the parlour was a chamber, and over that a garret. The doors of these two rooms which opened on to the staircase he had blocked up, and the only way of entering them was through trap doors in the ceilings, which were securely fastened down, the windows of the parlour and chamber over being barred.

At length the constables managed to force an entrance into the garret through its window, where they discovered a large quantity of machinery and everything necessary for the making of forged coins. Descending through the trap-door into the chamber beneath they found a printing press, etc., for forging notes. In the parlour underneath they arrested Booth. He was brought to trial on 31 July and 1 August 1812 at Stafford Assizes when he was condemned to death, and his accomplices to transportation.[1] In accordance with the custom of the time he was executed on gallows set up in front of Stafford Gaol, and in the presence of thousands of spectators. After receiving Holy Communion in the condemned cell where he was chained to the wall, his fetters were struck off, and his arms were bound to his sides. Accompanied by the chaplain, carrying his Prayer Book, he walked to the place of execution, prepared to meet his end, when a most distressing accident took place which is best described in the words of a contemporary[2]:

'The unfortunate culprit having been conducted to the platform, some time was passed in prayer, after which the halter was affixed to his neck and the cap drawn over his face. On a signal given by himself that he was ready to meet his fate the platform suddenly dropped, when, awful to relate, the rope, not being properly fastened to the fatal tree, slipped off and the poor malefactor fell to the floor, a distance of eight or ten feet. Notwithstanding the height of his fall, his great weight, and the defenceless situation in which a man whose arms are pinioned is placed, he did not appear to be bruised. He lay for a few moments apparently stunned and insensible, and on recovering his senses did not utter the least murmur or complaint, but resumed with additional fervour his petitions to the Throne of Grace, enquiring with much solicitude for the worthy clergyman already alluded to, and who with great promptitude again attended him.

'A full quarter of an hour elapsed before the drop was again prepared, when he submitted once more to his fate with a resignation which seemed to increase with his protracted sufferings. In the hurry and confusion occasioned even in the mind of such a personage as Jack Ketch, by the distressing

---

[1] A pamphlet, "The Trial of William Booth who was tried at Stafford, Friday, July 31, 1812, for forging and money making.'
[2] Pamphlet printed by J. Drewery, op. cit.

accident which had happened, the drop, which had fallen in the first instance with the utmost facility, met with some impeachment in the general confusion, and the unhappy Booth gave three signals by dropping his handkerchief before he was launched into Eternity.[1]'

Ullenhall Church. (O'D)

[1]The writer is indebted for much of the information about Booth to Mr. John Free's article in the *Birm. Weekly Post*, 12 Nov., 1932.

WOOTTON WAWEN

PRIOR to 1915 St. Peter's at Wootton Wawen was the mother church of Henley and until 1861 of Ullenhall. A full account of this exceptionally interesting building is given in the writer's book on that place but it may be well to repeat here that between the years 723 and 737 Aethelbald, King of Mercia, gave twenty hides of land there for a monastery,[1] which in those days would probably be a small establishment of monks, or perhaps more likely of secular clerks, who ministered to the surrounding district. It may have come to an end in the Danish wars but the spot was sacred to the Christian religion and it is more than likely that the Saxon Church was built on or near its site. Of this church three-fifths of the central tower remains and has been assigned to the period 1035-42. As it has an archway in each wall there can be no doubt that the original plan of the building was cruciform. It is one of the most interesting survivals in Warwickshire and the only example of Saxon ecclesiastical work in the county with the exception of parts of the nave at Tredington.

The church, as it exists to-day, exhibits almost every successive style of architecture besides many unusual features and is deserving of close study. George Gilbert Scott described it as ' an epitome in stone of the history of the Church of England.' Its ancient monuments and library of chained books of 16th and 17th century theology are also notable features.

Soon after the conquest, Robert de Stafford gave the church of Wootton and an endowment of land to the Benedictine Abbey of St. Peter of Castellion of Conches who established a small Alien Priory here. This Priory with all its possessions was bestowed by Henry VI on his new foundation, King's College, Cambridge in 1443.[2]

Wootton Hall,[3] the ancient home of the Smiths and Smythes, is an attractive mansion standing not far from the church. It is of Italian design in stone built mainly in 1687 with apparently an older building incorporated in its western portion. During last century it was often let and the writer feels that the following letter written to him in instalments in 1937 by Capt. Hubert Berkeley, who lived there during his father's tenancy of it more than seventy years ago, will be of interest to readers :

' With reference to your Wootton Wawen book, pages 38-40, when the Tempests left the Hall, Mr. Ferrers of Baddesley Clinton and Lady Chatterton lived there from 1867 to 1869. Then my

[1]Birch, *Cart. Sax.*, No. 157.
[2]*Wootton Wawen*, p. 41.
[3]A disastrous fire occurred to the upper part of the Hall in May, 1945.

father and mother, Mr. R. Berkeley and Lady Catherine Berkeley and their twelve children, 1869 to 1874. After that the old Duchess of Norfolk resided there for one year and she was followed by Capt. Haydock, who was succeeded by Capt. Wickham. The last-named married the widow of Sir Alfred Tichborne of Tichborne, Hants, mother of Sir Henry Tichborne (my school-fellow) defendant in the great trial.[1] Her first husband was brother of Roger Tichborne, lost at sea. You will notice that Sir Frederick Smythe would only let the house to old Catholics not to converts ; though Capt. Haydock was a convert, his wife was an old Catholic. Mrs. Fitzherbert[2] was brought up in Wootton Hall and lived there a great deal even after her marriage to the Prince Regent.

'The Carington heart[3] was in an old heart-shaped oak box lined with velvet and enclosed in an inner box covered with velvet. Mr. Wm. Keyte found it in a cupboard in the stone-floored room at the very top of the back stairs. At last not knowing what to do with it he put it in a grave when he was burying some one in the Catholic cemetery.

'The concealed staircase from the priest's two rooms went up to the attics and also down to the housekeeper's room, in the thickness of the wall.

'We were always told the ghosts of two monks walked on the path past the old plague pit at the corner of the public cemetery where the path goes down to the Traveller's Rest. I never saw them, but our butler did and also Haydock's servants.

'The Maypole was set up near the Bull's Head and was decorated on both May Day and Wake Day, when it came down. I think it was the pole of a rick sheet. The children carried about a little one, a long pitch-fork decorated.

'Wootton Wake,[4] from 1869 to 1874, was mostly at the Bull's Head and Navigation Inns, and included a donkey race from the former to the latter. There were also stalls selling food and sweets in the churchyard.

'You mention the Waterloo man but not the Trafalgar man. The former lived in the second house beyond the school on the Henley side. My grandfather, the third Earl of Kenmare, who was also an old Waterloo man, used to talk to him about Quatre

[1]In 1869 the title and estates were claimed by a man from Australia who asserted that he was Roger, elder son of Sir James Tichborne. After a trial lasting 9 months he was found to be Arthur Orton, son of a Wapping butcher, and was sentenced to 14 years' imprisonment. Before he died he admitted his identity.

[2]She was Maria Anne Smythe and was morganatically married to the Prince Regent (George IV) in 1785. The Prince of Wales' feathers may be seen in one of the bedrooms.

[3]Thought to be that of Lord Carington, murdered at Pontoise by his valet for his money, 21 Feb., 1664-5.

[4]Held on the feast of St. Peter and St. Paul, patron saints of the Church, 29 June.

Bras and Haye Sainte while we listened.   The Trafalgar man died
before we left and is buried on the west of the path.

   ' The parson was Mr. Brookman who lived in the vicarage all
our time.   He was most friendly with my father and Father Morrell,
the priest, and was a smart little man with well-made breeches and
boots and had good horses.   He was a hard-riding, hunting parson.
We knew of no other at Wootton.[1]

   ' Please forgive me for writing thus to you but your delightful
book sets me thinking.'

Henley-in-Arden Football Club in 1891. (WI)

[1]Evidently the then vicar the Rev. E. D. G. M. Kirwan was non-resident.

ABOVE: The gentlemen dressed as ladies in 1890 and challenged them at hockey. (WI) BELOW: The Quoit Club won six out of seven matches in 1905; back row: C. West, T. King, H. Hodges, A. Stokes, F. Moore, W. Hadley; front: A. Lowe, O. Coppage, J. Yarwood, G. Lowe and F. Harris. The lad is unidentified. (O'D)

Public Hall, Henley=in=Arden.

PROPRIETORS:
THE HENLEY-IN-ARDEN PUBLIC HALL AND INSTITUTE LTD.
MANAGING DIRECTOR: MR. W. ERNEST NELSON.

OPENING PERFORMANCES.

Monday Afternoon, January 4th, 1909, at 2=30.
Tuesday Evening, January 5th, 1909, at 7=30.
Wednesday Evening, January 6th, 1909, at 7=30.

PRICES OF ADMISSION—

AT OPENING PERFORMANCE ON MONDAY AFTERNOON, JAN. 4.

Reserved Seats 3s. and 2s.

Unreserved Seats 1s.   **Gallery 6d.**

(Doors open at 2 o'clock).

AT EVENING PERFORMANCES ON JAN. 5 AND JAN. 6.

Reserved Seats 2s. 6d

Unreserved Seats 1s.   **Gallery 6d.**

(Doors open at 7 o'clock).

Seats may be booked at MR. ROBERT HERRING'S, *98, High Street, Henley-in-Arden, where plans of the Hall may be seen.*

Stage Director	- - - - - MR. W. ERNEST NELSON.
Musical Director	- - - - - MR. FRANCIS MORTON.
Leader of Orchestra	- - - - - MR. A. B. CALLAWAY.
At the Piano	- - - - - MRS. MORTON.

The Public Hall was opened in 1909 — the result of an initiative by Dr W. E. Nelson. (WI)

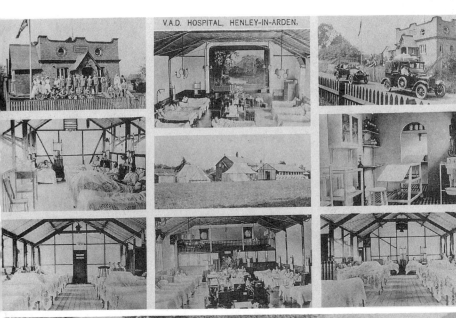

V.A.D. HOSPITAL, HENLEY-IN-ARDEN,

ABOVE: From 1914 to 1919 the Public Hall was used as a VAD hospital until it reverted to its original use and in 1947 was renamed the Memorial Hall. (O'D) BELOW: This was the ambulance, behind the dressing station. (WI)

XXV

ABOVE: On 19 July 1919, the 1st Henley-in-Arden Girl Guides assembled — back: Hilda Symonds, Nora Rhodes, Nellie Maine, Miriam Woodward, Rhoda Stocks; front: May Sumner, Mary Townsend, Mary Yearsley, Nel Carrington, Florie Beard, Kath Timms, Ida Bates, Alice Hemming and Grace Richards. BELOW: Christmas 1939 — J. L. Mason & Son's magnificent display of over 400 turkeys and 21 brace of pheasants. (Both O'D)

INDEX OF PERSONS

Two of the records in the Appendix have not been indexed: Henley Hearth Tax Roll, 1663 (p. 173) and Certificates for using Hair Powder, 1797 (p. 175). These are omitted to save space at this time.

The letter *n* after a number indicates a footnote.

Dalton, John, 139, 140 ; Oliver, 175.
Dane, Tho., 177.
Danfor, Widow, 26.
Dann, Jas., 87.
Dartnell, G. R., 98, 99 ; Mr., 102 ;
 Maj. Gen. Sir J. G., 99.
Darwin, Chas., 41 ; Erasmus, 41.
Dashwood, Eliz., 40.
Davies (Davis), Jane, 124, 145 ; Mrs.,
 143, 144 ; Miss R., 90n.
Dawn, John, 171.
Delves, Eliz., 39.
Devon, Thomas, Earl of, 6.
Deyster, John, 68, 170.
Diamond, Dr. W. B., 98.
Dodsley, Publisher, 120.
Dolfin (Dolphin), Herebert, son of, 179 ;
 Matt., son of, 179 ; Tho., 137.
Dolman, Miss, 94, 142 ; Mr., 94.
Dorell, W. H., 177.
Dormer, Hon. Frances, 124, 131.
Dorset, Marquis of, 39.
Doughty, Rev. John, 117, 118.
Dudley, Arms, 14 ; John, Lord, 71 ;
 Lord Guilford, 37 ; See Earls of
 Warwick.
Dugdale, Jas., 42n ; Sir William, 4 et seq.
Duroure, Count, 131 ; Countess, 131.
Durvassal, 18 ; John, 169 ; Roger, 169.
Dyer, Wm., 179.

East, Chas., 102.
Easterbrook, Canon W. J., 50.
Eberall, John, 89.
Edkyns, Alys, 177.
Ellis, Rev. John, 98, 184.
Ethelbald, xi.
Evans, Jas., 86n.
Eyr, John le, 179.
Faber, Ric., 4.
Fairfaxe, Tho., 57.
Faukener, le, 18.
Fauks, John, 48.
Fayrer, Dr., 81, 98, 102.
Fenys, see Say, de.
Ferrers, Mr., 166.
Fieldhouse, Ernest Fran., 42 ; Miss N.,
 15 ; W. J., 29, 42, 70, 71, 177.
Fifhyde (Fifhide), Wm., 44, 51.
Fisher, Jos., 86n.
Fitz-Gerald, Sir Jas., 123.
Fitzherbert, Mrs., 167.
Flower, Fran., 86.
Ford, Mr., 102 ; Sarah, 97n.
Franklin, Benj., 129.
Freeman, see Clayton.
Freno, Roger de, 169.
Freville, Arms, 52, 53 ; Baldwin, 36,
 39 ; Joyce, 39 ; Mgt., 39.
Fuleswel, Adam de, 179.

Fulk the Armourer and Edith his wife, 4.
Fuller, — 37.
Fullwood, Edmund, 176 ; Joan, 162 ;
 John, 162 ; Lady, 175 ; Rob., 162.
Furnival, Mgt., 35.

Gaches, Rev. Daniel, 62, 78, 98 ;
 Mary, 62.
Galton, Darwin, 41, 42 ; Sir Francis,
 41, 42 ; P.M.E., 42 ; Sam. John, 41 ;
 Sam. T., 41.
Garrick, David, 119 ; Geo., 119.
Gaunter, Ric. le, 169.
Gaveston, Piers, 34.
George IV., 167n.
George, John, 133.
Gibbs, Alice, 77 ; Benj., 98 ; E. L., 107 ;
 Mary, 98 ; T., 7n ; Tho., 77.
Gilbert (Gilebert), Mr., 138 ; Rob., 179.
Glocestria, Milo de, 1.
Gloucester, Thomas, Duke of, 35.
Godfrey, Jos., 70.
Golafre, John, 169.
Goosetree (Goostrye), Edw., 23 ; Rob.,
 177 ; Wm., 23, 47.
Gosnel (Cosnel), Tho. 67.
Graves (Greaves), John, 134 ; Jos., 137 ;
 Richard, 120, 140.
Gray, Tho., 104.
Green, J. W., 101.
Grenburgh, Domina de, see Mountfort,
 Roisa.
Gretenok, Ric. le, 179.
Grevyll, John, 6.
Grey, Lady Jane, 37, 38.
Griffin, Mr., 46.
Guinness, Mr. and Mrs. R. D., 15.

Hall, Harry, 82 ; Mr., 94 ; Rev. Tho.,
 47, 98, 144.
Hancok, Wm., 170.
Handy, Rob., 107.
Hannett, John, 54, 55, 60, 75, 80, 81,
 86, 101, 106, 107, 127 ; Books by 106.
Harcourt, Edw., 89 ; John, Lord of, 33.
Harding, John, 86n ; Tho., 86n.
Harecourt, Alice de, 30.
Harewell (Harwell), Arms of, 52 ;
 John, 170.
Harmon, Wm., 7, 38.
Harper, Agnes, 177 ; Edmund, 177 ;
 John, 170-172, 177-8 ; Mary, 177 ;
 Wm., 177.
Harris, Simon, 13.
Harrison, Humph., 26 ; Wm., 107.
Harrope, —, 180.
Hartwell, Tho., 66n.
Haselholt, John de, 169.
Hawkes, Harry, 28, 71 ; Jos., 82.
Haydock, Capt., 167.

INDEX OF PLACES AND GENERAL.

The Perambulation of Ullenhall, 1640 (p. 180) and the Survey of the Manor of Barrells, 1681 (pp. 182-3), both in the Appendix, have not been indexed, to save space at this time.

The letter *n* after a number indicates a footnote.

INDEX TO ILLUSTRATIONS

(Figures in brackets refer to the nearest preceding text page)

SUBSCRIBERS

Presentation Copies

xxxix